Cross-Cultural Counseling

A C A S E B O O K

Clemmont E. Vontress
Jake A. Johnson
Lawrence R. Epp

CROSS-CULTURAL COUNSELING

10 9 8 7 6 5 4 3 2

American Counseling Association
5999 Stevenson Avenue
Alexandria, VA 22304

Director of Publications
Carolyn Baker

Publishing Consultant
Michael Comlish

Cover art by Donna Coleman

Cover design by Jennifer Sterling, Spot Color

Library of Congress Cataloging-in-Publication Data
Vontress, Clemmont E., 1929–
      Cross-cultural counseling: a casebook / by Clemmont E. Vontress, Jake A.
  Johnson, Lawrence R. Epp.
        p.   cm.
  Includes bibliographical references and index.
  ISBN 1-55620-210-5 (alk. paper)
      1. Cross-cultural counseling. 2. Cross-cultural counseling—Case studies.
I. Johnson, Jake A. II. Epp, Lawrence R. III. Title
BF637.C6V66   1999
158'.3—dc21
                                          98-49420
                                            CIP

TABLE *of* CONTENTS

ABOUT *the* AUTHORS

Clemmont E. Vontress, PhD
Dr. Vontress is considered one of the pioneers of the multicultural counseling movement. For nearly 30 years, he has been an esteemed counselor–educator at several leading universities. In 1997, he was recognized by the American Counseling Association Foundation as being one of the profession's most distinguished counselors. He was the first African American to achieve tenure and to be elevated to the highest professorial rank of Professor Emeritus of Counseling in the Department of Counseling, Human, and Organizational Studies by George Washington University in Washington, DC.

Jake A. Johnson, EdD
Dr. Johnson is an assistant professor of education and the coordinator of the guidance and counseling programs at Bowie State University in Bowie, Maryland. He currently serves as president of the Maryland Association for Multicultural Counseling and Development. He is also a psychotherapist in private practice, in which he counsels multicultural families, adults, adolescents, and children.

Lawrence R. Epp, EdD
Dr. Epp is a psychiatric therapist in the East Baltimore Mental Health Partnership of the Johns Hopkins Hospital and in private practice with the Phoenix Counseling Service in Owings Mills, Maryland. He served for 2 years as Clemmont E. Vontress's graduate assistant at George Washington University in Washington, DC. He is president-elect of the Maryland Association for Multicultural Counseling and Development and is a visiting lecturer at Bowie State University in Bowie, Maryland.

CASE CONTRIBUTORS

Amani Aridi, EdD (Candidate)
Ms. Aridi is a doctoral candidate in the Department of Counseling, Human, and Organizational Studies at George Washington University. She completed her undergraduate work at Howard University and holds a master's degree in educational measurement and research from Johns Hopkins University. She is considered an incredibly gifted counselor by her peers.

Myung Ho Cha, EdD
Dr. Cha was a graduate of the doctoral program in counseling in the Department of Counseling, Human, and Organizational Studies at George Washington University. He is currently a counselor, organizational consultant, and instructor of counseling in Korea.

Daisy C. Espinosa, MA
Ms. Espinosa is a graduate of the master's program in rehabilitation counseling at George Washington University and is currently a mental health counselor in Virginia and a patient advocate at the George Washington University Hospital.

Eirini Gouleta, LPC
Ms. Gouleta has a master's degree in education from a university in her native Greece and a master's degree in education in counseling and development from George Mason University. She practices mental health counseling in Washington, DC, and Virginia.

Charles Grausz, MA
Mr. Grausz is a graduate of the master's program in school counseling at George Washington University and is currently a school counselor in Virginia.

Susan V. Greynolds, EdD (Candidate)

Ms. Greynolds is a doctoral candidate in the Department of Counseling, Human, and Organizational Studies at George Washington University and is a psychotherapist in private practice at the Professional Network Group in Washington, DC.

Cheryl D. Haas, MA

Ms. Haas is a graduate of the master's program in community counseling at George Washington University and is currently manager of public communications with the American Counseling Association and a psychotherapist in private practice at the Professional Network Group in Washington, DC. She was a past president of the George Washington University chapter of the Chi Sigma Iota Counseling Honor Society.

Morris L. Jackson, EdD

Dr. Jackson is community programs officer at American University and an adjunct professor of counseling at George Mason University in Virginia and George Washington University in Washington, DC.

Victoria A. Sardi, EdD (Candidate)

Ms. Sardi is a doctoral candidate in the Department of Counseling, Human, and Organizational Studies at George Washington University. She was a past president of the George Washington University chapter of the Chi Sigma Iota Counseling Honor Society, a recipient of the Thomas J. Sweeney Leadership Award, a Leader in Counselor Education Fellow, and a recipient of the Outstanding Service to the Chi Sigma Iota Chapter Award.

Calvin E. Woodland, EdD, PsyD

Dr. Woodland has served as a high-ranking administrator in several state hospitals and universities while simultaneously maintaining a private practice as a clinical psychologist.

FOREWORD

Peter R. Breggin, MD

This book arrives on the professional scene at a critical time in the life of counseling, psychology, and the entire field of mental health. It breathes new life into a field that is in danger of expiring.

Most mental health disciplines are kowtowing to the medical model and medication. They are adopting the most superficial of 20th-century values—scientism, the application of simplistic physical principles to human life. Unwittingly serving the interests of the pharmaceutical industry and psychiatry, they have allowed their more profound understanding of human nature and human progress to be replaced by simpleminded genetic, biological, and medical concepts. Although these physical concepts may seem modern, they are in fact rooted in 18th- and 19th-century psychology and psychiatry, with their emphasis on mimicking the physical sciences while enforcing authoritarian control and suppression.

Tragically, counselors and other therapists are forsaking their more inspired roots in humanistic and existential psychology. When faced with difficult clients or stressful therapy situations, they refer their clients to pill-pushing physicians. In turning to medical doctors and medications to bail themselves out, they abandon the human relationship and communication as the most effective methods of helping people in distress.

As a result of this ultimate reliance on simplistic pharmacological solutions, the fields of psychotherapy and counseling are losing their verve as well as their sustaining values. Like ships without rudders, counselors and therapists without principles will run aground and sink.

Meanwhile, some courageous leaders among counselors and therapists continue to gain their strength and inspiration from more profound humanistic and existential values. This book reflects two of the most positive aspects of counseling as a profession: first, a firm footing in philosophical and psychological principles and second, an empathic understanding of individual clients.

The authors also emphasize perhaps the single most important principle in human existence: We are all more alike than different, more similar in our humanity than unique in our individuality, and ultimately in need of the same respect and love as all human beings. Phrases in this book such as "the sameness of human beings" and "universal culture" remind us that cross-cultural counseling at heart is simply good counseling that is conducted between two or more individuals with many shared values and mutual respect.

In *The Heart of Being Helpful: Empathy and the Creation of a Healing Presence* (Breggin, 1997), I viewed cross-cultural therapy through the lens of basic needs that are common to all human beings. Neither race nor culture can truly separate individuals. Individuals of any race or culture are as likely to meet their soul mates in a seemingly different culture as in their own. In my clinical work and in my professional and personal life, I often find that my closest, most fulfilling relationships evolve with people of very different backgrounds from myself. This book further develops the principle of cross-cultural empathy and shared values with a clear statement of principles and many lively stories that illustrate those values.

Not only progress in counseling but also human survival itself depends on the realization that we are all members of the same family. This book is a contribution not only to the fields of counseling and psychology but also to human understanding.

Cross-Cultural Counseling: A Casebook is worth reading for both its thoughtful explication of fundamental principles and its vital, sometimes enchanting, stories of real people. It will inspire professionals and educate students.

Although I am a psychiatrist, I am proud to teach in the Department of Counseling at Johns Hopkins University. It is my belief that counseling, along with humanistic psychology, remains the hope for the future for empowering clients rather than controlling them. These more humanistic, existential disciplines also hold in their hands any contribution that psychology and counseling may make to human progress. Counseling, with its educational, existential, and humanistic thrust, is carrying a torch that remains in danger of being extinguished. This book helps to keep the flame alive and gives new life to it.

May 1998
Bethesda, Maryland

Cross-Cultural Counseling

Cross-Cultural Counseling

By nature, human beings are wanderers, always wanting to see what is over the horizon. In venturing from their habitats, they encounter contours of the natural environment, life forms, and concomitant behaviors that they have never seen before. Curious, they want to know why things are so different from what they have always known. It was this curiosity that prompted the beginnings of global exploration and the discipline of *anthropology*. The curious wanderers began to catalog what they saw in new lands. When Europeans set foot on the African continent for the first time, they were struck by the dark-skinned people they saw and their "unusual" way of life. To protect themselves as they ventured among beings whom they perceived as "savages" and "cannibals," they were forced to find out as much as they could about the "strange" people inhabiting the "Dark Continent." They commissioned and sent forth "scientists" to bring back information about the Africans and their customs. A new research technique began that came to be known as anthropology, or the description of ethnic groups or tribes.

Margaret Mead and other anthropologists shocked Western sensibilites with their descriptions of tribal peoples whose behaviors seemed exotic and promiscuous. Their descriptions of cultural differences published in journals and textbooks in this country and abroad were fascinating to consider but had little practical meaning to the average person. In due course, social work as a profession developed in the United States. Academic social workers began to study cultural differences at home in somewhat the same way anthropologists were doing in exotic lands. Although their research was interesting, it had little direct application in terms of how clinical social workers could adapt their techniques of helping to those who were perceived as "culturally different" in American society. In a sense, the research was used mainly to protect clinical social workers from harm as they made "home visits" in the ethnic enclaves of impoverished immigrants and former slaves, in somewhat the same way the anthropological researchers in Africa served to protect the physical well-being of colonists who sought to plunder riches and assume the ownership of land without the violent objection of native Africans.

It is only in recent years that an understanding of culture and cultural differences has been used to help people directly. The change in how academicians used a knowledge of culture and its application coincided with the advent of the *counseling movement*. As a helping profession, counseling, unlike psychology and psychiatry, was less "scientific." Its practitioners came from undergraduate programs in education, sociology, philosophy, religion, social sciences, and many other disciplines new to helping. These individuals were more willing to apply the insights gleaned from these other disciplines, along with psychological insights, to construct a more holistic vision of the client.

Fortunately, for many people who heretofore felt like outsiders in their own country, a group of professionals called *cross-cultural counselors* or therapists now exists. These counselors apply their understanding of culture to help clients who very often encounter problems in living because of their real or perceived cultural differences. That is, people who are perceived to be different by members of the dominant cultural group in the United States are not always in reality different from those who perceive them as such. For example, middle-class African Americans are more like middle-class European Americans than are middle-class Russian-born White Americans, even though the similarity and dissimilarity usually are not recognized by White Americans in general. In the minds of many White Americans, similarity of skin color presupposes a cultural similarity, which is only a very superficial and misguided form of analogy.

The purpose of this book is to define culture from the perspective of existential philosophy and to explain how counselors and therapists in general can apply their understanding of culture to help people with problems in living, no matter where they were born. To accomplish this objective, several case studies of clients representing many different cultural, racial, and ethnic backgrounds are presented so as to illustrate the subtle dimensions of counseling culturally different clients.

THE CULTURAL BEING

As shown in Figure 1, human beings are products of their genetic endowments and life experiences. At conception, their destiny is already determined in part by the intricate DNA helix that exists in every cell. However, the final shape of that destiny is influenced by an individual's life experiences. Human genetics and life experience intermingle as they are filtered through five cultural layers. The first layer is the *universal culture*, or the way of life that is indicated by the physiology of the human species. People are conceived in a given way, they consume nourishment to live, they grow into adulthood, they contribute to the welfare of the group, and they grow old and die. These and other ways of life are invariable dimensions of human existence. They, therefore, may be called universal culture.

Human genetic endowments and life experiences are also shaped by the ecosystem and the demands that it makes on one's way of life. Climatic conditions, indigenous vegetation, animal life, seasonal changes, and other factors determine how people interact with nature and themselves. Obviously, people who must use dog sleds to commute to the grocery store see life differently than those who need only to pluck their nourishment from trees and plants in their backyard. Imagine also what it must be like to live several months of the year in complete darkness and how such an existence would affect daily activities. For these and other reasons, it seems tenable to posit the existence of an *ecological culture*, the second layer of the cultural filter.

The third layer of the filter is the *national culture*, which derives from the fact that a stable community of people share the same territory, heritage, language, economic system, government, and allegiance to a way of life for which they are willing to die if necessary. Although people born abroad may join the community, they must fit into the culture that was already established by earlier generations. In other words, they are expected to become *acculturated*, or to take on the culture of their adopted country. In large measure, schools serve as primary institutions of acculturation for young people. However, everybody needs to learn to negotiate the culture of the host country. They must learn its rules and regulations, many of which are sanctioned by law. The social demands and expectations that provide self-direction for individuals in one country usually are inadequate to ensure comfortable adjustment in another.

The fourth cultural layer that helps to make people into the persons they are is the *regional culture*. Many countries manifest distinct regional differences in terms of language, dress, customs, and other ways of life. Regional differences exist for various reasons. In large countries, different climate zones influence how people negotiate environmental differences. In other countries, proximity to the borders of neighboring countries contributes to a blending of cultures along the boundaries. Regional cultural differences are also often by-products of military conquests and political annexations.

The fifth and final layer in Figure 1 is called *racio-ethnic culture*, mainly because racial and ethnic groups usually reside in separate communities where they perpetuate their way of life. Separatism is especially true in countries where racial attitudes are such that racially and ethnically different people feel unwelcome in the dominant group's community. For example, in Paris, there are sections of the city where Africans live, another where Arabs reside, and others where various other ethnic groups settle in their own neighborhoods. In New York, the same phenomenon is observed: Not only is there a Harlem where African Americans reside, but there is also a Spanish Harlem where Spanish-speaking people of color live and perpetuate their culture. It is unnecessary to debate whether people choose voluntarily to live among their own cultural group or whether they are forced by the larger society to do so. The results are the same: a racio-ethnic culture that is transmitted from one generation to another. Although people may relocate to other communities, usually their cultural roots remain in the community of origin.

THE CULTURAL DISTILLATE

As can be seen in Figure 1, individuals are distillates of a cultural filter consisting of five layers. The filtering continues throughout their life span. At each developmental stage, their genetic endowment interacts with life experiences to determine the nature of their existence. This ensures that each human being is distinctively different from all others. As Vontress (1979, 1996) pointed out, individuals embody four dynamically interactive "worlds," which can be described best in the language of German existentialists. First, there is the *Eigenwelt*, that "private realm" of the human personality that cannot be experienced or completely understood by another person. Second, the *Mitwelt* suggests that what people are is a product of their relationships with others. In fact, many observers would say that nobody is really him- or herself. Instead, they are composites of other people, primarily their parents, siblings, and peers, who shaped their personality just as their

Figure 1. An Existential Model of Culture.

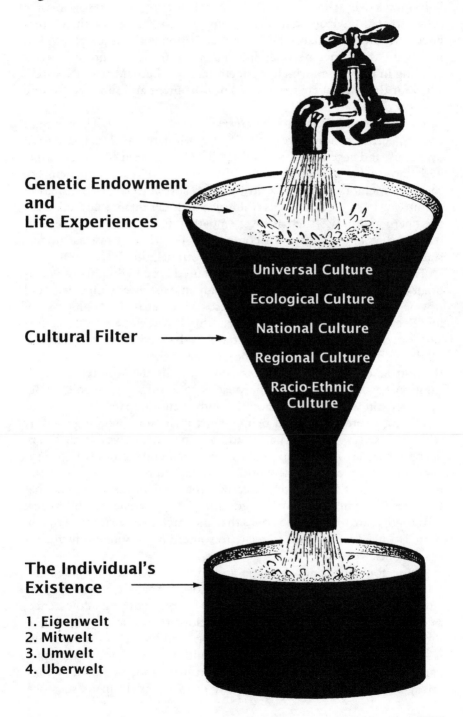

Genetic Endowment
and
Life Experiences

Cultural Filter

Universal Culture

Ecological Culture

National Culture

Regional Culture

Racio-Ethnic
Culture

The Individual's
Existence

1. Eigenwelt
2. Mitwelt
3. Umwelt
4. Uberwelt

genes directed their physical characteristics. Third, the human being is influenced by the *Umwelt*, or natural environment. How people relate to that environment directly impacts the nature of their existence. Although the natural environment often is taken for granted, it makes the difference between life and death for thousands of species residing in its bosom, which is affectionately called "Mother Nature." Without the natural environment's nourishment and support, no one would exist.

Fourth, humans relate to the *Uberwelt*, or spirit world. They require the respect, direction, love, and affection of parents, elders, departed love ones, and potent spiritual entities. The spirit world connects people with those who, although "come and gone," still reside in them because of memory, genetic contributions, and cultural indoctrination (Vontress, 1996). Perhaps this realm also includes intangible feelings of the "here and now," such as love, empathy, devotion, respect, and altruism, that bind the human community together in mutual understanding with a powerful, if unseen, "emotional glue."

The existential model of culture presented here highlights the paradoxical complexity and simplicity of human existence. Culture should not be viewed separately from the rest of life—it is the "compass" of life. Because people cannot live to adulthood without a set of practices and procedures that are designed to guide their existence, they require a culture for their orientation in the world and their survival. The tub at the bottom of the model is used to communicate the notion that acculturation has a purpose. That purpose is to ensure that people live as best they can while they develop through their life span.

During existence, human beings must maintain a working rapport with themselves; that is, they need to know themselves at all times. Second, they are obliged to establish and maintain a rapport with others because they exist in the world of others and require their love and respect. Third, it is absolutely necessary that individuals recognize that they are a part of the animal kingdom and are governed by biological systems that are similar to the ones that animate other creatures. Fourth, there is a need for humans to relate to something or somebody greater than themselves.

These four needs are dynamic and interactive. Each may demand fulfillment more strongly at one period of life than at others. For example, the need to learn about one's self is urgent during adolescence, as one's body quickly changes as it develops reproductive organs. Although the need to relate to others is a powerful force throughout life, it is especially demanding during early adulthood, when individuals prepare to assume adult roles and initiate intimate and, we hope, lifelong linkages with members of the opposite or same sex. In many societies, people seem to be more in touch with their spiritual selves toward the end of their existence than at other stages of their existence.

In general, everything that lives manifests a predictable chronology of existence. It is conceived, sprouts, bears fruit, shrivels up, dies, and returns to nature to be recycled. This sobering and inevitable cycle also occurs with human beings. The tub at the bottom of Figure 1 suggests that human existence is a continuous and changing movement. During youth, human existence flows quickly and abundantly. As people age, the flow of life (genetic expression and life experiences) slows, but the evaporation process continues unabated until the tub of life is empty. No one escapes from life alive, nor can its flow be slowed or reversed. Peering at the tub where our existence ends and evaporates emphasizes the preciousness of each moment of life.

THE CROSS-CULTURAL CLIENT

According to the model of culture presented in this book, everybody is similar and dissimilar to everybody else at the same time. After all, all human beings are cultural products of the universal culture. As such, there is a global similarity in terms of how people manage their existence. They become progressively culturally different as their genetic endowments and life experiences pass through filters beyond the universal culture. The model suggests that older people, women, people with disabilities, and gay men and lesbians are not culturally different from other people with whom they have been socialized. Their existence has been filtered through the same cultural layers as others in the ecological, national, regional, and racio-ethnic environments. In spite of their age, gender, physical condition, or sexual orientation, it is a disservice to label these individuals as culturally different when they may not perceive themselves as being different in this manner from the rest of the community.

The special issues of age groups, genders, persons with physical challenges, and sexual minorities deserve treatment under specialties other than "cross-cultural counseling" where they can receive more than superficial coverage. Groups that are not recognized as cultures may argue that the issues they grapple with are so profound and alienating that it makes them feel as if there is a cultural gulf between them and others. Although their feelings of alienation may be as real as those of recognized cultural minorities, to cast too broad a net of what it means to be culturally different could potentially make everyone culturally different and deprive this term of its distinctive meaning.

The essence of cultural difference lies in the multiplicity of layers of cultural influence that are shared by a group. A cultural group is not a synthetic, or human-made, linkage of individuals who share a common issue. It is an evolving, multigenerational group into which its members are born and then bear forever its physical and psychological markings. It is better to avoid the slippery slope of expanding the definition of culture and to stick with those groups who are traditionally so defined, whose issues have been neglected historically and now demand renewed attention as our nation evolves into a multicultural society. It would not do justice to either cultural or generic groups to dilute their issues together into an indistinct hodgepodge.

Counselors are advised to ask clients if cultural differences contribute in any way to their presenting problem. For example, it is untenable to assume that every African American client is automatically a cross-cultural client. Take the case of John Jones, a 28-year-old Black man who presents himself to his counselor complaining of anxiety in his new job at a prestigious law firm where he is a recently hired associate. He experiences panic attacks each time he makes a presentation on the job. As an infant, John was adopted by a wealthy White family and grew up in an all-White neighborhood. He was the only Black student in his elementary, junior high, and senior high schools. He matriculated at Harvard College, where he graduated with honors. He went on to study law at the University of Virginia and graduated in the upper quarter of his class. Should his race or cultural background be considered in helping him with the anxiety that he experiences on the job? Cross-cultural counseling is not intended to create cultural issues where they do not exist but to heighten sensitivity when they do.

Cross-cultural counseling is a helping device that can be used when cultural, racial, or ethnic differences present a potential area of misunderstanding in the process of psychotherapy. Cross-cultural dyads may consist of an African American counselor and a White client, an Asian American therapist and an African American client, a European American therapist and a Latin American client, an African American counselor and a Japanese foreign student, or any other combination of interactants. Cross-cultural group therapy often is more problematic than dyadic helping, because the leader cannot always control the multitude of possible interactive responses and response styles in groups consisting of a diverse cultural and socioeconomic mixture. Even though counselors may consider themselves to be good students of a particular foreign culture, their knowledge may in fact be restricted to a given socioeconomic or ethnic group in the culture. They may be unaware that mixing upper-class clients from countries with rigid class structures with lower-class clients from the same countries is apt to create a great deal of embarrassment for all parties and guarantee therapeutic failure for the group.

ORGANIZATION OF THE BOOK

This book is organized in two parts. Part 1 consists of three chapters in which the theoretical groundwork is laid for part 2. In the introduction, an existentially based theory of culture is offered, the cross-cultural client is defined, and the format of the book is described. In chapter 1, several constructs that may affect cross-cultural counseling are discussed. In chapter 2, the existential basis of cross-counseling is described. In part 2, 10 case studies of culturally different clients are presented. In each case, the client is introduced, the client's history is presented, and three analyses are provided. The first one is from a *conceptual perspective* using recognized psychological and cultural concepts, the second is from an *existential perspective*, and the third is based on the *diagnostic model* presented in the fourth edition of the *Diagnostic and Statistical Manual of Mental Disorders* (*DSM–IV*; American Psychiatric Association [APA], 1994). After the case analysis, a brief discussion is provided so as to enable the reader to understand the rationale for each analysis. Finally, each case presentation is followed by discussion questions that are provided to encourage students and other readers to consider the complex aspects of each case. Although each case is based in general on facts from real case files, careful attention was taken to conceal the identities of the actual clients.

CHAPTER ONE

Culture and Counseling

During the past 30 years, counselors have come to recognize the impact of culture on therapeutic relationships, diagnoses, and the techniques they use to help clients. In the 1950s and 1960s, counselor–educators generally considered counseling to be counseling; that is, they believed that theories and techniques that worked with one group of clients would work with another, regardless of cultural background (Jackson, 1995). One indication of how far the helping professions have departed from this position is the *DSM–IV*, which has been prepared to "incorporate an awareness that the manual is used in culturally diverse populations in the United States and internationally" (APA, 1994, p. xxiv). Although significant advances have been made in recognizing that clients are reflections of the cultures in which they have been socialized, a theoretical framework still does not exist to help counselors work effectively with clients who do not fit comfortably within the worldviews of the American psychoanalytic, cognitive–behavioral, or humanistic approaches to counseling.

Three or 4 decades ago, social workers, psychologists, counselors, and counselor–educators began to call attention to the problems they encountered in working with the "culturally deprived," "culturally disadvantaged," and "Negro" clients. In the 1970s, the literature that described the dimensions of the problems presented by such clients increased (Jackson, 1987, 1995). At the same time, some universities introduced graduate courses to enhance the effectiveness of counselors working with the "culturally different," as D. W. Sue (1981) called clients who deviated from the cultural mainstream. These courses are now required by the various accreditation bodies in counseling and psychology; however, students often complete them feeling more dissimilar from their culturally different clients than similar, because the courses convey reams of factual information on cultural differences that make it seem impossible to bridge the differences. Students often come to the faulty conclusion that only persons of like cultures should work together therapeutically; this belief has even become embodied in "Afrocentric" counseling theories.

What these courses offer is essentially a "groups approach." In other words, as there was in the 1960s, today there is a tendency to generalize about the characteristics of a minority group in graduate classrooms, at professional conferences, and in journal articles and books. Even though Americans of Hispanic, African, European, Asian, and indigenous descent continue to become total participants in and reflective of the national culture, it is often assumed that cultural differences between ethnic groups are readily distinguishable and easily described. It is our contention that although there are some shared values within ethnic groups, there is a danger of stereotyping ethnic groups if counselors expect too rigidly a given set of behaviors from them. Approaching cross-cultural clients with a stereotype can cause as much misunderstanding as approaching them with stark ignorance of the cultural values they hold.

The purpose of this chapter is to (a) offer a perspective that recognizes that although human beings are dissimilar, at the same time, they are more alike than different; (b) list and describe some concepts that affect cross-cultural counseling; and (c) indicate some implications of these concepts for counseling clients who are not fully assimilated into the host culture.

CULTURE

Culture is simultaneously visible and invisible, conscious and unconscious, cognitive and affective. Although most of it is out of sight and mind, it provides human beings with their most essential qualities, which are transmitted throughout the life cycle through socialization. Culture is the sum total of a people's beliefs and procedures for negotiating environments at each stage of existence (Vontress, 1986b). Most people are products of five concentric and intersecting cultures: (a) universal,

(b) ecological, (c) national, (d) regional, and (e) racio-ethnic. The cultures are neither entirely separate nor equal. The most foundational, the universal, which is biologically determined, influences all others.

No matter what the conditions under which people live are, people still must adjust to the fact that they are human beings. For example, African Americans are first of all culturally alike because they are members of the human species. As such, they share the biologically dictated behaviors of all members of the human group. Second, they are forced to adjust to the same climatic conditions as do all other Americans. Third, as members of the national culture, they take on the behavior, attitudes, and values of Americans in general. Fourth, they are influenced by the culture of the region in which they live. Thus, Marcus, a native of rural Alabama, is apt to betray his roots by the manner of speech that is peculiar to that region. Fifth, because of Marcus's African ancestry, European Americans are apt to react to him as if he were inferior, a fact that leaves psychological scars on him and members of his group (Vontress, 1986b).

This concept of culture suggests that everybody is multicultural in the sense of being composed of multiple cultural influences rather than being "culturally monolithic." It also limits the groups that may be classified as culturally different to those who share traits that have been recognized traditionally as "cultural"—that is, ecological, regional, national, or racio-ethnic traits—rather than those who share a universal characteristic. Therefore, women, gay men and lesbians, people with disabilities, and older people are not considered culturally different because they are socialized in the same families and under the same cultural influences as their male, heterosexual, able-bodied, and younger siblings and relatives. Although their forced or voluntary segregation from their families or privileged circles gives them the flavor of a separate "subculture," we would like to discourage thinking of these groups as culturally different, because such a strong label is alienating and not reflective of how these groups think of themselves. To make the stages of human development, gender, disability, or sexual orientation into distinct cultural groups is to magnify the natural differences within groups. It would mean looking at all differences through a microscope rather than within their natural contexts.

Counselors must also guard against *ethnocentrism*—the tendency of the inhabitants of modern cultures to belittle those from less technologically advanced ones. Because the majority of the people of the world live in what some writers refer to as "folk" or "primitive" societies, counselors need to understand that the distinguishing feature of these societies is not a lack of "collective intelligence" but rather a different set of social priorities (Wade, 1993). Many of these societies, while admiring technological achievement, seem to place greater emphasis on human relationships and spirituality and, thus, are not experiencing the breakdown of societal norms that now blights technological cultures, as reflected in their rampant crime and violence, drug abuse, juvenile delinquency, disrespect of authority, road rage, and disintegration of the two-parent family, among other social ills.

Loomis (1940), Redfield (1947), Becker (1950), and Tumin (1973) are among the early social scientists who offered classic studies of primitive and advanced cultures. These scholars made Americans appreciate that their culture is large, heterogeneous, urban, industrial, literate, and secular as opposed to being small, homogeneous, rural, agricultural, nonliterate, and sacred. At the same time, it is important to recognize that societies throughout the world are in a state of change. An American arriving in West Africa for the first time, for example, would be struck by the mixture of folk and modern cultures (Vontress, 1991). Therefore, it is untenable to generalize about any cultural group. Students of culture are advised to view on a continuum dimensions of culture that are subject to change as a result of such factors as economic advancement, television, political shifts, and international relations.

CULTURALLY RELATED CONCEPTS

Culture is a paradoxical idea. It should be viewed as simultaneously fixed and dynamic. Although many aspects of the human environment are transient, there are both natural and human-made objects that have been standing for many generations. Mountains, trees, rock formations, and the great pyramids of Egypt are examples of permanent fixtures that contrast with the transitory life forms whose generations successively witness their beauty and majesty. Although there is general continuity in each cultural group, generational replacement produces a great deal of tension and change in politics, fashion, and social values (Moles, 1967). Therefore, any concepts that are used to help people understand culture must be viewed as partial ideas advanced to understand a complex and ever-changing whole. The concepts listed below should be understood in this light. They are briefly defined, and their implications for cross-cultural counseling are discussed.

Acculturation

Acculturation is the process of becoming adapted to a new or different culture. It usually suggests that the new arrival or socially excluded individual adopts the language, values, attitudes, dress, and behavior of the host culture. As Fischer (1965) pointed out, becoming like "the others" also implies duration. That is, it takes people a while to adjust to a new culture. Young people tend to acculturate more quickly than their older cultural peers do (Turner, 1986). The related concept of *assimilation* conjures up the image of the human organism unconsciously absorbing surrounding stimuli. Because culture is cumulative, it seems tenable to conclude that young people in a host culture or community are apt to become like the people in that community more quickly than their older relatives who have been socialized during their formative years in their native cultures.

An obvious implication is that the more clients are acculturated, the more counselors can feel comfortable using theories and techniques that they use generally with U.S.-born clients. However, they are faced with the problem of having to determine the level of acculturation that is presented by each client. There is no single index for doing so. For example, a client may speak perfect English but have little or no understanding of the values, attitudes, or affective dimensions of the host culture. Counselors need to develop an easy yet effective way to find out the degree to which culturally different clients are similar to people in the host culture. They may require new counselees to write structured cultural autobiographies in which they reveal dimensions of themselves, such as (a) place of birth, (b) school attended, (c) languages spoken at home, (d) places traveled, (e) U.S.-born friends, (f) languages spoken, and (g) as many other items as are needed to obtain a thumbnail sketch of the person. As can be seen in Table 1, the items for the autobiography should be selected to sample the client's culture. The information in the essay helps the counselor determine which theoretical approaches might be appropriate to use with specific clients.

Autoplasty Versus Alloplasty

Two concepts that have been useful in understanding approaches to helping culturally different clients are autoplasty and alloplasty. The combining form *auto* derives from the Greek *autos* and means "self." *Allo* derives from the Greek *alias* and means "other." The combining form *plasty* comes from the Greek *plastos* (form) and refers to the means of promoting growth, development, and change. Finding the most appropriate solutions to problems that are encountered by culturally different clients is challenging, as Draguns (1989) pointed out. Should clients change themselves to accommodate the host environment (autoplasty)? Or should the environment change itself to promote the adjustment of the culturally different client (alloplasty)? For example, John Washington, the only African American student in Mrs. Jones's 10th-grade English class, is sent to the counselor by the teacher, who writes that he is "indifferent to learning." The student indicates to the counselor that it is not so: The teacher has an unconscious racial bias.

Table 1. Outline for a Cultural Autobiography

1. What is your name, birth date, and place of birth?
2. What is your cultural or national heritage?
3. What was the cultural mix of the schools that you attended?
4. What was the cultural mix of the religious institutions that you attended?
5. What was the cultural mix of the neighborhood where you grew up?
6. What trips abroad have you taken?
7. What foreign languages do you speak, read, or write?
8. What is the cultural mix of your workplace?
9. Do you ever participate in social or recreational activities with people who are racially or culturally different from yourself?
10. Have you ever worked around people in the military or civilian sector who were different racially, culturally, or both?
11. Have you ever had racially or culturally different teachers, professors, or both?
12. Do you now or have you ever taught, supervised, or otherwise been in charge of racially or culturally different people?
13. How do you feel around people who are racially or culturally different from yourself?
14. What academic courses have you had that are related to racial or cultural differences?
15. What other experiences have you had that would help a person understand your level of exposure to racial or cultural differences (e.g., a spouse or intimate friend who is racially or culturally different)?
16. What type of climate do you feel most comfortable residing in?

What does the counselor do? Tell John that he should "kowtow" to the teacher to pass the class (autoplasty) or confer with the teacher to determine whether she is sensitive to John's racio-cultural background (alloplasty)? Sometimes cross-cultural issues have no specific resolution except to lend moral and emotional support to the culturally different client.

International students new to the United States present similar problems. For example, some complain to their advisors that they are unaccustomed to taking multiple-choice examinations on which they obtain low scores. Should counselors help them learn how to take such examinations (autoplasty) or should they inform professors of the dilemma, hoping that they will adjust their teaching methods (alloplasty)? With the autoplastic approach, counselors attempt to help by getting clients to change themselves; with the alloplastic one, they try to get the system or its agents to make adjustments in the interest of clients. Because people act on their environments as environments act on them, counselors generally find that they use both the autoplastic and alloplastic approaches to help culturally different clients. However, counselors often discover that persuading systems to change in culturally insensitive and bureaucratic organizations is a challenging undertaking that requires much skill in advocacy and some degree of patience.

Collectivism Versus Individualism

Collectivism and individualism are concepts that have been widely discussed and contrasted in social science (Triandis, 1994). Collectivism refers to social systems in which individuals submit to the interest of the group, which may be the family, ethnic leaders, the community, work colleagues, the nation, or other affiliations that provide a sense of belonging for the person. On the other hand, individualism suggests societies in which the needs, desires, and aspirations of individuals take precedence over those of such groups as the family, kinship clan, and community at large. Although the concepts often are presented as opposites, it is probably more correct to view them as indicators of general tendencies and inclinations that can coexist in the same individual depending on the issue or circumstance (Carrithers, 1992; Dube, 1988). With the intense and constant movement of people from one nation to another, it is no longer tenable to hold to fixed views regarding transients. People who are individualistic in one country often become collectivistic in another and vice versa, for various reasons. For example, in developing countries in which agriculture is the primary means of subsistence, people benefit from being neighborly. In capitalistic societies where individuals often live and work in impersonal environments, others who do not contribute significantly to the fulfillment of one's immediate needs are seen as competitors rather than compatriots (Fischer, 1965).

In collectivistic societies, the head of the family assumes a powerful and respected role. In individualistic ones, household heads exert much less influence over family members, especially adults. Cross-cultural counselors need to ascertain the extent to which clients are products of individualistic versus collectivist socialization. It is a good practice to ask clients whether there is someone at home or elsewhere who should be consulted regarding the presenting problem and its solution. To enter into counseling without respecting the head of the family may impact negatively the outcome of counseling. Whatever recommendations are decided on in counseling may be rejected by family authority figures unless they are consulted early in the counseling process.

Cultural Intuition

Cultural intuition is the immediate knowledge, sensation, and rapport that counselors often experience when they relate to clients from their own culture. It is the empathy a person feels for a cultural peer. As a result, there usually is increased ability to relate to clients and to determine the nature of their presenting problems. This concept should not be interpreted to mean that counselors external to the native cultures of their clients are unable to empathize with them: People are all multicultural in the sense that they share commonalities at some level of experience. For example, the existence of Americans is influenced by a common ecology, economic system, network of bureaucratic procedures, media, and the like. As such, Americans are socialized to respond spontaneously to certain cues to which people reared in other countries do not respond. Therefore, there is a national cultural intuition that enhances the rapport and mutual comprehension of one American for another. Likewise, on the racio-ethnic cultural level, people who grow up in the same racial or ethnic community generally sense the feelings, thoughts, and knowledge of their cultural peers more quickly and spontaneously than do outsiders.

Although cultural intuition is a human phenomenon, the uncanny ability to know what another thinks, wants, and feels without knowing the origin of the power is especially prevalent among homogeneous groups that are unaffected by outside influences (Moles, 1967). In such societies, each person is a veritable template of the other. Even so, cross-cultural counselors must guard against countertransference or unconsciously generalizing their own experiences onto clients who are in fact different from them in many ways because they were socialized in culturally different families and communities. People are alike and different at the same time.

Direct Versus Indirect Intervention

In helping clients, counselors talk to them face to face or interact with someone else on their behalf. In the United States, counselors usually talk directly with clients who have problems, especially adult clients. On the other hand, in many cultures that are external to the American society, the head of the family assumes responsibility for all problems in the unit. If a family member has a problem, the head of the household consults the helper on behalf of the entire family, not just the person who is perceived to be the "identified patient." In collectivistic societies, individuals do not have problems, families have problems, which in turn reflect negatively on the head of the family, who feels responsible for the entire unit (Triandis, 1994; Vontress, 1991).

Indirectness seems to be more pronounced in traditional collectivistic societies than it is in individualistic counterparts. For example, in West Africa, parents and other adults in extended families socialize children by reciting fables, riddles, and maxims that are designed to inculcate important lessons. When the children become adults, they are apt to consult traditional healers who use the same indirect intervention strategies to communicate suggested solutions to problems presented by clients (Vontress, 1991). Indirect intervention refers to counselors working through one person to assist another. It also refers to indirectness in terms of the language and techniques counselors use to help their clients. In general, U.S.-born people are apt to be "up front" in communicating with people. However, in counseling culturally different clients, direct communication styles may be considered offensive.

Emic Versus Etic Perspective

In recent years, cross-cultural counselors have recognized the importance of emics and etics. Emics are ideas, behaviors, items, and concepts that are culture-specific. Etics are ideas, behaviors, items, and concepts that are culture-general or universal, as discussed by Triandis (1994). However, the term *etic* is used frequently to describe the prevailing or dominant culture to which a culturally different client must adapt.

Basically, counselors need two pairs of "spectacles" through which to view the experience of their culturally different clients: an "emic" pair that allows the counselor to empathize with the client's specific cultural worldview and an "etic" pair that allows the counselor to understand what his or her own cultural worldview is and what demands it makes on those who must adapt to it. The etic spectacles often are the most difficult to acquire, because much of our awareness of our own culture is unconscious and, ironically, more accessible to "outsiders" who have not been immersed in it. The emic spectacles can be gained by learning about the client's culture through outside reading, by visiting the culture, or, at the very least, by asking the client to produce a detailed cultural autobiography (see Table 1).

The most difficult question is which perspective counselors should assume in diagnosing problems that are presented by culturally different clients. That of the client's culture (emic) or that of the dominant or universal culture (etic)? For example, in working with African American clients, should counselors consider the cultural demands and expectations of the community in which clients live (emic) or should they judge African Americans by the European, middle-class values that many professional counselors hold (etic)? Or perhaps there is a third alternative—a universal standard by which the behavior of oppressed peoples can be judged across all cultures (etic)? These are difficult and controversial philosophical questions.

In our view, the cultural perspective that is most reasonable for counselors to take depends on the extent to which clients are able or willing to negotiate the dominant American culture. This is a very practical stance. For example, an emic perspective may be the appropriate view to take with recently arrived refugees who are unfamiliar with American society. Although minimally fluent in English, their way of thinking is still "colored" by their culture of origin until they assimilate to their host culture. In like manner, an etic perspective may be the appropriate view to take with Black graduates of an all-minority high school on their first day on a predominantly White Ivy League campus. Although they may feel uncomfortable in a "White culture," it may seem patronizing to them if the counselor assumes that they do not understand the dominant culture of their university or their situation as minorities. In other words, adaptation in human cultures is a euphemism for conformity. Whether an emic or etic perspective is assumed is often based on the client's ability or willingness to adapt a part of him- or herself to the dominant culture.

Historical Hostility

People are cultural extensions of their forebears (Fischer, 1965; Wade, 1993). Even though much of the past is no longer a conscious part of people's present existence, it continues to impact their relationships with others, especially those whose ancestors were participants in the earlier history. For example, because of slavery, many African Americans harbor unrecognized negative feelings toward European Americans (Vontress & Epp, 1997). In like manner, many Native Americans are unable to forgive and forget the atrocities that were inflicted on their people by European settlers who pushed them off their ancestral lands. The inability of cultural progenies to forgive usually is related to the perception that the people who mistreated their forebears continue to mistreat them (West, 1993). The hostility they feel has been passed down through generations. It therefore may be called *historical hostility*.

The phenomenon can be observed in many parts of the world. In Africa, old ethnic rivalries caused parts of the continent to be drenched with blood and set in motion the exodus of thousands of refugees fleeing the murderous attacks of adversaries whose hatred for them goes back many generations. In Europe, the slaughter and displacement of people in former Yugoslavia is another example of historical hostility being vented against people who are long removed from the events of the past that first triggered the hostility. In the Middle East, old hostilities continue to simmer and threaten to explode at any time. Therapeutic phenomena, such as resistance, transference, and the reluctance of clients to self-disclose, often are manifestations of events that are buried in the cultural histories of counselors and clients.

Holistic Versus Monistic Diagnoses

Societies differ in terms of what people perceive to be problems in life, their causes, and who should be consulted to remedy them (Fischer, 1965). In general, in modern and technologically advanced societies, human problems are categorized into four groups: physical, psychological, social, and spiritual. Each category has its own set of specialists who are trained to deal with individuals' complaints. In the United States, individuals consult physicians for biological problems; counselors, psychologists, and psychiatrists for psychological concerns; social workers and related experts for social difficulties; and ministers, priests, rabbis, and imams for spiritual guidance.

In traditional societies, human beings and their problems in living usually are understood holistically. For example, in West Africa, individuals seek the counsel of a single healer for problems ranging from a broken toe to perceived conflict with a deceased relative (Vontress, 1991). They also consult the healer when they are concerned about the yield of their crops. Mainly animists, they perceive problems in holistic terms: Everything in one's environment is related. To understand problems presented by clients, healers in traditional Africa seek to understand their relationship with nature, other people, themselves, and the spirits they consider important in the conduct of their lives. American counselors who focus exclusively on the psychological dimension of their clients' lives must recognize that in many cultures, the social, physical, and spiritual dimensions of a person's life are just as important as the psychological. Therefore, they are advised to search for ways to explore these dimensions with clients from "holistic" cultures.

Personalism

Personalism is a perspective on life that maintains that the person is the center of intrinsic value (Lavely, 1967). According to this perspective, people are more important than what they do to earn a living or the material things they possess. In general, collectivistic societies in which individuals live interdependently in small communities encourage the development of reciprocal, interpersonal alliances (B. Mounier, 1992). Neighbors inquire daily about the well-being of families and the individuals in them. In contrast to industrialized urban societies, privacy in a collectivistic society is not a cherished value. Individuals are less apt to be split into two personas—one private and the other public. Each person is unique, irreplaceable, and worthy of respect and attention.

As a cultural ingredient, personalism has implications for counseling culturally different clients. First, clients may annoy counselors with personal questions that seem inappropriate. For example, clients may ask counselors if they are married, if they have children, or how old they are. Such questions usually are signs of respect: Clients want to indicate that they value counselors as human beings. Second, personalism has implications for diagnosis. Individuals are considered to be more than a set of traits that can be inventoried and added; each is a dynamic presence that responds to the same environments differently at different times. Viewing clients as a static, sum total of inventoried traits and facts is apt to cause many culturally different clients to resist taking tests and accepting the results as indications of who they are.

Introspection and Self-Disclosure

Introspection and self-disclosure are closely related concepts. Introspection refers to the self looking within to discover and evaluate the content that is housed there. In counseling, it is assumed that the content and insights derived from introspection will be shared with the counselor. The revealing of the self to others so that they may know that self is called *self-disclosure* (Chelune & Associates, 1979). Counselors need to recognize that in many collectivistic societies, people are socialized to submerge the self in the interest of the group. In such cultures, it may be considered impolite or unhealthy to focus on the self. Instead, the person is considered to be a part of the whole. On American college campuses, international students from family-centered societies often write the family name first and their given name last on official documents.

However, some clients may not self-disclose for other reasons. For example, lower-class African American men may resist revealing personal content unless they perceive their audience to be persons of goodwill. Although they are able to introspect, what they discover about themselves may be so painful that they do not want to share it with anyone. Historical hostility can also keep such clients from self-disclosing with a counselor whose ethnicity symbolizes a historical oppressor. In fact, clients have been known to generalize this hostility to African American counselors whom they perceive to identify with European Americans.

Cultural Anxiety

Life is a series of events taking place in different venues populated by people and a variety of natural and human-made objects. In large measure, socialization of the young in any culture is designed to teach individuals to manage different problems, situations, and expectations as they move through the life span. Because parts of the world differ in terms of climate, soil, terrain, and food, it is understandable that cultural groups develop a variety of patterns of behavior that are required for survival. Their survival skills put them in good stead as long as they remain in their native cultures; however, when they travel to strange lands, they are likely to experience uneasiness because of their unfamiliarity with expected behaviors and roles in the host culture.

In coming to the United States, many individuals from collectivistic societies that are characterized by interdependence among family members are overwhelmed by anxiety. Back home, relatives validate their personality and status in the family and community. People know where to go, what to do, and who to see when they need information, diversion, support, and objects destined to enhance the quality of life. In living abroad, these same individuals may lose the sense of community that is basic to well-being. Being alone in a foreign country for the first time, sojourners often are obliged to make a multitude of unaccustomed daily decisions by themselves, use public transportation, eat strange food, and communicate in a strange language. Although international university students may come from upper-class families, on American campuses, they are just "foreign students," who in fact may be treated as simpletons simply because their ability to use English is less than perfect. Therefore, their anxiety is understandable. It is generated by the strangeness of the host culture. It may be referred to as *cultural anxiety.*

The symptoms of cultural anxiety often are misdiagnosed because they are reported as somatic in persons from nonpsychological cultures. That is, individuals often complain of headaches, eye strain, constipation, inability to sleep, and other physical problems. Although living far away from their family members, these individuals usually communicate with family members by telephone. Counselors who intervene to help these individuals adjust to American culture should ask them about the advice they receive from their parents and other significant adults back home, whom their culture recognizes as the repository of appropriate advice. Such inquiries can enhance the rapport with clients and contribute to the effectiveness of therapeutic interventions with them.

Cultural anxiety approximates the *DSM–IV* (APA, 1994) diagnostic category of separation anxiety (309.21). It also resembles the homesickness that many American college students experience. However, it is a much more intense feeling for individuals residing in a totally new culture in which most of the cues and responses acquired during socialization back home serve little purpose. To some degree, racial and ethnic minority group members who are citizens of the United States experience cultural anxiety when they move from the comfort and support of their communities to mainstream cultural environments. Those who have been socialized in integrated settings before going away to college usually fit in well on most campuses.

IMPLICATIONS FOR COUNSELING

It is antitherapeutic to stereotype clients who appear to represent national, cultural, or racial groups. People with ancestral roots in Europe, Asia, Africa, the Middle East, the Americas, and other parts of the world defy the simple classifications that their superficial racial characteristics would indicate. Their forebears, in adjusting to the natural and social requirements for living, all evolved behavioral differences so as to adapt to their region of the continent, but many of these differences can be lost to subsequent generations who are socialized differently. Differences in socioeconomic status, religious beliefs, and educational attainment further confound one's ability to stereotype an ethnic group member.

American racial and cultural minorities also elude precise definition. For example, wealthy Hispanics, regardless of their country of origin, are different from Hispanics from rural villages in Central and South America. Those who are of the third and fourth generations should not be compared with people who are recent immigrants. In the case of American Indians, it is unreasonable to compare similar individuals from different tribes or those who live in cities with people who still reside on reservations. In counseling Asian Americans, it is important to recognize that individuals of Japanese, Chinese, Vietnamese, and Indian descent are apt to be as different from each other as they are from Anglo clients. Although African Americans have dark skin pigmentation, that is often where the similarity ends. There are cultural differences resulting from educational and economic advantages that set upper-, middle-, and lower-class African Americans apart.

Perhaps more important are differences in terms of African Americans' perception of themselves vis-a-vis White Americans. Four rough categories may be observed. First, there are *monoculturally White* African Americans who may be offended if they are reacted to as other than "just an American." Second, some individuals appear *equicultural*, in that they are equally comfortable around White and Black people. Third, there are *biculturals*, who appear to prefer one racial group over the other but who can function between both. Finally, for various reasons, many Black people seemingly reject association with White people whenever possible and may identify with an African culture that is more unfamiliar than the Anglo culture. These individuals can be referred to as *monoculturally Black*. Note that these categories are not just limited to African Americans but can be applied to all minority groups who must survive in the midst of the dominant European American racial group. There are clearly monocultural Asians, bicultural Arabs, and equicultural Latinos who have assumed these adaptive strategies as minorities in the United States.

What is important to appreciate is that individually expressed cultural differences, not generalizable group differences, risk affecting all aspects of counseling, including (a) the relationship, (b) the diagnosis, and (c) the intervention.

The Relationship

Even though it is untenable to generalize about group similarities and differences as they relate to psychotherapeutic relationships, it is useful to recognize that some clients in all cultural groups respond to counseling differently because of their socialization. For many clients, the idea of introspecting and self-disclosing is cause for high anxiety. For others, historical hostility or prejudice toward the counselor's cultural or racial group may impede the establishment of effective rapport. For numerous reasons, other clients from countless backgrounds may expect a friendly, relaxed, and personal relationship with their helpers, an expectation that might be threatening to counselors who perceive helping as a scientific enterprise demanding a prescribed social distance between interactants. Potential clients present too many perceptions and expectations of helpers to forewarn counselors of each possible cultural pitfall. Instead of relying blindly on therapeutic relationship prescriptions, therapists should realize that the therapeutic relationship, as modeled in Western counseling textbooks, is imbued with cultural assumptions that may need to be altered creatively to serve the culturally different client.

The Diagnosis

There are several things to keep in mind when diagnosing clients who are external to the mainstream culture. First, ascertain whether assessment tools and procedures that are used normally with dominant group clients are appropriate for culturally different counterparts. Second, decide whether to diagnose from an emic or etic perspective, or both. That is, should the yardstick for "normal" be based on the expectations of the individual's immediate cultural group (emic) or those of the community at large, extending beyond the client's racial or cultural neighborhood (etic)? In most cases, people can assume multiple cultural worldviews in a single day, but one usually predominates as the most comfortable. Therefore, both the emic and the etic perspectives may need to be considered at the same time, although the client may assume one worldview most of the time. Even so, the focus of therapy always depends on the nature of the presenting problem and the "cultural spectacles" through which the client is viewing the problem. Third, determine whether a purely psychological assessment is sufficient or whether the diagnosis should be based on social, physical, and spiritual considerations as well. Each client must be viewed individually, not in stereotypical terms.

Intervention

Historically, counseling in the United States has placed considerable responsibility on clients to help themselves. Counselors' imposition of their own values and expectations on clients has been discouraged. Counselors are taught not to "think for" clients but to help them think for themselves. However, expecting help seekers to solve their problems is not normal for people from collectivist cultures in which authority figures usually influence rather directly the lives of others. Therefore, on their arrival in this country, it is understandable that individuals would anticipate the type of intervention to which they have become accustomed. Further, culturally different people may be more comfortable talking to counselors if they can bring other family members or friends with them to the consultation. Counselors are advised to determine during the first interview what clients expect from them in terms of the outcome and style of intervention. Do they prefer to (a) work things out for themselves with a minimum of assistance from the counselor, (b) work cooperatively with the counselor, or (c) be authoritatively directed by the counselor in the search for a solution to the presenting problem?

SUMMARY

For over 30 years, psychotherapeutic professionals have demonstrated continued interest in the impact of culture on the process and product of counseling. Dictating the behavior of all human beings, culture consists of five interacting influences—the universal, ecological, national, regional, and racio-ethnic—all of which contribute to the personality of every human being. As people move from one cultural venue to another, they face adaptation challenges. In trying to help cultural outsiders, counselors are also faced with a series of potential obstacles that should be considered in their work. In this chapter, these have been discussed under the following subheadings:

- acculturation,
- autoplasty versus alloplasty,
- collectivism versus individualism,
- cultural intuition,
- direct versus indirect intervention,
- emic versus etic perspective,
- historical hostility,
- holistic versus monistic diagnoses,
- personalism,
- introspection and self-disclosure, and
- cultural anxiety.

Finally, some specific recommendations are presented to help counselors relate to, diagnose, and intervene effectively on behalf of culturally different clients.

DISCUSSION QUESTIONS

1. What is your definition of culture? How does it impact counseling?
2. Is the "groups approach" useful in cross-cultural counseling?
3. Define the American culture. How does it determine your behavior?
4. Have you ever traveled abroad? How did you feel in a strange culture?
5. How would you go about establishing rapport with a culturally different client?
6. How does your culture determine your personality?
7. What are some aspects of the American culture that may affect foreigners in a negative way?
8. If American-made tests are inappropriate to use as diagnostic tools with culturally different clients, how, then, will you diagnose their problems?
9. What are some things that you can do to grow as a cross-cultural counselor?
10. Would you feel comfortable consulting a racially or culturally different counselor for help with your own problems?

CHAPTER TWO

An Existential Foundation for Cross-Cultural Counseling

Since the beginning of recorded history, people have sought to understand the human condition. How did they get here? What is the purpose of life? Where do they go after death? How do they live a virtuous life? What responsibility do they have for themselves and their fellow human beings? Through the ages, philosophers have addressed these and other concerns that continue to trouble humans. In ancient Greece, Socrates, in considering some of these questions, counseled troubled souls to know themselves in order to cope with their existence. The Stoics of the same historical period advised people to master their emotions through the power of logical reasoning.

In 19th- and 20th-century Europe, the search to understand the human condition came to be known as *existentialism*. Søren Kierkegaard (1813–1855), Martin Buber (1878–1965), Gabriel Marcel (1889–1973), Martin Heidegger (1884–1976), and Jean-Paul Sartre (1906–1980) are among the philosophers who wrote about the grim aspects of the human condition that are seldom addressed directly. In due course, these and other writers were classified as existentialists, even though they often held disparate views regarding the human journey through life (E. Mounier, 1947). The reason for the dissimilarity is that existentialism is an attitude and an approach to understanding human beings rather than a specific philosophical school or theory, as May (1967) pointed out. It was out of the European view of the human condition that Boss's (1963) *Daseinsanalysis* (existential analysis), Frankl's (1967) logotherapy (therapy through meaning), and other existential approaches to counseling and psychotherapy emerged.

The existential approach to counseling may be the most applicable to the culturally different. It is grounded in the universal characteristics of human beings, is comprehensive in outlook, and shares core beliefs with the world's major cultures and religions rather than reflects the provincial theory of a given person, time, or place. Indeed, the existential approach is not culturally neutral: There are certainly the biases of its upper-class, European proponents disguised within its ideas. However, of all the counseling theories available, it comes the closest to describing the universal human experiences of love, courage, suffering, anxiety, and death that transcend the boundaries dividing cultures. Thus, the existential approach, although not a perfect foundation for cross-cultural counseling, may be the best available.

THE UNIVERSALITY OF LIFE ACROSS CULTURES

Whatever our culture, race, or station in life, we all must acknowledge the transitory nature of our existence and imbue our brief lives with meaning. Existential counseling's aim is to help clients courageously face life's brevity and its inherent meaninglessness—the twin dilemmas of existence that unsettle our tranquility and lie at the epicenter of life's critical issues (Yalom, 1980). As clients often strain to articulate, Sartre's (1972) character from *The Flies*, Roequentin, poignantly expressed the anguish of not knowing his reason for being, as he saw his life as incidental to the unfolding world around him: "I was in the way," he bemoaned (p. 173). Like Roequentin, clients feel caught in the shuffle of a frenetic existence with no "compass" to guide them.

Existential counseling is probably the most useful approach to helping clients of all cultures find meaning and harmony in their lives, because it focuses on the sober issues each of us must inevitably face: love, anxiety, suffering, and death. However, existential counseling is not a process of morbid rumination or a philosophy of resignation—as it is often misconstrued. Rather, it ultimately seeks to develop and enhance our relationships with ourselves, others, nature, and our spirituality. It hopes to accomplish these objectives through a Socratic dialogue between counselor and client, based in equality, where both participants share their life experiences and acquired wisdom, comfort and challenge each other, and devise a plan for better living. The focus is primarily on the client, but the existential perspective honestly recognizes that the counseling relationship also benefits the counselor.

The philosophical principles cherished by existential counselors are very similar to those espoused by philosophers through the centuries, the world's major cultures and religions, and even other theories of counseling. Yet existential counseling is largely credited to European thinking, linked to names such as Camus, Sartre, Binswanger, Kierke–gaard, and Jaspers. American scholars, such as Frankl, May, and Yalom, have popularized this outlook as well as elaborated on its principles. Even Carl Rogers (1980/1995), who is often assigned to his own philosophical school, unknowingly may have promoted existentialism's tenets, as he confessed in later life: "At the urging of my students, I became acquainted with Martin Buber (first in his writing and then personally) and with Søren Kierkegaard. I felt greatly supported in my new approach, which I found to my surprise was a home-grown brand of existential philosophy" (p. 39).

We believe that other counselors already follow existentialism either unknowingly or through practicing counseling theories, such as Gestalt, Adlerian, or reality therapy, whose tenets were grounded in existentialism but whose names do not reflect this foundation. In fact, it is our contention that existentialism is not simply a provincial European philosophy, but its core beliefs are embedded in the fabric of every culture and philosophical system, meriting their characterization as universal.

UNIVERSAL VALUES AND EXPERIENCES

Although human cultures across the world possess starkly different characteristics, we can think of them as sharing the same basic philosophical building blocks. Many of the world's philosophies have concerned themselves traditionally with how people interact with and exist in the physical world, how they interact with others, and what values and beliefs they ought to adopt. Binswanger (1963) proposed that human beings exist in three distinguishable but inseparable worlds, which he coined in his native German (with English equivalent) as the *Umwelt* (physical world), *Mitwelt* (public world), and *Eigenwelt* (private world). To understand human beings fully, he thought that counselors should examine their client's functioning in each of these three worlds. Later expounding on Binswanger's ideas, van Deurzen-Smith (1988) argued that the former did not pay sufficient attention to the "spiritual world," or the world of values. She proposed that this fourth world be a central focus in the later stages of counseling, and she named it the *Uberwelt* or, literally, the "overworld."

The basic tenets of existential thought are illuminated best through discussion of the four worlds in which Binswanger (1962) and van Deurzen-Smith (1988) believed human beings exist. Although this may be a simplistic approach to describing the complexity of human life, this model offers a useful system for conceptualizing human existence. The essential message of existential philosophy is that when one of these worlds is neglected, it will come into focus and lead to an imbalance in one's life. We use examples from cultures around the world to show the universality of this model.

Umwelt (Physical World)

The *Umwelt* is the support system for everything that lives. It consists of the air, water, soil, sun, vegetation, animals, mountains, valleys, and everything in the universe on which humans depend for survival. Human existence is defined by the fact that people are a part of nature. They are subject to its physical laws just like all other creatures (Funk, 1982). According to Staniforth (1964), each part of the universe may be the reflection of a single living organism that is united by a common energy. The symbiotic coexistence of humans and their natural environment may be expressed more passionately by Eastern philosophers than by their Western counterparts, with the notable exception of Henry David Thoreau, who left an urban existence for the rustic pleasures of his Walden Pond. Pachuta (1989), a Chinese physician, recommended that humankind destroy all artificial barriers between itself and nature to maximize health and well-being. In many parts of Africa, people believe that they, like plant and animal life, are intimately connected to the natural world and would perish if this relationship were severed (Vontress, 1991). In Eastern and Western thought, the belief can be found that humans are at their best when they are in harmony with nature.

The biological self, composed of common molecules of water and carbon, is the living embodiment of nature in us. Health, sickness, and aging are universal concerns, although only Western cultures seem to regard advancing age negatively and to worship youth unduly. Yet there is no physical reality that is more universally understood and feared than death. Death is truly a universal, physical experience and a dark specter for all humanity. Although it is recognized globally as a given of human existence, its finality and bleakness have not been accepted at face value by all. Throughout many philosophies, death has been reframed as a sharp passage to another existence. One will find benevolent interpretations of death as early as the Greek philosophers, ancient Chinese Taoists, Islamic theologians, and African animists. These writings each have the intensity of existential thought as they attempt to confront the bitter reality of the human condition.

A few examples will illustrate the solemnity of this early existential thought. Epicurus (c. 271 BC/1994) soberly expounded on how to die well through living an active and pleasing life. Mohammed, in translating the writings of Allah, noticed how the metaphor of death runs though all human endeavors. He remarked, "We can interpret death and living in even more senses than day and night: death physical, intellectual, emotional, and spiritual" (Ali, 1983, p. 129). The African animist Ranginya reflected on the meaning of death and came to excuse it as "nature's way of easing the congestion in the universe" (Oseghare, 1992, p. 95). Lao Tsu (1972), the originator of Taoism, did not harp on death by itself but saw it as one pole of the Tao, or creative force of nature, whose wisdom in creating, destroying, and recreating he encouraged his followers to humbly respect.

Death is the conclusion of our physical existence. Before our final exit from the physical world, we lead a life that is supported and constricted by the givens of the physical environment. Existentialists often say that we are "thrown" into existence like clay heaped on its sculpting wheel, awaiting shaping by the whimsical and random forces of our environment. Our bodies make intimate contact with this world while our senses interpret it with unique perceptions. We attempt to cope with the world's obstacles by increasing our fitness and agility, and we often preserve its poignant beauty through our arts. It may be a bold leap of inclusion to call physical fitness and art timeless existential concerns, but their persistence since ancient times makes one wonder whether these epitomize, at a nonintellectual level, the existential quest to appreciate, master, and connect one's self spiritually with the physical world.

Mitwelt (Public World)

Even though individuals are separate, unique, and self-contained, they cannot exist without others. The infant cannot survive without the help of its parents, and a small human group such as the family needs to be cohesive to defend itself against other groups, animals, and forces of nature. Quite apart from the advantages that accrue from society, individuals normally delight in each other's company. Contact with human beings is the stimulus that elicits emotional and visceral reactions (Dewey, 1959). The reactions of others in the family, school, community, and other collectivities to which people belong play a significant role in defining their individual and collective identities (Watts, 1996). Both sexuality and language imply that individuals are incomplete by themselves (Macquarrie, 1972/1977). Although the human body contains several complete systems (nervous, alimentary, respiratory, etc.), it has only half of a reproductive system and is thus incomplete without another person of the opposite sex. Language evolved to enable individuals to communicate their personal thoughts to others. They need to transmit to one another not only their ideas but also their hopes, fears, and aspirations that impact the whole group (Donceel, 1961). As Plato pointed out long ago, the individual is related to the community as the cell is related to the body: One cannot exist without the other (Brett, 1963).

It would seem that cultures emerge from an inherent need for humans to avoid isolation and loneliness. We are born into a family group, are socialized in different groups throughout life, and often spend our lives trying to find the group in which we fit most comfortably. However much some people may deny the necessity of significant contact with others, we are group creatures by design. This close proximity to others, which forms a significant part of our daily existence, beckons us to ponder thoughtfully how we may improve these interactions, lest they become mechanical and empty. This quest to improve human relationships is age-old and universal.

Ancient philosophies and traditions have revolved around the quest for the ideal principles of human behavior. Plato (Hamilton & Huntington, 1987) believed that a society functions best when its citizens are ranked by class. His model of social life was inherently elitist, which is antithetical to the egalitarianism of most existential thought. However, his writings contain the honesty about the human condition that existentialism admires. The ancient Muslim scholars carefully circumscribed every aspect of social life through the *Shar'ia*, or legal code, whose tenets were aimed to promote social harmony, given the complexity of human beings (Bielefeldt, 1995; Sardar, 1993). Traditional African societies orally passed on philosophical principles on human conduct that emphasized the existential concept of responsibility while at the same time promoted reasoned discussion that was designed to build solidarity and consensus.

Philosophical debate regarding human conduct continues into the present, especially because the public world is the most powerful in its influence on psychological adjustment and happiness. It is here that we suffer most, as our fellow human beings can both love and hurt us and often do the latter within the context of their proclaimed love. Human beings have a prickly, porcupine quality to them: They can prick us with their sharp quills if we are not cautious (Freud, 1921/1955). As Sartre (1972) wrote in his play *No Exit*, the location of hell is not a fiery furnace in the netherworld; it is "other people" in the here and now (p. 61). It is among our fellow human beings, whose love and respect we desire but cannot always obtain, that we are most vulnerable. This predicament has been a central focus of the existentialists, if formally, and of all humankind in our sober and reflective hours.

Eigenwelt (Private World)

Although *Eigenwelt* is often translated simply as personal identity, it connotes much more than that. The human body consists of thousands of intricate mechanisms working in harmony. Set in motion even before birth, many of them monitor the human organism's internal and external environments throughout life. The monitoring system is composed not only of sensors that permit humans to see, hear, taste, smell, and feel but also of countless reflexes that automatically respond protectively when the organism or parts of it are threatened. In addition to the inherent tendency to protect themselves from physical assault, humans tend to guard against psychological harm. In interpersonal relationships, when psychologically assaulted by others, they generally are quick to counter with "defense mechanisms" in order not to feel hurt.

Human feelings, whether physical or psychological, register in the brain of a single individual and therefore are specific to that experiencing organism. No matter how intimate people are with others, it is impossible for them to share their deepest and most private thoughts and feelings (Lindenauer, 1970): They are individual products of uniquely different environments (Fromm, 1976), and their distinct constitutions cause them to experience the same milieu in a different way. Even members of the same family are necessarily different and existentially alone in the world. They have no recourse but to come to terms with the solitariness of their own existence (Frankl, 1967). This requirement of life causes many people a great deal of uneasiness.

The *Eigenwelt* implies uniqueness and separateness. Individually, people have their lives ahead of them. They are faced with their freedom. This means that they are obliged to make decisions about their lives, to discover who they are, to search for meaning, and to take decisive action based on what they know about themselves. No matter what others think or wish, in the final analysis, each person must face life and death alone. This aloneness is a source of *existential anxiety*—a chronic feeling of nervousness—that is an intrinsic part of the human condition (Bugental, 1976).

By ourselves, we construct a personal wisdom for living, which sometimes occurs at unexpected moments of insight. Van Deurzen-Smith (1988) guided her clients toward introspection to help them realize "a fuller grasp of [their] experience and to become able to embrace the paradoxes that [they] may [have] previously tried to side-step or evade" (p. 87). When we are persuaded to travel into the abyss of our psyche, we are forced to look at both our good and our bad qualities, even our potential for evil. The experience can be painful, but transcendental, as we surpass the understanding of reality in black-and-white dichotomies.

All of us are good and bad, innocent and guilty, beautiful and ugly. Deep reflection leaves us humbled through perceiving the world as many hues of gray.

The premium existentialists place on introspection is doubly held by Eastern cultures. According to the ancient Taoists and Buddhists, individuals lose their psychological identity when they become blown like a reed with each passing fad and interest of the masses. They become alienated from their "original nature"—the inborn voice of their conscience that tells what is best for them. To return to their "original nature," Taoists and Buddhists believe that one must heed this inner voice and know one's self through meditation and self-reflection. The ancient Chinese text the *Tao Te Ching* expressed this idea eloquently, "He who knows others is wise; he who knows himself is enlightened" (Lao Tsu, 1972, p. 117). Like the Western injunction, "Be true to yourself," the Eastern philosophies believe that "sagehood" evolves from abiding by one's conscience without the display of arrogance or self-importance. In both East and West, there is no royal path to living, only the path that suits one's self.

Uberwelt (Spiritual World)

The *Umwelt*, *Mitwelt*, and *Eigenwelt* were coined by the Swiss psychiatrist Ludwig Binswanger (1962). Emmy van Deurzen-Smith (1988), a British psychologist, felt that Binswanger had been remiss in not including in his description of existence what is to her the most important environment, the spiritual world, or *Uberwelt*. Therefore, she added it to complete Binswanger's model. According to her, human existence cannot be explained completely. People continue to search for an understanding of themselves and the mysteries of the universe. Unable to know the "unknowable," they need to relate to forces that are greater than themselves. They require the respect, direction, love, and affection of parents, teachers, elders, departed loved ones, and spiritual entities. The spirit world connects individuals to people who, although "come and gone," still reside in them through memory, genetic contributions, and cultural indoctrination. In many cultures, departed ancestors are considered invisible and valuable members of the family. Their wisdom sustains and directs the lives of the living (Masolo, 1994).

Spirituality usually is thought of as a component of religion, not psychotherapy. However, existential counselors believe that a holistic view of the client must include the spiritual dimension. In both modern and primitive societies, religious beliefs greatly influence one's interpersonal relationships and perspective by imposing a meaningful system on daily living. Ironically, Western psychotherapists, wishing to make their discipline "scientific" and still paying homage to the atheism of their patriarch, Sigmund Freud, eschew the exploration of their clients' religious beliefs. The consequence of this practice is that it imposes a psycho-therapeutic system of *moral relativism* on the client, which challenges his or her religious system of meaning. Although in certain instances, loosening the rigidity of beliefs can be liberating, a life without absolute moral principles can be ambiguous and anxiety provoking, as all moral choices become equivalent.

Since the earliest of times, religions have attempted to fill a moral vacuum in a universe with no prescribed set of values. Christianity, Judaism, and Islam, among the most concrete in their tenets, offer their sacred texts, the *Bible*, the *Torah*, and the *Qu'ran*, as handbooks for coping in each of the existential worlds (Netton, 1992). By contrast, primitive Africans, lacking a codified text, believed that an invisible universe of spirits helps the living navigate life's decisions (Okolo, 1992). Similar to the Africans, if less apt to personify the spirit world, the ancient Chinese believed that there is a mysterious spiritual force, the Tao, within all creation that will lead us to truth—if we pay attention to it.

Across the world's religions, both primitive and modern, we dis-cover the common belief that there is a spiritual entity beyond our perception in which resides the meaning of our universe and our indi-vidual existences. Whether this force is supernatural or scientifically ex-plainable, most human beings demonstrate a need to understand this aspect of reality. Existential counseling respects this need, whose ex-pression usually is restricted to religious activity. For within existential-ism, the spiritual is not otherworldly; it is a constant and legitimate concern, which influences mental health in the here and now, especially in the face of life's wonders and tragedies.

THE BALANCING OF THE FOUR WORLDS

In recognizing the four worlds of human existence, we outline the ex-pansive outlook of existential counseling. The existential counselor is a macroscopic and holistic thinker who sees beyond specific maladaptive behaviors to find the imbalances among the client's four worlds that produce and maintain his or her emotional disturbances. Like the exis-tentialists, Huff (1993) noted that Islamic scholars were sensitive to the interrelationship of spiritual and public life in which the former checks the moral transgressions of the latter. African traditional healers were cognizant of the entwinement of the spiritual and public worlds and believed that mental health derives from "living in harmony with one's fellow humans . . . the ancestors, spirits, and creator in the invisible realm" (Diallo & Hall, 1989, p. 80). In the Islamic and African worldviews, if one's spiritual world is misaligned, it will have an impact on the public world and vice versa.

Buddhism may entwine the spiritual and physical worlds so as to make them indistinguishable. In Buddhism, the spirit of the Buddha is in the physical world itself, even pervading inanimate objects, such as a stone or a rose. As Shaku (1987) remarked,

> [The] Buddhist God is not above us, nor below us, but right in the midst of us; and if we want to see him face to face, we are able to find him in the lilies of the field, in the fowls in the air, in the murmuring mountain streams; we can trace his footsteps in the sea, we can follow him as he rides upon the storm; we can meet him in the bush; indeed, wheresoever we may turn, we are sure to be greeted by the smiling countenance of the author of this universe. (p. 48)

In religious iconography, the omnipresent statue of the Buddha symbolically represents the coexistence and integration of the spiritual nature of the Buddha in the ordinary material of stone. This is an important metaphor, because it reminds Buddhists that spirit and matter are not separate entities; they are two poles of all reality, the inseparable yin and yang.

These are just a few examples pointing to a universal belief in the interaction of the existential worlds. Viewed as an organic whole, the different worlds are like the developing petals of a flower. For a young sapling to bloom fully, each petal must grow and integrate into the single entity of the flower. As van Deurzen-Smith (1988) applied this notion to counseling, "It is not possible to work exclusively in one [existential] sphere and neglect all the other aspects. Though clients frequently emphasize their struggle in one particular dimension, it is usually essential to ensure that difficulties in living get worked through on all four dimensions" (p. 88).

Existential counseling recognizes that life is an intricate balancing act. The physical, public, private, and spiritual worlds each require attention or their neglect will form a hungry vacuum that cries out for emotional nourishment. Van Deurzen-Smith (1988) recommended that an individual has to be able to harmonize successfully the various existential worlds to form a meaningful and balanced lifestyle. Because of differing life circumstances, certain individuals will find this task easier than others because the random meeting of sperm and ovum ensures great variations in the intellectual, emotional, and material endowments we come into the world with. We arrive on different planes, and fate deals us different life spans in which to unfold our existential possibilities. Some people will experience long and harmonious lives; others will face brief and nasty struggles ending in an unfair death. The goal of the existential counselor is to help clients face whatever existence fate bequeaths them with courage, hope, and a striving to find meaning in life's suffering.

However unequal our existence in the four worlds is, each of us inevitably moves toward death, where all humans find their ultimate equality. We cannot stop time: The sifting of the hourglass's grains is the most rigid and unmerciful aspect of living. Yet this irrevocable movement enriches life and reminds us of the short chronological boundaries to our existence. Yalom (1980) believed that the striving to transcend death is the creative force behind our monuments, inventions, books, artistic creations, and the like—all that is conceived to gain individual immortality through the realm of ideas or materials. Some, however, become stuck in the past so as to distract themselves from their movement toward death, with the sad by-product that this retrospective existence hampers their creativity and enjoyment of the present. It is easy to blame the past for life's unhappiness; it is harder to find the courage to move forward and make the best use of the time remaining within the four worlds of existence.

THE BUILDING BLOCKS OF AN EXISTENTIAL RELATIONSHIP

Throughout the history of professional counseling in the United States, authorities have devoted more attention to the helping relationship than to any other aspect of the therapeutic enterprise. Some writers and theorists have made the relationship the essence of counseling itself. The emphasis on the relationship has highlighted numerous problems in cross-cultural counseling because, in the United States, clients from "lower status" racial, ethnic, socioeconomic, and national backgrounds often are unaccustomed to relating to their "higher status" counselors as equals. They often feel uncomfortable in a cross-cultural counseling relationship because they feel that they are being judged by someone who is affluent, more educated, and perhaps unfamiliar with the moral compromises and complexities of a less privileged existence.

In a few instances, culturally different clients may desire an unequal relationship with their counselor, owing to their culture's belief that professionals are wiser and able to provide accurate advice. Although professionals do possess a wellspring of useful information, and clients may accord them the deference of a respected elder, or even a "guru," it is important for the counselor, irrespective of the client's attribution, to maintain a posture of "philosophical equality" with the client. Culturally different clients may wish to defer to the opinions of their counselor, but it is detrimental to the human spirit when the counselor does all of the thinking for the client. Achieving some degree of "individuation"—to borrow a term from Jungian psychology—in personality may be a universal developmental task, which is revisited at each of life's stages as choices must be made regarding the person we are to become. It should be no different in the counseling suite.

The existential counseling relationship strives to approach what Buber (1970) called the *I–Thou rapport*: a deep fellowship stressing honest sharing and mutual regard. It would not be an overstatement to characterize this relationship as one that generates a platonic exchange of love, akin to what the Greeks called *agape love*, but which Boss (1963) chose to label "psychotherapeutic eros," without intending to imply the romantic element that the word *eros* would suggest. Although underemphasized in other counseling theories, existential counseling sees the sharing and generation of loving feelings as a powerful therapeutic force that is essential to all significant relationships, not simply the therapeutic. Satir (1988) expressed love's value most powerfully: "Without loving and being loved, the human soul and spirit curdle and die" (p. 141).

The existential counseling relationship is a natural one, devoid of psychological distancing. The counselor is not a blank slate awaiting projection in the Freudian schema. In fact, the therapist's interpretation of transference is peripheral to this encounter because existential counseling assumes that seeking parental relationships or friendships with a therapist is a natural striving, disguising the very human desire for connection, bonding, and love. To be effective facilitators of such authentic relationships, therapists must be truly willing to help others as a "calling." They must be at peace with themselves as imperfect and mortal human beings who can draw honestly on their own experiences and frailties and be unafraid to share these with their clients.

The existential counseling relationship is undergirded by four philosophical concepts that contribute to the equality between counselor and client: (a) death, (b) empathy, (c) psychotherapeutic eros, and (d) I–Thou rapport. They are interrelated in that they highlight the sameness of human beings. Their focus is on similarities that bind people together, not differences that set them apart.

Death

Everything that lives must die. The awareness of this simple fact should help counselors to keep things in proper perspective as they relate to their clients. May (1967) admonished that the inevitable sweep of the "Grim Reaper" for all who live is the ultimate source of human humility. His coming for humanity puts everybody in the same boat, regardless of their cultural or racial background. Counselors' awareness of death is the strongest bond of mutuality they have with their clients.

Unfortunately, people who deny the reality of death often are the same ones who deny the sameness of human beings. Although others die, the possibility of their own death is remote in their minds.

Empathy

The concept of empathy claims considerable attention in classrooms of counselors-in-training: They often are warned about the dangers of becoming emotionally involved with clients. Actually, empathy came into English as a translation of the German word *Einfühlung*, which means "one feeling" (Anikeeff, 1951). Ochanine (1938) pointed out that this common bond that humans have for one another is natural. Jaynes (1976) indicated that it is certainly a part of human consciousness to "see" into the consciousness of others, to feel their hurt and their sorrows. Empathy is the feeling of unity and emotional involvement with and resemblance to fellow human beings, such that one has the desire to live in harmony with them (Angeles, 1981). In the existential counseling relationship, differences based on class, race, nationality, culture, possessions, education, intelligence, taste, and other grounds that have caused people to discriminate against others are pushed into the background. Counselors relate to clients as fellow humans just like themselves.

Psychotherapeutic Eros

To specify the closeness that should exist between the counselor and client, Boss (1963) used the concept of psychotherapeutic eros to communicate a love relationship. He distinguished this love, however, from the love of parents for their children, love between two friends, love between a priest and his flock, and love that exists between the sexes. Rather, it is a spontaneous unselfishness, respectfulness, and reverence for the client's existence and uniqueness. Existential counselors love their fellow human beings as they love themselves. They are personalistic in the counseling relationship. That is, they consider the person to be more important than anything else in life, including role status, class, money, or attractiveness. They do not distance themselves professionally from their clients. According to Gross (1978), psychotherapeutic closeness increases the likelihood of successful counseling. In other words, it is important that clients feel that their counselors appreciate them deeply as fellow human beings.

I–Thou Rapport

Buber (1964) succinctly described the nature of the existential encounter. He discussed three modes of relating to others: (a) I–It, in which the individual relates to the other as if the latter were an object, thing, or instrument; (b) I–You, in which the person relates to the other respectfully but with a distant formality; and (c) I–Thou, in which one life opens to another, such that there can be significant human sharing. The I–Thou relationship is one in which there is direct, mutual, present interaction rather than possession. Counselors are world citizens who commit themselves to helping their fellow human beings through life. They do not allow cultural, national, or racial ideologies or conflicts to loom large in their encounters, for to do so is to encourage cultural defensiveness on the part of their clients.

In sum, the existential counseling relationship is a natural and caring one. Although ironic in a profession that prides itself on its caring and humanism, Vontress noted how radical the notion of a caring therapeutic relationship is to the professional counseling community:

> Over the years, my colleagues have come to see me as an iconoclast because I reject the notions of therapeutic objectivity and professional distance and declare them to be anti-therapeutic. Instead, I espouse Medard Boss' (1963) ideal of therapeutic eros. I believe that we must genuinely care about our clients as fellow human beings. I have come to despise the professional games and bureaucracy that we dispense as our means of helping others. No wonder clients often come to hate counseling centers; these organizations often reflect the insensitivity of the client's world instead of offering a place of refuge and healing. (Epp, 1998, p. 12)

Being an existential counselor would seem to mean having the courage to be a caring human being in an insensitive world.

DIAGNOSIS

In counseling, diagnosis is the process of identifying the client's issue or illness along with its etiology and prognosis (Gough, 1971). It is the most important aspect of counseling because a problem needs to be defined before it can be solved. Because existential counselors are most concerned with the human predicament, they mainly are interested in finding out how each client is coping with or handling existence. To do this, they may use common existential themes, such as diagnostic foci or human dimensions, to explore the client's mode of existence, which usually determine the kind and degree of problems clients encounter in living. Some of these concepts are (a) self-knowledge, (b) authenticity, (c) becoming, (d) courage, (e) meaning, (f) harmony, (g) death, and (h) responsibility.

However, in using such a diagnostic procedure, therapeutic professionals need to recognize that life consists of opposites and contradictions (Lowen, 1980). That is to say, to understand and appreciate the negative, it is imperative to experience the positive (Ricken, 1991). To know what it is "to be" assumes knowledge of what it is "not to be" (Watts, 1996). Human beings are a complex mixture of opposites: sanity and neurosis, rationality and irrationality, good and evil, aggression and compassion, and so on. As a result of life circumstances, upbringing, and, perhaps, biology, some individuals have learned to keep these polarities tilted in the positive direction. But it is a naive conviction that some people live without pathology or evil—all people live by managing their negative polarities so that they do not hurt themselves or others. In diagnosing presenting problems and personalities of their clients, counselors should resist temptations to classify people and their struggles with the human condition into simple categories of praise and blame or health and sickness. The existential terms defined and discussed below should be viewed as nonjudgmental.

Self-Knowledge

Individuals are unique in their innate qualities or what they make of themselves once they arrive in the world (Frankl, 1967). Their great challenge is to continue to discover the secret forces within themselves as they journey through life (Staniforth, 1964). At each stage of their development, they are equipped to relate to the natural, social, personal, and spiritual forces that impact their lives. However, to benefit from life's growth opportunities, they must know themselves. This imperative suggests that they pay attention to what their particular nature requires of them. Zimmer (1951/1974) pointed out that people possess both strength and wisdom. Unfortunately, these often are hidden in the deepest recesses of their minds. Sometimes, knowledge of self is so remote from personal recognition that clients resist any attempt to expose themselves to themselves. Even so, the search for the authentic self is a worthwhile quest because people who do not know themselves do not know what to do with their existence: They are likely to go through life letting others make choices for them. Those who permit this eventuality are apt to be alienated from themselves and those who direct their future.

Developmentally speaking, human beings who know themselves best are those who disclose themselves easily to others (Jourard, 1964). Their fellow human beings are confidants with whom they are unafraid to reveal their weaknesses and imperfections. Because the demands of life continue to change as people grow through the life span, it is important to recognize that the acquisition of self-knowledge is a never-ending process. Every change, challenge, and transition requires introspection. In fact, self-knowledge today does not guarantee self-knowledge tomorrow, and self-knowledge at home does not guarantee self-knowledge abroad.

Authenticity

Authenticity comes from the Greek word *authentes*, which means "one who acts with authority" or "what is done by one's own hand" (Reese, 1980, p. 41). It is one of the main concepts of existentialism (Wild, 1979). For example, Macquarrie (1972/1977) indicated that existence is authentic to the extent that individuals mold themselves into their own image. Bugental (1965) echoed this notion when he declared that people are authentic to the degree that they live in harmony with themselves and nature. Unfortunately, few people have the courage to live according to their own dictates (Lowen, 1980). Too many of them "become inauthentic" by allowing external influences to define their existence: They adopt roles and put on facades as if to reject their authentic selves.

Inauthenticity has implications for mental health. First of all, hiding the true self from others produces anxiety (Hadas, 1958): There is always the fear that others will discover what is hidden. Second, inauthentic people are apt to be passive, tiptoeing through life, anxious about making waves (Koestenbaum, 1971). Because they are afraid to allow their natural unfolding, they can never actualize their true potential (Fromm, 1976). They are living in *bad faith*, as Sartre (1996) put it, for they continually deceive themselves about their true character. Third, inauthentic people often are unable to relate to others (Macquarrie, 1972/1977). Although they want to make contact with their fellow human beings, they are unable to do so because they feel that they cannot trust them. According to a Chinese saying, "If you cannot trust yourself, you cannot trust anyone else" (Watts, 1995, p. 24). Fourth, inauthentic individuals may never be sure of their own happiness because they need others to authenticate it (Delamarre, 1996). They are unsure of their successes in life because they need positive feedback from others to validate them.

People can be authentic in any society, whether it is individualistic or collectivistic. In individualistic cultures, individuals generally are socialized to elucidate their uniqueness and to individuate themselves from others. Their authenticity is self-centered. Society encourages them to be independent and self-reliant. In collectivistic communities, individuals are less individuated. They derive their personal identities from groups, especially their families and the persons heading them. In writing their names, they place the family name first and the given name last, a practice that reflects their identities. In other words, what it means to be authentic in one culture may be different in another.

Becoming

The idea of becoming or unfolding has a long history. According to Buddhist, Hindu, and other Asian views of nature, no matter what form life takes, it is a series of changes (Puligandla, 1975; Watts, 1995). The Greeks held a similar view. Aristotle indicated that nature is not a thing, but a process (Brett, 1963): Growth is a series of minute increments and the final product is their result. The Stoics, in discussing how nature unfolds, pointed out that a plant grows, blooms, produces seeds, "moves," and changes according to the intentions of its nature (Annas, 1992). In relating this phenomenon to human beings, existentialists point out that people are never fixed or defined once and for all but are always changing as they move into the future (Flam, 1970). Human development is, as Hall and Lindzey (1957) posited, an unfolding of the original undifferentiated tissue that congealed in the womb. The ultimate goal of unfolding is the realization of selfhood. So long as they live, people are forever inventing themselves (Sartre, 1996). They are never finished products.

Becoming is so much a part of human existence that individuals who attempt to resist the flow of nature are apt to encounter difficulties in life. According to Selye (1956), life is largely a process of adapting to the immediate surroundings at any given time. A perennial give-and-take has been going on between living matter and its inanimate environments, between one living being and another, ever since the dawn of life in the prehistoric oceans. The secret of health and happiness lies in a successful adjustment to the ever-changing conditions of life. The penalties for failure in this great process of adaptation are stress, disease, and unhappiness.

Although life is anxiety producing, it requires continuous movement and change until the final destination—death—is reached. Understandably, some individuals become immobilized by this fact of life. They become "stuck," existentially speaking. Unable to continue unfolding as life requires, some individuals appear indecisive, develop phobias, manifest symptoms of depression, or narcotize themselves with drugs to eradicate their fear of becoming. Like the rose, human beings move from seed to a beautiful, if thorny, flower and then wither into the soil, providing nutrients that nourish the next budding seed. Each stage of life has a meaning and integrity of its own that must be lived fully but then mourned and let go of to allow movement to the next stage.

Courage

Courage derives from the Latin word *cor*, which means "heart" (Servan-Schreiber, 1987). The derivation suggests that it is both an emotion and a strength that plays a significant part in determining human behavior, even though its role often is unrecognized. May (1975) posited that courage is the capacity to confront life as it is. The primary confrontation is the recognition and acceptance of the fact that human beings are products of nature. As such, they, like everything else housed in the natural environment, must die. Once this reality is accepted, people are released from the potentially immobilizing fear of death (Koestenbaum, 1971). Knowing that their "days are numbered," they let free their existence. There is no time to waste on trivia. Recognizing their aloneness, they reach out to others, even though there is always the possibility of being rejected or hurt in the attempt to achieve a meaningful and intimate coexistence with fellow travelers (May, 1975).

Courage gives individuals the will and determination to introspect and to accept themselves as they really are (Bedford, 1972). They do not need to adopt roles that are foreign to their nature or to lead inauthentic lives (Lowen, 1980). They realize that people do not get out of the world alive no matter who they are or how they present themselves to others. Everybody is in the same boat, heading for the same destination—death. So why pretend to be "larger than life"? Finally, courage enables people to search for a "higher power." They are not reluctant to admit that there are forces in the universe that are greater than themselves. Therefore, they use their internal strength to connect with these exalting aspects of existence.

In some cultures, individuals are ennobled by the teachings and memories of their ancestors. In others, human lives are fulfilled by the belief in a supreme being. In any case, people need to submit to something or someone who is perceived to be more powerful than themselves to derive courage and protection. However, for many people, it appears easier to reject than to accept personally anything that is "unscientific," no matter how powerful and mysterious the phenomenon may be. Frankl (1967) believed that atheism cannot offer the security and direction of a transcendant being but instead can lead to a host of psychological difficulties as one becomes rudderless in an amoral and godless universe.

Meaning

Meaning in life is a primary concern of existentialists. Funk (1982) declared that human beings seek an object of devotion to satisfy an intrinsic need. Bulka (1979) maintained that the search for meaning is the main motivational force in people. He pointed out that people are spiritual beings whose differentiation from lower life-forms is rooted in the *Uberwelt* (spiritual world), or the uniquely human need to imbue life with meaning.

Frankl (1975) posited that there are several reasons that meaning is important in the lives of individuals. First, according to him, the more people are absorbed by something or someone other than themselves, the more they become themselves. Second, meaning provides a rhythm for human existence (Frankl, 1967). It gives people a reason for the routines of their daily lives. Consistent and uniform patterns of life provide them with a uniformity and predictability that seem basic to mental health (Staniforth, 1964). Third, meaning makes individuals feel that their presence on earth has contributed to the common good of the human community (Puligandla, 1975). Fourth, a reason for being reduces the tendency of people to engage in self-destructive behavior (Lowen, 1969). Imbued with a reason for being, they want to prolong life as long as possible. Fifth, meaning reduces the wear and tear on the human organism. Committed people often are unaware of the efforts of their enterprises. Their strivings produce a spiritual fulfillment, not physical and mental distress (Frankl, 1967). This is not to say that individual strivings eliminate all physical stress. However, meaningful pursuits reduce the time it takes for the body to restore itself after each exertion (Ofman, 1976).

Admittedly, meaning in life is important, but how is it achieved? There are several ways to answer the question. First of all, individuals must find ways to discover what creates meaning in their lives (Servan-Schreiber, 1987). Second, meaning is not a one-shot deal. According to Bulka (1979), it is a composite of all of life's experiences. He maintains that meaning can be a product of almost anything, even suffering. Finally, whatever meaning individuals find in life comes from themselves (Kopp, 1972). People are imbued with meaning in their lives to the extent that they take responsibility for themselves (Koestenbaum, 1971). Each day, they give birth to themselves again. Do they resume yesterday's agenda or do they take another route to achieve their goal in life (Sartre, 1996)? The answer is probably a little of both. Learning from their mistakes, they are able to make corrections each day they live.

Meaning in life has implications for existential diagnosis. When counselors ask clients about meaning in their lives, it is clear that they want to know something about the quality of their inner experiences, as Klinger (1977) pointed out. That is to say that meaning in life is a very subjective and pervasive quality that defines a person's whole existence. A life devoid of meaning is probably a life that can be characterized as despondent and neurotic (Watts, 1995). It is no surprise that Maslow (1971) reported that drug addicts and alcoholics are people who are depressed and basically bored with life. Usually, boredom comes from being unable to find meaning in intimacy with other human beings (Klinger, 1977).

Harmony

The word *harmony* comes from the Greek word *harmos*, which means "a fitting together or joining." It is a combination of parts into an orderly or proportionate whole. The idea has played a modest but continuing role in worldwide philosophy throughout the ages (Reese, 1980). The Greek Epictetus advised people to "go with the flow" if they wished their lives to be tranquil and serene (Edman, 1944/1972). The Stoics, in recognizing the deleterious effects of stress on the human body, advised individuals to "let go" of their worries (Hadas, 1958). A little respite and relaxation restore the mind's energy; unrelieved mental exertion results in dullness and languor. The Romans stressed the importance of *mens sana in corpore sano*—a sound mind in a sound body (Wolff, 1976).

In somewhat the same way, existentialists invite humans to maintain harmony in their lives by establishing and maintaining rapport with the *Umwelt* (natural environment), the *Mitwelt* (interpersonal environment), the *Eigenwelt* (self-system), and the *Uberwelt* (spiritual world). People are at their best when they enjoy and benefit from nature rather than try to harness it to suit their immediate needs. Consider the therapeutic effects of birds chirping in the trees, a brook gurgling downstream, mighty ocean waves lashing against the shore, a manicured lawn, or a bouquet of roses thrown to a young woman on the wedding day of her friend. Individuals also cannot survive outside the *Mitwelt* (world of others). Without the care and love of parents or other significant adults, children would not reach adulthood. Other people are what give individuals their identity, companionship, support, love, and psychological well-being throughout life. The *Eigenwelt* (the self-system) is basic to a harmonious existence. Although individuals are housed safely in a self-contained system, they must maintain contact psychologically, physically, and morally with the outside world. Failure to do so means that they are cut off from a large part of their existence that can be fulfilled only by rapport with fellow human beings. The *Uberwelt*, or spiritual life, is everywhere in whatever lives. Individuals are connected by genes and socialization with the long historical chain of life, as Carl Jung suggested by his construct *collective unconscious* (Rychlak, 1981). In fact, many people do not separate life on earth from the hereafter. Masolo (1994), for example, observed that traditional Africans are not only concerned with happiness in this life, but with happiness in the hereafter as well. From an existential perspective, the good life is one that is balanced—in harmony with forces of nature, others, self, and other known and unknown forces that impact existence.

Death

In general, death is a powerful, although often unspoken, concern of human beings. According to Moulyn (1982), it is a major fracture in human existence. The dread of dying and death is ever present in the psyche. Recognizing this pervasive anxiety, Socrates was among the first philosophers to point out how unfounded the dread is (Ricken, 1991). To him, it reflected how inclined humans are to prejudge the unknown. Sharing his views are most believers in Islam, who do not fear death because they accept life as a transitory gift. Taoist philosophy teaches a similar view of death and emphasizes that it should never be denied (Watts, 1995). The Stoics in ancient Greece declared that humans should welcome old age and death because they are a part of the normal course of nature (Hadas, 1958). In spite of these views, in modern Western civilization, especially in the United States, death has been repressed (May, 1967). Most Americans consider death to be obscene, unmentionable, pornographic, and to be avoided if at all possible. When people die, they usually are dressed up as if they were still alive.

From an existential perspective, death stands out as an important consideration because it embraces the whole of life (Nauman, 1971). Existence is full of death and dying. The world can be likened to a great rail or airline terminal with people arriving and departing all the time. Nobody plans to stay long. Although some individuals stay longer than others, eventually they all depart. The point to keep in mind is that the terminal of life is not meant to serve as a permanent abode. All travelers are en route to their final destination, which is death. Existentialists counsel that without death, life would have no meaning: Only one who is aware of death lives intensely. Epicurus, another ancient Greek, felt that it was unhealthy and pathological to deny death (Annas, 1992). According to the teachings of Zen Buddhism, only individuals who come to terms with their death derive ultimate fulfillment from their existence (Suzuki, 1959). In traditional Africa, life is made more complete when it is lived in conjunction with its anticipatory counterpart (Elungu, 1984).

It would appear that people who accept their eventual death are more courageous than those who deny it. They are decisive, can make choices, and are more likely to implement them, for they realize that their days are numbered. They want to make good use of each day they live. The recognition and acceptance of death enable individuals to establish priorities. They do not want their lives to be consumed by trivia. Imbued with humility, people who know that they are en route to their demise learn to live harmoniously with fellow travelers. They do not "put on airs," pretending to be somebody they are not (Morano, 1973). In other words, confrontation with death liberates the human spirit. People have nothing to be afraid of and no reason to be timid or to feel inadequate or inferior anywhere anytime. They are free to live fully as nature intends.

Responsibility

Responsibility is basic to the cohesiveness of the human group. People, like other species, are endowed with the herd instinct. The individual is incomplete without others. Parents feel responsible for their children because they are extensions of themselves. Members of families and other enduring and interacting collectivities come to feel a sense of responsibility for one another because of the interdependency that generally develops in goal-oriented groups (Sartre, 1996). Mutual responsibility is more obvious in extended family societies than it is in individualistic ones in which individuals often give the impression that they do not need anybody.

Mutual responsiveness in the human community leads to unity, which in turn contributes to purpose, strength, and self-protection. It is so basic to existence that Glasser (1965) referred to irresponsible people, not neurotics or psychotics. Irresponsible behavior is a threat to the welfare of the group. People usually expect parents, teachers, officials, politicians, and other public servants to be responsible—to hold the public trust. Individuals derive happiness, fulfillment, and advancement in life to the extent that they manifest responsibility in the interdependent roles they play (Frankl, 1967). Responsibility, therefore, is an important diagnostic focus. Counselors should help clients ascertain the degree to which they are living responsibly.

Existential Diagnosis

The concepts discussed above are not all of the existential ideas that could be offered as yardsticks to determine how well clients negotiate their existence. Writers who have come to be known as existentialists do not analyze human existence the same way. Therefore, the diagnostic framework presented in this chapter should be viewed as one of many possible approaches that might be used to diagnose from an existential perspective. Regardless of which one is used, existential counselors need to consider how they can accommodate their diagnoses with the *DSM–IV* (APA, 1994) diagnostic codes and categories that usually are required by managed health care organizations.

Appendix F of the *DSM–IV* lists 397 diagnoses and codes. Because only eight existential diagnostic constructs are provided, readers are likely to want more diagnostic directions. First of all, the existential constructs are holistic. They recognize the physical, psychological, social, and spiritual dimensions of human existence. Although the *DSM–IV* recognizes the psychological (Axes I and II), the physical (Axis III), and the social (Axis IV) causes of psychiatric problems, it omits entirely the spiritual forces in people's lives. Using only a few diagnostic categories, counselors should be able to determine rather quickly the general nature and source of presenting problems. With this information, they can then assign specific *DSM–IV* categories and codes that are required by insurance companies. The following examples may be instructive. Code 296 (major depressive disorders) suggests in existential terms problems that are connected with courage and existential anxiety. Code 301.6 (dependent personality disorder) evokes existential constructs such as self-knowledge and becoming because such problems usually are products of socialization. Code 307.0 (stuttering) suggests the existential ideas of self-knowledge, becoming, and courage because this speech problem often is related to early socialization and anxiety concerning parental affection and support. Most existential counselors will not experience difficulty ascertaining which *DSM–IV* categories and codes are most appropriate once they have conceptualized an existential diagnosis.

RECOMMENDATIONS AND PROGNOSIS

Usually, after diagnosing the client's situation, counselors decide what ought to be done, by whom, and to what extent. In psychotherapeutic professions, these decisions are referred to as recommendations or *treatment plans*. Helping professionals are also expected to predict the probable outcome of the recommended intervention. This step is often called *prognosis*. With the advent of managed health care, therapists often are required to indicate how many counseling sessions are needed to achieve the therapeutic goals listed on the treatment plan. Although these procedures may be discussed as separate aspects of helping, they are, in fact, inseparable because counselors should not consider implementing a therapeutic idea without simultaneously considering its consequences. However, it is vain to believe that counselors can predict in a scientific fashion a client's fate: The human psychology can unexpectedly surprise and disappoint us.

Because existentialists usually think of therapy as a counselor–client partnership, it is important to involve the help seeker in the development of treatment plans and timetables. To do this, clients need to understand that they will help their counselor formulate a tentative diagnosis of their condition at the end of the first visit. Every effort should be made to communicate with clarity the areas of life on which individuals need to focus therapeutic attention. Once clients understand and accept the analysis of their situation, they can then work to improve themselves.

INTERVENTION STYLE

Existential counseling is a voyage to self-discovery not only for clients but also for their counselors, who invariably see a little of themselves in each of their clients. The main goal of therapeutic encounters is to engage individuals in a personal struggle to confront the areas of "stuckness" in their lives (R. E. Johnson, 1971). To do this, counselors should be flexible in style, varying their therapeutic approaches from one client to another and from one phase to another in the treatment of the same client (May, 1991). Vontress argued that existential counseling surpasses the superficiality of Rogerian reflection of feeling—the repetition of "How do you feel?"—and aspires to learn "How do you live?":

> I had the great honor of conversing with Dr. Carl Rogers on several occasions; and to this day I hold the highest respect for him. . . . While I think the elements of his approach form the foundation of any good therapeutic relationship, I find the remainder lacking in philosophical sophistication. I say this with great reverence for Dr. Rogers who was not a philosopher but a practitioner of keen insight. . . . Existential philosophy fills in where Rogers left off. It defines the issues that must be broached in a counseling session in broad strokes: love, death, suffering, and meaning. When these issues are confronted, I believe the results of counseling will be more enduring than the haphazard work on the issues the client struggles with at the moment. (Epp, 1998, p. 4)

The specific technique, approach, or style to be used should be based on the uniqueness of the individual. Existential counselors are necessarily artists who are creative, individualistic, and fluid in their work and who have a spiritual connection with each client. They reject the notion that psychotherapy is a science embodying facts, principles, and methods that must be memorized and applied in a standardized way to all clients (May, 1991). In fact, Ungersma (1961) indicated that helpers who emphasize techniques too much run the risk of becoming technicians, not therapists; their clients in turn become machines to be manipulated in accordance with prescribed techniques. In a sense, a scientific approach to psychotherapy often can be unwittingly antitherapeutic.

Perhaps the simplest way to communicate the existential intervention style is to refer to it as a Socratic dialogue. As readers may recall, Socrates, the ancient Greek philosopher, had a knack for getting individuals to discover themselves and to live according to the content of their self-discovery (Wolff, 1976). He was convinced that the surest way to attain reliable knowledge was through the art of a disciplined conversation, in which he acted as an intellectual midwife (Stumpf, 1975). He would confront people with various points of view on topics under discussion and try to bring into focus their strengths and weaknesses. Out of this experience, he hoped that individuals would develop their own wisdom and resulting direction in life, giving birth to a new self (A. H. Johnson, 1977). Socratic dialogues did not always end in clear-cut answers for individuals (Rychlak, 1979). Sometimes the hard questioning would trigger ideas in the mind of students that would take time to understand. This approach to knowledge of self was called the *maieutic*, or hatching, method.

In essence, existential counselors, like Socrates, do not use a bag of tricks to get their clients to explore their existence. If they have a technique, it is their focus on the unique existential struggle of each client. As dialecticians, they look for difficulties that impede the unfolding or becoming of individuals and help them to discover the reason for their "stuckness" (Christian, 1977). There is no one way of doing this. How counselors "do their job" depends on the uniqueness of the interactants. Counselors must ask themselves how they can know and enter the worlds of their clients (May, 1967). Once they are inside, the most important question then becomes "Now what do I do?" The answer to this self-inquiry resides in the heart and mind of the counselor, not in a recipe box of techniques. Vontress warned during an interview

> I do not know whether all counselors are equipped to be existentialists, however simple this philosophy may sound. Being an intimate friend, in a therapeutic sense, is emotionally draining for the counselor while healing for the client. In my opinion, counseling techniques . . . are not for the client's benefit but for the counselor's. They are a structure for the therapeutic interview as well as the filler, or white noise, to use when the counselor is unsure of what to do. Sigmund Freud, in my opinion, acted like a blank slate and free associated with his clients, because that was the degree of intimacy he could tolerate. In truth, his clients didn't need a blank slate nor a word game but a loving human being to hear their personal struggles. (Epp, 1998, p. 6)

The central agent of healing in existential counseling is the therapeutic personality of the counselor (Frank, 1961) who relates to the client as a fellow traveler. In graduate schools, many counselor–educators view counseling as a science, which justifies the teaching of techniques that are designed to put counselors-in-training in good stead in relating to clients. Unfortunately, culturally different clients often do not "see" the science or understand the techniques. They see and understand only the helper there with them—the other human being—who can not substitute technique for true caring because phoniness, superficiality, and indifference are recognized by members of every human culture.

THE EXPERIENCE OF EXISTENTIAL COUNSELING

Existential counseling posits that there are no right or wrong choices in life, only choices that are right for the individual (van Deurzen-Smith, 1988). However, it adds a sobering realization to this neutrality regarding decision making: Once a choice is enacted, it is irrevocable. This is why existential counselors believe that when one makes decisions, he or she should do so thoughtfully in order to be able to accept the consequences and to minimize the inevitable regret of foregoing other choices.

The existential counselor does not promise a remedy to unhappiness. Existence, from the existential viewpoint, is riddled with suffering, which is normal and often acts as a catalyst for positive change. Vontress believed that

> it is not useful to think of one's life in the black-and-white categories of suffering or joy. Life is obviously both; and it is through the experience of both that we can make this distinction, which allows us to take pleasure in our periodic moments of joy. But suffering is not sheer pain without meaning; it is often the most precious teacher in admonishing us not to revisit the past actions that brought the suffering upon us. In essence, without suffering, there would be no growth; and without joy, there would be no reason for growth. One complements the other. (Epp, 1998, p. 8)

Breggin and Breggin (1994) also ennobled the role of suffering in life:

> It's a truth communicated by Judeo-Christian and Eastern religions that the road to salvation must pass through suffering. The Buddhists say you cannot get to peace without passing through passion—passionate suffering. Have you ever read a biography or an autobiography of anyone whose life seemed worth recording—without discussing the depths of their emotional suffering? To rid ourselves of the option of suffering is to rid ourselves of ourselves. (p. 241)

In this light, what modern psychiatric diagnosis labels as mental illness—conditions such as depression and anxiety—are not wholly pathological but developmental in being by-products of living in a painful world. We are never completely free of these negative emotions nor would we wish to be, for psychological pain is the most memorable teacher. Without it, we would repeat our mistakes endlessly. This is why existential counselors often are reluctant to recommend that clients be placed on the popular antidepressant medications because these drugs may only mask the pain that serves as the impetus to the client's self-reflection and change. Of course, too much psychological pain is injurious and should be addressed medically if necessary, but the effort to narcotize all pain, even at the client's solemn request, enables the "stuckness" in development that initially incited the pain.

The existential counselor attempts to model and promote authenticity in the client. Being authentic is the culmination of a process in which one defines the direction of one's life and musters the courage to follow it. But reaching this end point can be an internal struggle that requires the counselor's support. Often in life, authenticity means generating one's own value system in the face of the competing values of one's family or cultural group. Yet existentialists often are depicted wrongly as rebellious individualists, when in fact they would condone only values and behaviors that are sensitive to the needs of others—those that would be called "responsible" in the existential lexicon.

In existential counseling, the specter of death is used as a spur to encourage the client to reflect on his or her choices and authenticity. Individuals who deny the reality of death often are those who treat others insensitively because they see life as an endless game in which others exist as objects to be manipulated. When life is perceived as eternal, the interaction with others becomes trivial and the moments of human contact lose their preciousness. Only by reminding the client of his or her mortality does the finitude of life come back into perspective and each momentary encounter increase in value. The same medicine is good for the counselor. Vontress implored, "Death is the common leveler. When the counselor recognizes that he or she is as mortal as the client, all the facades of superficiality, superiority, and inequality that may enter the counseling relationship dissolve and counselor and client interact with equality and genuineness" (Epp, 1998, p. 12).

Once the reality of death is recognized by the client, the counselor must facilitate the search for meaning. Death and the meaning of life are existential twins; in the face of inevitable nonbeing, human beings innately seek the meaning of the brief time they have. The Gestalt psychologists discovered many years ago that participants could not tolerate an incomplete or ambiguous figure: They had to imbue these with some perfect shape or meaning (Frank, 1961). The same process goes on within each of us at a philosophical level. We each must find some ideal to follow, or we feel incomplete and lack self-esteem. The search for meaning is an individual odyssey as manifold as the diverse human personalities who seek it.

SUMMARY

Existential counseling is a rich philosophical approach to psychotherapy that shares many of the same tenets with the world's major cultures, religions, and both Eastern and Western philosophy. It is this fact that makes it a universally applicable theory of counseling. However, existentialism subtly challenges the other counseling perspectives in its expansive view of life through the four worlds and through its belief that a narrow focus on cognitions, feelings, or psychodynamics in the therapeutic relationship addresses only a narrow slice of existence. Ultimately, the existential counselor wishes to explore concertedly with the client all of life, not simply the random issues that emerge in session, whose transient importance may only fade into the background of the larger scheme of life that went unexplored.

DISCUSSION QUESTIONS

1. Should counselors engage clients in discussions of the spiritual aspects of their lives?
2. What is the difference between existential anxiety and neurotic anxiety?
3. As an existential counselor, what is your position regarding the use of Prozac and other antidepressants to help people with problems in life?
4. How does one reconcile professional distance with empathy? Which of the existential concepts should counselors emphasize in their work?
5. What is the role of tests in existential counseling?
6. Existential counseling is sometimes thought to be similar to Rogerian counseling. Discuss the similarities and differences.
7. Do you think that existential counseling is appropriate for all clients, regardless of their cultural background?
8. Some writers maintain that existentialism originated in Europe. Do you agree?
9. Why is meaning in life so important to the psychological well-being of human beings?
10. How can existential counselors adjust to the diagnostic requirements of the *DSM-IV*?

Case Studies of Cross-Cultural Clients

INTRODUCTION TO PART TWO
Case Analysis

The case histories in this book are analyzed from three different perspectives: (a) conceptual, (b) existential, and (c) the *DSM–IV* (APA, 1994) perspectives. The three-pronged approach is used to encourage counselors to look at cross-cultural clients in as many ways as possible in order to understand them, to decide on a productive treatment plan, and to predict the outcome of intervention strategies.

The value of the case method, which is commonly used in law schools, is that it presents clients in their complexity. Counseling textbooks often are guilty of depicting human problems in very simple and monolithic terms; unfortunately, these problems often are "sanitized" for use in the classroom, which robs students of a proper preparation for dealing with clients from dysfunctional homes or amoral subcultures, and those who present issues "where there are no right answers." No specific amount of factual information makes a cross-cultural counselor: Cross-cultural counseling is a way of thinking or, more succinctly, an openness to different modes of thinking. The cross-cultural counselor is one who can metaphorically hold up a kaleidoscope and understand that each combination of color and shape is no more beautiful than the other, just different.

THE CONCEPTUAL PERSPECTIVE

In analyzing or diagnosing clients from a conceptual perspective, counselors recognize that human beings organize their lives around certain *universal concepts*, or patterns of behaviors, that are taught by cultures generally to provide stability and consistency in people's lives. Before birth, human organisms are attached to the wall of their mothers' womb, which nourishes and sustains them. On entering the world, they are attached to a cultural group that serves a similar purpose: It shapes and molds individuals to adjust comfortably to a specific social order. It is visible and invisible, conscious and unconscious, cognitive and affective. It provides the proverbial concepts, which others have called rules, mores, or psychological principles, that people live by.

Most people are born into and socialized by a single culture that becomes their lifeline. They think, speak, and act according to the dictates of their native culture. If for any reason they leave that culture, they are apt to experience difficulties being "away from home." Acculturation, alienation, collectivism versus individualism, cultural anxiety, and historical hostility are just a few universal concepts that have implications for counseling culturally different clients. The concepts of Western psychology can be joined with these to form a more comprehensive understanding of the client, because notions such as Oedipal dynamics, sibling rivalry, and repression, although having cultural variations, also speak to universal issues of humankind.

In diagnosing from a conceptual perspective, counselors are advised to focus on cultural differences as expressed in these *non-culture-specific concepts* rather than on "group stereotypes," which incorrectly specify that members of groups behave in a predictable manner. The advantage of using non-culture-specific concepts is that this approach emphasizes that all cultures consist of individuals who present a continuum of cultural behaviors. For example, there are members of collectivistic societies who are very individualistic, even more so than some members of individualistic societies. Analyzing culturally different clients with "concepts" rather than "blanket stereotypes" honors the individuality of the client.

The reader will see that the conceptual approach can be difficult in a world that loves labels and differentiation among groups. As soon as a client reveals that he or she is Jewish, African American, or Hispanic, these labels conjure up all kinds of expected characteristics and behaviors that distinguish these groups as unique. Language and logic through creating categories and subcategories may fuel the creation of the stereotypes that we all know are inaccurate but seem to exist to give some meaning to the labels and categories a system of language engenders. In the cases presented, although a conceptual approach is strived for, the reader may see remnants of the groups approach throughout, as groups and group characteristics are discussed. However, it is our hope that we consistently emphasize that although a group of people may share a given label and a set of defining characteristics, no individual embodies the stereotype of the group, and individuals within the group may differ among each other as starkly as the stereotypes lead us to believe that individuals differ between groups.

THE EXISTENTIAL PERSPECTIVE

When diagnosing from an existential perspective, counselors recognize their clients as individuals who are confronted with the challenges of an uncertain and often painful world. Self-knowledge; authenticity; becoming; courage to be; meaning in life; perspective on death; existential anxiety; responsibility; and rapport with nature, others, and self are among the constructs that serve as diagnostic foci to analyze each client's being in the world. How people measure up on these broad indicators of existence usually predicts the nature of the psychosocial problems they present to counselors, psychologists, psychiatrists, and other psychotherapeutic professionals.

THE *DSM–IV* (APA, 1994) MODEL

The *DSM–IV* provides a multiaxial approach to diagnosing clients. Each of its five axes refers to a different set of information that is designed to help therapists to plan treatment and to predict outcome. The multiaxial system is meant to promote holistic thinking, yet, sadly, many practitioners record the required information in a perfunctory manner but do not take the time to reflect on the possible impact of the different axes on the client's functioning. A formal diagnosis in this model takes this form:

Axis I	Clinical disorders Other conditions that may be a focus of clinical attention
Axis II	Personality disorders Mental retardation
Axis III	General medical conditions
Axis IV	Psychosocial and environmental problems
Axis V	Global Assessment of Functioning (GAF; 1–100 points, with 1 indicating a life-threatening mental illness, 50 indicating serious symptoms, and 100 indicating superior functioning)

In cross-cultural counseling, Axis IV information is extremely useful because it provides information regarding psychosocial and environmental problems that may affect the diagnosis, treatment, and prognosis of mental disorders that are noted on Axes I and II. The potential problems are grouped together in the following nine categories:

1. problems with the primary support group,
2. problems related to the social environment,
3. educational problems,
4. occupational problems,
5. housing problems,
6. economic problems,
7. problems with access to health care services,
8. problems related to interaction with the legal system, and
9. other psychosocial and environmental problems.

The problems listed above are stressors that have the potential for producing psychological difficulties that may be indicated on Axes I and II. For example, economic problems in disadvantaged communities in the United States often produce a ripple effect, creating a variety of psychological and social problems. In some cases, life is so difficult that many people without jobs, housing, and access to medical services may be perceived to be suffering from low-grade depression or dysthymic disorder, which often is attributed to a biological origin instead of to more obvious social factors. Ironically, today, biology is easier to manipulate through medication than age-old social problems that seem refractory to political pressures and, even, the passage of time.

The *DSM–IV* is an important tool for counselors and other psychotherapeutic professionals to use with their cross-cultural clients. Clinicians need to understand the relationship between psychosocial and environmental problems and Axes I and II designations. Understanding multiaxial interactions requires information that is related to stressors that are endemic to various communities and the way in which cultural outsiders may react to them. However, it must be emphasized that the *DSM–IV* predominantly reflects the mental phenomena found in Western cultures. It is important to understand that culturally different clients may not manifest depression or anxiety in exactly the same way as Westerners or have a "psychological language" to describe their feelings. Often persons who are unfamiliar with Western psychological terminology present somatic symptoms as their evidence of mental illness while not knowing how to conceptualize or describe the sadness or tension they may be feeling.

CHAPTER THREE

A Girl Named India: The Challenge of Living Within a Culture of Violence

INTRODUCTION

With curly orangish-black hair draping over her forehead, India is a light-skinned and freckled adolescent of African and Mexican American parentage. At the impressionable age of 13, she lives on a corner in North Philadelphia that is known for its drive-by shootings, street-side junkies, emaciated prostitutes, and aesthetic unsightliness. The trees in her neighborhood have all withered from automobile smog, and the children are limited to one playground where used syringes are littered in the protective gravel, creating the possibility that a child could fall from the swings or monkey bars and be infected accidentally with HIV.

India's dress is casual and appropriate, characterized by loose-fitting blouses and jeans with dark colors and designs but clearly unreflective of her poverty. She does not appear emotionally invested in her appearance, nor does she care to attract the attention of boys with the flashy or immodest styles that her precocious adolescent peers flaunt. She appears plain and reticent but gives the initial impression of being far older than 13.

Her mental health counselor, Anna, is her cultural antithesis: White, Ivy League educated, and Jewish. If Anna is ever in India's neighborhood, it is within the security of an automobile, speeding quickly by. If India is ever in Anna's neighborhood, it is to admire its beautiful square and its well-kept rows of townhouses. India and her therapist are so different from each other that it might be wondered whether they can connect in the deep, caring way required for successful psychotherapy. Anna wonders whether her empathy will be perceived as genuine because her life never encountered the social and racial obstacles that India's did. She feels as though she and her client will face each other as if they are inhabitants of two different planets. India is also the first client Anna ever counseled as a beginning intern.

PRESENTING CHALLENGE

At intake, India reported feeling "anxious and unloved," as well as an array of fears and anxieties that included the fear of fire at night, the fear of her parents dying, the fear of sleeping on her back, and the need to sleep with her mother. Some of these fears she justified with credible explanations: She claimed that some teenagers had set an abandoned car ablaze across from her home, which caused her fear of fire and her compulsion to sleep in her street clothes should she need to escape quickly. She also claimed that she saw her stepsister die on her back after being mortally wounded by a stray bullet, which caused India to avoid sleeping on her own. She could not explain why, at the age of 13, she still slept with her mother, except to uphold its legitimacy as a family custom.

The clinic's psychiatrist evaluated India and offered a tentative diagnosis. He believed that India's symptoms resembled a condition called generalized anxiety disorder, whose essential feature is "excessive anxiety and worry for a period of at least six months about a number of events or activities" (APA, 1994, p. 432). As therapy progressed, India disclosed new symptoms—shortness of breath, overheating, anxiety attacks, headaches, fatigue, irritability, imaginary companions, nightmares, and transient phobias—which would exceed this diagnosis and suggest other syndromes. India's condition could not be confined to a single diagnostic category.

CASE HISTORY

Family Dynamics

In the first meeting with India, Anna planned to clear her mind of any theoretical bias and to simply facilitate a description of the issue. Her goal was to build rapport and to try to understand India's worldview in the spirit of a Rogerian counselor, not to confront, direct, or interpret.

When India began talking, Anna realized that her plan would need to be altered. India spoke quickly in a rambling fashion and made trivial and commonplace events the center of discussion. Anna had trouble following India's logic and deciphering her "Spanglish" (Spanish–English) dialect. She crystallized India's issue as having no friends and being bored, but Anna wondered whether she had probed deeply enough. She realized that she would have to be more directive and structured in India's therapy or it would lead nowhere.

The second session with India focused on her African American mother. Anna had predicted that this would be a sensitive topic because "feeling unloved" by her mother was the issue that had brought India into therapy. India spoke about her mother with mature acceptance of her personality, which she described as cool, indifferent, and disposed to being alone. These adjectives did not add up to a grotesque or abusive parent—India's mother was no monster—but to a parent who did not know how to instill a feeling of love or worth in her daughter. Even when asked by India, her mother could not easily affirm her love; in fact, she found the request ridiculous. Anna tried to assure India that her mother loved her but had difficulty expressing it. India's strained facial expression articulated her reply: How can my mother love me and not show it?

India would describe a childhood centered around her Hispanic father, Miguel. She fondly remembered their strolls together through shopping malls and their friendly teasing with one another. Whenever India mentioned her mother, the same bitter memory was recounted: the two watching soap operas on television in the kitchen without any verbal interaction. India does not understand why her mother became emotionally withdrawn. When pressed to guess or search for a precipitating event, India resistantly stated, "She's always been that way!" Apparently, India's mother felt that "she was excluded from the family," possibly because of India's fusion with her father. She had even threatened to move into her own apartment. India recalled the arguments between her parents, with each trying to enlist her reluctant support. Anna aimed to probe deeper into India's parents' relationship, but her line of inquiry would be eclipsed by India's need to digress into her fantasy.

Fantasy Life

Fantasy tends to be rich in a child's early years but gradually diminishes with age. At 13, India's life was filled with fantasy and pretend play, which seemed to indicate immaturity. Anna listened with great amusement as India described how she would mousse and style her dog's hair, have him wear an old Dick Tracy hat and John Lennon sunglasses, and position him on the front porch of her home to be displayed to pedestrians so as to confuse them about his canine identity. India confessed that her dog was better than a human friend because he "knows how to keep a secret." At some level, she may have preferred him to a human friend because he was so filled with energy and life. India inserted at the end of the session that she had experienced a trying succession of deaths, with her godmother passing away just recently.

India's painful disclosure would unfold no further. By the next session, she skirted the issue of death entirely and chose to describe how her daytime fantasy became incorporated into her nightmares. Anna wanted to move away from the analysis of dreams and fantasy and return to discussing India's fear of death, but India lived in her imagination. The only way to bring out her issues, Anna thought, was to explore the meaning of India's dreams in an attempt to discover why her dreams and fantasy were more enticing than reality.

India feared sleeping in the dark. Shadows on the walls were transformed into frightening lizards, bats, and dinosaurs in her dreams. She revealed recurrent dreams about people "coming up her stairs" and slashing her with kitchen knives, then leaving her on her front porch. She dreamed about "walking down steps" and the steps transforming themselves into the mouth of a "dirty sewer rat" that devoured her alive. She dreamed about walking through a subway station, concrete fragments falling on her, burying her alive. India believed that her nightmares could predict the future.

While recounting her nightmares, India had inadvertently returned to the theme of death, whose metaphor pervaded her fantasy. Over the past 2 years, India had experienced the deaths of her grandfather, stepsister, great-aunt, godmother, and three friends. Her great-aunt died the moment she had summoned India from the upstairs to "run to the corner to buy a pack of Camel cigarettes." She could vividly recall her great-uncle warning her, "Don't come up the stairs," lest she see her great-aunt's lifeless body. India linked her trouble sleeping on her back to having witnessed her stepsister die on her back after being mortally wounded by a feuding drug dealer's stray bullet, although India claimed that she had an intellectual understanding that a person could die in any position. At the end of the fourth session, India confided her deepest fear that "if my parents die too, I'll be alone in the world."

India's nightmares were not predicting the future but reflecting her current anxieties. It was obvious that each was centered around death—being buried alive, slashed with knives, and so forth—which merely reflected her daytime fears. Anna noticed that the passage up or down stairs was always related to tragedy. She offered the explanation that these images may be linked to her great-aunt's death, which was revealed "while going up stairs." India resisted this interpretation and insisted that the stair image stemmed from her falling down her best friend's steps as a little girl, injuring her wrist. Her rival interpretation showed Anna that India had accepted her belief that her dreams could not predict the future but instead reflected her immediate feelings.

By the fifth session, India was seemingly cured of her phobic symptoms through her newfound insights. She was now sleeping in her own room, had confessed to reclining on her back, thought less about possible fires, and had even come out of her seclusion to go on a trip to Atlantic City, New Jersey, over the previous weekend. She even claimed insight into her mother's aloof behavior. Anna was convinced that she could start planning India's termination of therapy, but physical complaints—headaches and colds—surfaced as the psychological issues disappeared.

India recounted a dream reflecting this odd conversion. She told her counselor that she dreamed of falling endlessly into a dark sewer. Anna usually would help clients attach their own meaning to dreams, but when they were baffled, as was India, she offered suggestions. She told India that falling could signify that an aspect of one's life is out of control, because the sensation of falling implies helplessness and fear. She asked India whether any problem in her life was making her feel "out of control." India immediately responded that her colds had become persistent and tenacious; she believed that she had lost control of her health. She also disclosed that she was having two to three headaches a day and was coping with the pain by taking aspirin.

Physical Pain and Imagination

The sixth and seventh sessions of India's therapy focused on new physical complaints, which began to multiply. India reported panic attacks that would come and go without an identifiable thought or trigger— although they often appeared when she was alone in her house. These were characterized by a racing heartbeat, sweating and overheating, dry mouth, dizziness, and headaches that were localized in the back of her head. She feared that she may have contracted HIV/AIDS because she remembered that she had gotten a blood transfusion when she was little and that she has drug-resistant acne. In her supervision class, Anna speculated whether India was "somatizing" her issues, displacing her fears into physical symptoms. Her university supervisor, Dr. Fromberg, found the idea provocative. She suggested that psychological issues are a form of "pain" that can become physical. Nevertheless, Dr. Fromberg felt that a physician should examine India to rule out a real physical illness before Anna jumped to any novel conclusions regarding India's symptoms.

Before Anna could focus on that task, India disclosed another facet of her psychological life: the existence of an imaginary companion. India called this person Indella (a combination of the name India and the name Marabella), who she claimed has lived in her mind since the age of 9. Indella possesses all the characteristics that India lacks. She is smart and funny and does not let her mother annoy her. She goes out a lot, has many friends, and can be mischievous. India controls when Indella is present but fears that Indella could one day control her personality. Was India developing a psychosis? Or was Indella the repressed young woman that India yearned to be? Anna did not sense that India was out of touch with reality, just trapped in a violent neighborhood where it was safer to use one's imagination than to play with one's peers in the streets.

India's mother did not support her daughter's therapy. She refused to take India to a doctor to investigate the physical symptoms. The junior high school's health clinic became alarmed at this decision because India was presenting herself daily at their offices. The school nurses had done all that they could do; India needed the examination of a medical specialist. The necessity became apparent when India revealed that she was taking as many as three tablets of aspirin a day to soothe her headaches. Her mother was asked to come to school to discuss this practice, which she reluctantly did. Anna was asked to participate in the meeting with the school nurses and India's mother in order to express the concerns of the community mental health clinic.

The experience of meeting India's mother was both fascinating and unsettling for Anna. She had heard much about India's mother, but her behavior surpassed Anna's expectations. India's mother presented herself as a relic of the 1960s, dressed in a white turtleneck, Annie Hall sunglasses, a beret with a slanted felt tip, and a carved Black Power fist dangling from her neck on a leather strap. She lurched over the desk where the meeting was held, nervously swaying back and forth, but peered intently at her questioners. In her responses, she was very defensive: She claimed she did not have enough money to take India to a doctor and confirmed without embarrassment that she and India were sharing the same bed. As Anna observed the mother's behavior, she kept trying to form a diagnosis, but she realized that the mother was eccentric, not mentally ill. India's mother left promising to take India to a doctor, and everyone naively believed her.

For 2 weeks, Anna lost contact with India. She was staying out of school because her headaches had become painful and enduring. Despite this fact, the mother had another change of heart and decided not to take India to a doctor. Anna was confused by the mother's reversal and its implied insensitivity. The school consulted child protective services concerning a medical neglect investigation. With the threat of this proceeding, the mother was persuaded to make a doctor's appointment for India. However, she made the appointment a month and a half away, despite India's unrelenting complaints and overconsumption of pain relievers.

India stopped coming to her sessions after this meeting. Anna did not know whether India's mother advised her to stop coming or whether this was a decision India made on her own. Anna did not hear from India for 3 months; then, one morning when she arrived at the clinic, Marsha, her site supervisor, informed her that India was in the hospital because she had miscarried a baby. Both Marsha and Anna were shocked and sped over to visit India in the maternity ward. India was sedated and sleeping at the time of the visit, so they could not learn anything about the father or why she had not even told Anna that she was pregnant. Anna called India several times at the hospital subsequent to their visit, but India never returned her calls.

CASE ANALYSIS

Conceptual Perspective

Anna tried to elicit India's issues using simple Rogerian positive regard and reflection coupled with dynamic interpretations of her fantasy. By the third session, she identified fragments of different issues— mother–daughter conflict, fear of death, and loneliness—but no unifying theme to pursue and unravel. Anna had developed a "wild interpretation" of India's behavior, which she presented to her site supervisor and faculty internship supervisor. Anna believed that India was sleeping with her mother to secure her mother's love before she dies because India had "lost the love" of so many significant figures through death and could not bear the loss of her most significant attachment. Anna also believed that India had secluded herself at home because her neighborhood was unsafe and, consequently, used her imagination for the safe recreation her community denied her.

In supervision class, Dr. Fromberg, the faculty supervisor, challenged the intern counselor's interpretation of India's symptoms. She dismissed Anna's speculations into love deprivation and urged Anna, if facetiously, to "tell India to get out of bed with her mother!" Dr. Fromberg explained that although one should be nonjudgmental, there are certain behaviors that are developmentally inappropriate. (India's sleeping with her mother was what most bothered Dr. Fromberg.) Anna immediately followed her advice, explaining to both India and her mother (over the telephone) that India must sleep in her own bed and be encouraged to "act her age" by socializing with her peers. India's mother was very receptive and, for a time, it seemed that India slept in her own room.

But India periodically returned to sleeping with her mother, and Anna speculated that it was due to the love deficit her faculty supervisor found frivolous.

Later in the semester, after Anna presented India's case a second time, her supervision class offered a new therapeutic direction. As Anna described India's symptoms—her wearing street clothing to bed, her sleeping with her mother, her nightmares, headaches, and so forth—the class responded in unison, "She's been sexually abused!" Anna was shocked and felt embarrassed that she could not see what was so obvious to her classmates. She remembered that Marsha, her site supervisor, and the attending psychiatrist, who was an expert on sexual abuse, had evaluated India and did not make this inference. India had denied sexual abuse in her intake interview. Did her behaviors indicate otherwise to those who were perceptive enough to understand them?

Dr. Fromberg believed that she had a theory that put all the pieces together. She explained that sexually abused children often sleep in their street clothes or with the nonabusing parent to shield themselves from their abuser. They often "somatize" their fears of the abuser into headaches or illness either to partly express them or to dissuade the abuser. Phobias and nightmares are also common among the sexually abused. Dr. Fromberg's explanation was persuasive. However, neither the psychiatrist, Marsha, nor the two therapists at the clinic's peer supervision meeting, accepted it. Anna was confused by the multiple interpretations of India's symptoms, but she did wish to explore whether the theory of sexual abuse ran a "common thread" through India's unusual behaviors.

Anna felt that the next step was to question India directly, if delicately, regarding past or present sexual abuse to see what feelings would be evoked. She told India a story about a girl who had been sexually abused and asked her if she could imagine how that girl might feel. India responded with only a quizzical expression. Anna then personalized the question by asking, "Has anyone ever touched you in a way you found offensive?" India denied any such occurrence but became withdrawn and irritated. Anna knew she had touched a sensitive nerve, because if the question were utterly ridiculous, she expected India to laugh it off or, at least, not become defensive. In response to Anna's remaining questions, India seemed to vacillate between denial and offering the rationalization that exposing an abuser would serve no purpose. Either India had been sexually abused or she felt that her therapist's line of questioning was misdirected and intrusive. Whichever was the case, Anna felt no closer to understanding India and, perhaps, had alienated her with probing questions into unusual life events that may never have happened.

In the absence of an accepted procedure for questioning adolescents about sexual abuse, Anna thought that she had done an adequate job. However, Marsha (her site supervisor) and the psychiatrist felt that she had asked "leading questions" and questioned whether it was appropriate to conduct a "sexual abuse investigation" in the middle of therapy. In their view, the client must be ready to disclose his or her abuse; the client cannot be forced or hurried. If the client has been sexually abused, a mental health counselor risks scaring the client away or discouraging the client from further disclosure. Marsha emphasized that generally it is harmful to ask a client a question before he or she is psychologically ready to answer it. Yet Anna felt justified in her questioning because she feared that waiting until India disclosed might do irreparable damage if she were being actively abused. To Anna, there appeared to be no right or safe decision.

Although India missed her next appointment, Anna's questioning did not scare her off: She returned 2 weeks later to continue her therapy. When she returned, she did not mention the previous session and continued as usual. Anna did not sense a change in their therapeutic relationship. It was as if the whole issue of India's sexual abuse had faded into the "ground" of her mysterious Gestalt. India's case resembled nothing Anna had studied in her graduate program in counseling. Like an abstract work of art in which one person can derive one interpretation and another a wholly different one, India's issues were a hodgepodge of psychological symptoms with different unifying themes depending on the perspective one wished to take.

The basic conceptual spectacles through which Anna could have better viewed India's array of problems was *holism*. This concept suggests looking at her problems in the aggregate instead of trying to reduce India's issues into exclusive and all-encompassing theoretical constructs or diagnoses, such as sexual abuse or anxiety disorder. India could not be classified within one theory or diagnosis; attempting to do so only seemed to address certain aspects of her problems and neglect others. Her counselor kept using psychoanalytic theory as her crutch in understanding India's issues, but she could have interpreted her issues through any theory. Anna appeared, in all honesty, simply fascinated by Freudian theory at the time.

Anna's supervisors, her supervision class, and Anna herself may have been guilty of *reductionism*. Although counselors need some map or theory to follow in treating their clients, maps or theories must be understood as artificial devices we use to help us understand our clients. Some counselors believe that their theories possess scientific validity instead of acknowledging that they may be simply tenuous hypotheses. As one can see from the case description, different individuals applied different theories to India's case, and all were probably right from their limited perspectives. Each erred by insisting that his or her theory was exhaustive instead of seeing that all the theories helped piece together the larger puzzle of India's life. Anna would have done better to explore each hypothesis regarding India's unhappiness rather than to search for a single reason provided by a single theoretical tradition.

Existential Perspective

Anna uncovered an important existential concern: India feared her parents' death and being left alone. It was interesting that India planned her sweet 16 party in 4 years, around the time she feared her father would die at age 75. India's morbid preoccupation regarding her parents' death was eerie and, undoubtedly, tapped into a gnawing and universal anxiety of parental death that Anna shared. Anna devised a quick thought-stopping exercise (merging existential and behavioral insights) to help India quell her ruminations regarding death. She asked India to state aloud her fear, "My parents are going to die. . . . My parents are going to die." Then Anna yelled, "Stop! Clear your mind!" and asked India to practice stopping this rumination herself. India was instructed to use this technique whenever the morbid fears returned.

Anna also taught India a guided imagery exercise to relieve her loneliness. Whenever India felt lonely, Anna instructed her to conjure up this soothing imagery: her two parents holding her tightly and cradling her, their love emanating like a warm, white light, engulfing her and making her feel secure and protected. Anna told India to breathe deeply of this imaginary light, then blow out all her fears and concerns. When Anna first demonstrated this guided imagery exercise to India, she placed her in a state of progressive relaxation. Her rationale was that the imagery would be associated with the feeling of relaxation. India found the exercise tranquilizing.

The behavioral exercises were simply a Band-Aid for the larger existential concern that simmered beneath India's symptoms. Within the dangerous community in which she lived—coupled with her cold and aloof mother—there was a glaring feeling that India was lacking in love. Love, in existential philosophy, entails a spiritual aspect that guarantees our belonging and security in our personal world. India's world felt terribly rejecting, not only of her but also of human life in general. She was surrounded by violence and cold-heartedness, and, in an ultimate sense, what she needed was to be regenerated with an enveloping sense of love. Her therapist's positive regard and empathy probably fulfilled part of this core human need. India may have become pregnant to create a baby who would love her unconditionally and who, in turn, she could love.

DSM–IV (APA, 1994) Perspective

India's symptoms could have produced a litany of diagnoses: depression, generalized anxiety disorder, conversion disorder, suspected sexual abuse, hypocondriasis, panic disorder, and social phobia, among others. Anna did not wish to downplay the importance of psychiatric diagnosis in helping to find an effective treatment for India, but India was constantly developing new diagnoses as the old ones subsided. Perhaps had Anna taken a medical model approach, she could have referred India for an anxiolytic or an antidepressant to relieve some of her symptoms. However, Anna had the intuition that India's symptoms were not as much reflective of a biological disease as they were a cry for help and love. Luckily, India was not referred: Given her reluctance to disclose her pregnancy, a psychiatrist may have inadvertently prescribed medicines that could have harmed her fetus (which unfortunately died, in any case).

Anna enjoyed speculating on whether India suffered from a psychotic disorder. Her site supervisor believed that India's imaginary friend, Indella, was a product of her loneliness, not evidence of psychosis. Anna herself saw Indella in Jungian terms as India's "shadow"—the side of herself she repressed but dearly wanted to express. She told her, "Indella is your imagination's way of saying 'You want a life!'" Anna predicted that "Indella will go away when you become Indella," but India was reluctant to integrate Indella into her personality. Occasionally, India would engage in an activity that was characteristic of Indella: inviting over a friend or relative, going to the mall, dressing up for school, and so on. But her pattern of change was cyclical: As soon as she expressed the "repressed Indella," she would quickly return to her old self with stubborn resolve and lost memory of the change.

Being presented with so many unusual symptoms, one might question whether Anna misdiagnosed a very sick girl. The real issue, however, may not concern misdiagnosis as much as cultural misunderstanding. India lived in a neighborhood that resembled a tragic cross between a third-world country and a battlefield. If one judges her symptoms by a suburban, middle-class standard, one misses that she was the victim of the trauma of her environment. One might assume that her symptoms were unusual, but they were not unusual for a young girl who lives under chronic and extraordinary stress. India was not mentally ill in a biological sense; her community was ill in a sociological sense. Anna did not wish to "politicize" psychiatric diagnosis, but she believed that such diagnoses were not beyond cultural influence. Anna felt that assigning India a serious label of psychopathology, when she is reacting as one would expect toward the traumatic circumstances of a violent culture, would only be an added injury to her condition. Anna chose to maintain the diagnosis of generalized anxiety disorder as the least stigmatizing rather than add on others, or choose a more serious diagnosis, as new symptoms emerged.

Anna was most hesitant about her university supervisor's and supervision class's diagnosis of sexual abuse. Although sexual abuse was a plausible explanation, Anna felt that it was also culturally influenced. Whether the conclusion derived from our profession's Freudian roots or our culture's obsession with sexuality, sexual abuse is sometimes used as an explanation for a client whose symptoms we simply cannot explain. If Anna had wholly accepted the class's theory, she would have had her client referred to a sexual abuse specialist. India later miscarried a baby, but it was believed that she had been engaged in a consensual sexual experience with a classmate who was the more likely source of her pregnancy than a child molester. Despite a pattern of symptoms that could be seen as indicative of sexual abuse, the client passionately denied sexual abuse, and her symptoms may have merely reflected her guilt and anxiety over becoming pregnant. If we take the client at her word, that she slept in her street clothes because she feared fires, not a sexual abuser, why would sexual abuse be the more plausible explanation, except that it is a professional and cultural fad to proclaim such a diagnosis?

Multiaxial Diagnosis

Axis I	Generalized anxiety disorder (300.02)
Axis II	No diagnosis
Axis III	No diagnosis
Axis IV	Lives within a violent and impoverished neighborhood
Axis V	GAF = 75 (current)

INTERVENTION STRATEGY

In all honesty, India's therapy with Anna resembled an ongoing polite conversation—sometimes exciting, sometimes boring, and often silly—but never approaching the miraculous psychotherapy that is portrayed in textbooks or movies. India talked and Anna listened, responded, made treatment plans, amended them, then threw up her hands and started over. The only consistency was Anna's empathy, positive regard, and patience. She invoked dream analysis techniques several times, which helped to clarify issues. But even when India's issues were unearthed, the exercises did little to change India's behavior. Anna assigned behavioral homework, which India briefly tried then ignored. Anna urged, coaxed, cajoled, supported, joked, and pounded her feet on the floor. India remained faithful to therapy but continued to distance herself from her mother and her peers and to live in her world of fantasy, although with a few intermittent episodes of improvement. Then India mysteriously dropped out of sight. What had psychotherapy done for her?

India's intern counselor had experienced more growth in herself than she had seen in India—at least she was learning to be a psychotherapist! Her site supervisor proposed in supervision, "When counseling is going badly, perhaps its objectives have been achieved." Anna thought about this intensely. India had stopped discussing her phobias (or, at least, she pretended they had been cured), although Anna realized that she still had them. India had stopped complaining about feeling unloved, although Anna knew that she still felt unloved by her mother. Her headaches had gone away, but Anna expected that they would with time. In short, India remained as she had entered therapy: phobic, lonely, and socially isolated—except she had a counselor! Anna could not quantify their relationship, but she knew that it had value because India kept returning.

Anna had to believe that India came to therapy for the encounter with her. Anna was no movie star or comedian, but within the harsh environment of North Philadelphia, she was someone to hear India's struggles, fears, and pain—to, perhaps, be a surrogate parent or friend. Anna played the human mirror that helped India look at herself: India "looked in the mirror" and found the image unappealing, yet accepted who she saw. Anna wanted to add happiness to India's life, but India chose the inner tranquility of self-acceptance. Perhaps Anna had succeeded in India's therapy in the mysterious, intangible way therapy sometimes succeeds. As Rogers (1961) phrased it, "We cannot change, we cannot move away from what we are, until we accept what we are. Then change seems to come about almost unnoticed" (p. 17). India's self-acceptance may have been the prelude to the change that would someday emerge, but which her counselor would sadly never have the satisfaction of witnessing.

DISCUSSION OF THE CASE

India's case would be overwhelming even for a seasoned practitioner. As Anna contemplated each of India's sessions, she felt fearful of reentering her labyrinth of fantasy, illness, and bizarre fears with no ball of string to lead India or herself out. She may have unconsciously ignored India's missed appointments, secretly planning her referral to a more experienced clinician who could pull India out of the morass of her family's dysfunction and not become flustered or discouraged as Anna had.

Anna realized that many counselors might criticize her for not referring India immediately to a more experienced therapist, but as one quickly learns in the real world, there are few places that an impoverished client can be referred. Anna sought expert supervision, and if she included the members of her supervision class, she may have had as many as 20 consultants involved in India's case. With all this advice, one might expect that India's condition would achieve a better result. Sadly, an unhappy life cannot be treated with the definitiveness of a biological disease. Counseling is seldom a smooth, linear, or rational process that ends in a "cure." It is a journey into the unknown, with many unexpected surprises and reversals, and it can offer only the chance of a better life, not the certainty of one.

It is hoped that India is doing well, but the last fragments of news were not promising: She had dropped out of junior high school with no intention of returning. India may have found a personal meaning in her psychotherapy, but she came with a power and momentum that was solely her own, over which her counselor had little control. Through the experience of the counseling process, Anna tried to teach India that a satisfying relationship is possible, and she hopes that the memory of their encounter will provide India with a template of the love and sharing that is possible between two human beings.

DISCUSSION QUESTIONS

1. Do you believe that Anna did an adequate job? Should she have taken a family therapy approach?
2. Do you think that India had been sexually abused? Or do you believe that she had a premarital affair that made her feel guilty, as Anna alleged?
3. What diagnosis would you have given India? Would you have referred her to a psychiatrist for medication?
4. Was India truly culturally different, as Anna argued?
5. Do you believe that Anna had no success with this client or that India truly gained self-acceptance?
6. Do you believe that the author's conclusions regarding therapeutic progress as being nonlinear and haphazard are accurate?
7. Do you think that Anna's cultural background was an unconsidered impediment in the success or failure of counseling?

8. What would you have done differently in this case? How would you have conceptualized India's issues?

9. Can we admire Anna for her honesty in portraying her experience of the client?

10. Was Anna a bit radical in her assumptions? Did Anna's theoretical bias function to the benefit or detriment of her client?

CHAPTER FOUR

The Dark Skin That Is Invisible to Myself: The Challenge of Racial Discrimination for a Blind Man

INTRODUCTION

A large and fairly heavy-set African American, Mike is a formidable presence within the small confines of a counseling suite. Although diagnosed as legally blind, he is a strikingly good dresser who exhibits an air of self-confidence, unfazed by his obvious disability. He is very intelligent and articulate and reveals a quick wit. Recently, he became a student at a school for the blind, where he hopes to gain skills that will help him become independent and make the necessary adjustments to his blindness.

His counselor is an Anglo American woman of Italian descent. She is warm and nurturing, with no pretense of arrogance, despite the fact that she holds advanced training in her field. Her style is very client-centered, although she blends the insights of other perspectives into her counseling strategy. The match of an African American and Anglo American may seem likely to yield the friction of historical hostility, but Mike's counselor deftly avoids the emergence of this phenomenon with her sensitivity, genuineness, and compassion.

PRESENTING CHALLENGES

Several challenges faced Mike. First, he revealed a striking lack of emotion regarding his blindness and virtually denied that he is blind. Second, his psychiatric history indicated some difficulty with impulse control and frustration with his many abortive attempts to succeed despite his disability and what he perceived to be a discriminatory culture. He came to counseling frustrated and angry, but beneath his outward hostility was an insatiable desire to move forward with his life.

CASE HISTORY

Family History

Born in 1921, Mike was the elder of two boys. He grew up in the infamous Eastside of Baltimore in a working-class community. "It was a totally residential Black neighborhood," he emphasized. "The only Whites we saw in our neighborhood were the firemen, the milkman, a few police, and the Metropolitan Life Insurance man." Mike described his home as "warm and loving." His mother, who was from South Carolina, had a junior college education and was a nursery school teacher. His father left supervising homework and educating the children to his mother. Mike referred to his mother as very well-read, compassionate, and wise. He revealed that most of his education inside the home came from her.

Although his mother is now deceased, Mike called her his best friend and spoke of her in the present tense. Mike was 26 years old when his mother died at the age of 45 of renal failure precipitated by hypertension. He saw her in "the last hour she was alive, and it was a very painful experience." For many years thereafter, Mike could not enter a hospital. He disclosed that he was "shaken quite a bit by the death" because he and his mother "always had a very strong, warm relationship, and she was very encouraging." He reminisced that he could always go to his mother with anything "personal, social, physical," and she would comfort him.

Mike felt closer to his mother than to his father. He explained that his father did not show emotion readily. He said that by his 20s and early 30s, he was able to understand his father's reserve, but he was never comfortable with it. Mike's father remarried when he was in his 60s, although his second wife died unexpectedly after several years of marriage. Mike's father retired to a veterans' home and is still there at the age of 96. Mike's father is part American Indian, but Mike is not sure how much Indian heritage he has, nor is he interested in this intriguing aspect of his family's lineage.

As a child, Mike experienced extreme sibling rivalry with his brother, Morris. He attributes the contentious relationship to his brother's dislike of his studiousness and his desire to improve himself. Morris, on the other hand, showed no interest in school and teased Mike by calling him a "smart aleck." Morris, who is a year younger than Mike, now lives in a nearby rowhouse. Morris is constantly struggling to overcome his alcoholism, which impedes his ability to hold a steady job. Earlier, he had a very serious car accident in which he lost his wife and child and badly injured himself. It was uncertain whether his drinking caused the tragedy, although the suspicion is that it may have been the primary cause.

Mike believed that his brother Morris "never adjusted psychologically and always needed a crutch—and booze was it." Yet Mike is relieved that Morris has pulled himself together somewhat with the help of his second wife, Tonya. Mike contends that he tries to maintain a good relationship with Morris, despite his shortcomings, because, he emphasizes, "Morris is my only brother." Mike claims that he and Morris speak frequently and that he is fairly generous with him in sharing clothing and money. Interestingly, Morris tries to maintain one point of superiority over his brother: He claims that his aged father likes him better.

Mike's most unusual disclosure was that his family owned a pipe organ that he learned to play. Mike also took tennis lessons while growing up, although this was not a sport that was played frequently by inner-city African Americans. His family had middle-class interests and aspirations without having the middle-class income that usually sustains them.

Marital History

At the beginning of counseling, Mike was reluctant to discuss his marriage, despite numerous attempts to persuade him to do so. At an unexpected moment, while reviewing a seemingly inconsequential episode of family history, he interjected, "There are things that happened at this point that I'm not going to mention . . . it had to do with my marriage, and I am not going to talk about it." His voice rose two octaves and his hands began to quiver. He continued to speak as he somberly lurched forward, "It will hurt too much to talk about . . . and I am not ready to deal with that kind of pain." His counselor assured him that he did not have to discuss anything he was not ready to reveal. Mike released a deep sigh of relief, an intense and thoughtful expression crossed his face, and then he confided, "I guess I could tell you about my marriage."

Mike was discharged from the military at the close of World War II. After returning home in 1945, he was reunited with his high school sweetheart, whom he resumed dating. They decided to marry and remained together for 4 short years, which culminated in a tumultuous breakup. Mike blamed "irreconcilable differences" for the separation and cast most of the blame on his wife. He considered her spoiled in desiring goods that they could not afford. He expressed that he cannot get along with a woman unless "she can reason and be objective."

Mike and his wife mutually agreed to dissolve their marriage in 1950. Mike was emotionally devastated by the decision, and he confessed that the experience of an unsuccessful marriage had a "negative impact on [his] ability to relate to other women." Mike had an idealistic vision of marriage, and that ideal was shattered forever. He hoped to find in marriage the respect and acceptance that the military, with its racism and social inequity, did not provide. Mike entered marriage frustrated and disillusioned by his military experience, and he could not tolerate an egotistical woman who cared as little for his happiness as the military did.

Mike would not discuss the three daughters who were the product of his marriage. That would hurt too much. But he did express the pain he felt when he saw other people with their families and the "joy they seemed to be experiencing." It was unclear whether Mike ever saw his daughters or salvaged any form of a paternal relationship with them, considering the animosity he felt for their mother. However, he disclosed that he had had such a "peaceful and loving" childhood that he never considered keeping his marriage together if it would result in constant turmoil between him and his wife. Mike believed that good fathers were with their children all the time, and he obviously did not fall into that category. Oddly, Mike remembered all of his children's birthdays, the dates of their first steps and words, and what they looked like while growing up, but he could not say whether he still had contact with them.

Educational History

Mike was an exceptional student. In elementary school, he received a citizen's medal from the Daughters of the American Revolution for outstanding scholarship. He attended one of the city's top high schools, where he excelled in many areas, especially foreign languages, mathematics, and music. He participated in his high school's band and competed on the tennis and swimming teams. Achieving the second highest grade point average in his class, Mike was selected to be the valedictorian in his high school graduation ceremony. His IQ of 137 placed him in the superior range of intelligence.

Mike would have finished high school earlier, but his father insisted that he not skip two grades, as was suggested by his teachers. In later years, Mike felt that this plan operated to his disadvantage. Had he been allowed to advance at his own rate, by the time of the draft, he felt that he could have been in his senior year of college, which would have allowed him either to acquire a student deferment or to enter the military as an officer candidate, enabling him to pursue a military career. In any case, Mike was drafted into the military after his 1st year in college and his education was abruptly interrupted.

After Mike finished his military service, he completed a bachelor's degree in business administration. Part of his motivation for achieving a college degree was to avoid becoming another unsuccessful young Black man in an unsympathetic White culture—another statistic flashed and forgotten in the daily news. For this reason, he chose to prove his ability in a predominantly White college. Mike was the only African American in his college class, and he enjoyed standing out in this way. He wanted "there to be no question of the quality of [his] education, because [he] got the same kind that the White people got."

Mike continues to distinguish himself in the school for the blind that he now attends. He feels funny about returning to school after such a long absence, but he gains satisfaction in demonstrating his academic superiority over the other students. He is constantly boasting about his academic abilities and considers himself one of the school's brightest students.

Work History

From the 2nd year of high school until his graduation, Mike worked during the summers and part time throughout the school year. While in college, he started his own accounting business and was able to solicit 10 clients for the services he offered. However, as the nation's economy began to falter, he lost most of his clients. Luckily, he quickly found a job in the federal government that enabled him to maintain his income level. When his marriage dissolved, he moved to California, where he held various progressively responsible positions in management. However, he expressed bitterness at the discrimination he encountered in the workplace that precluded him from fully realizing his potential.

Mike's favorite job was with a shipping company composed predominantly of White employees. He reported that "the company's comptroller had a high school education and was prejudiced and stupid." He mentioned, "I did not last long because the comptroller was adverse to me." Mike explained that this administrator repeatedly gave him poor performance reviews and once filed an erroneous grievance stating that Mike had fallen asleep at his desk on April 14th—the deadline for filing taxes with the Internal Revenue Service—when the truth was that Mike was working intensely in a huddled posture to get the returns out on time. The comptroller was never reprimanded for making the false report, nor did he apologize.

Fortunately, Mike was able to leave this company to return to work with the federal government and then a savings and loan on the East Coast. Ten months later, he began to develop glaucoma, which began as mild headaches and occasional sightings of halos around bright lights. To reduce the strain on his eyes caused by detailed accounting work, Mike terminated his employment with the savings and loan and began working for an insurance company. He worked there for the next 10 years but was finally forced to retire because of his failing eyesight. Sadly, the president of the company was about to offer Mike a high-level executive position, but Mike had to refuse it because his glaucoma had reduced him to almost complete blindness. Mike regretted that this unfortunate twist of fate had robbed him of the "break" for which he had long awaited.

Medical History

Mike suffered from diphtheria as a child, and this illness caused him to feel chronically weak and tired. However, he believed that being a weak child redirected his energies to reading and quiet games, rather than to sports and outdoor activities, which established the pattern for his later studiousness. While in junior high school, Mike acquired an interest in swimming and tennis that helped to develop his physical stature, but he never became a sports enthusiast or a star athlete.

Except for the onset of hypertension and severe headaches, Mike enjoyed good health while living in California. Mike's doctors in California could not discover the cause of his headaches. After returning to the East Coast, he was examined by a neurologist, who referred him to an ophthalmologist. This specialist was able to locate the cause of Mike's headaches in the eye strain attendant to diminishing vision. During an eye examination, Mike recalled being "asked to cover my right eye while looking through my left eye, and I found that I could not see anything. . . . The doctor told me that had I come to him a few weeks earlier he might have been able to save my vision." Mike was shocked by what he had heard. He remembers driving home while shaking in the car seat—a cold, moist sweat had soaked his undershirt.

Mike ruminated over the doctor's prognosis that he was destined to lose his eyesight to glaucoma. For 5 years, he felt mad and resentful about his condition and wanted to sue his doctors and the employers who had overtaxed his eyesight on their financial records, but he realized that his anger was misplaced. He now believes that he is "on top of it," but he will not share any fears or deep feelings about the prospect of total blindness. Mike retains a small visual field, but he is considered legally blind.

Mike also suffers from hypertension, as his mother had. He is also beginning to develop osteoarthritis—which causes pain and stiffness along his spine—but he claims that its chronic discomfort is not a problem.

Social History

Mike had as normal a childhood as could be expected living in a poor inner-city enclave. The fatigue and weakness caused by his diphtheria, however, made him very introspective, and he devoted a substantial amount of time to reading. His relationship with his only brother, Morris, was not close. Mike maintains that he had many friends, but he qualifies the sociability this would imply by confessing, "When you get right down to it, I guess I'm basically a loner." Mike has only spoken about one or two close friends in counseling. Sadly, his closest male friend died last year of an unexpected heart attack while carrying groceries up his front stairs.

Mike enjoys the company of women, and they enjoy the charm Mike exhibits in their presence. Currently, he has three close female friends, but he does not want to remarry because he is afraid that his disability would make him a burden to his wife. At the same time, he expressed that "if I did remarry, the woman would have to compromise and do things my way. . . . I think women are illogical and have no order in their lives." Mike's voice rose as he made his next point: "I feel a great deal of hostility at how women like to pry." He felt that "ladies are quite aggressive in their own way. . . . It's a myth that little girls are made of sugar and spice and everything nice." However, Mike claimed that he loves women, despite their shortcomings, and that 90% of his friends are female. But he emphatically tells his new female friends that "they have to debitch and make their own decisions instead of allowing other women to influence them."

Mike enjoys listening to jazz and classical music. He collects records and tapes and spends time escorting women to concerts, plays, movies, and dances. However, since the loss of his eyesight, he finds these activities confusing and stressful, and he is slowly becoming reclusive.

Mental Health History

Mike worries about his ability to control his emotions, fearing that he may be a ticking time bomb with an easily ignitable fuse. He traced the first suggestion that he could lose his control to his father's warning: "My father told me that if I did not try to control my temper, I would be in serious trouble someday." However, Mike's initial realization that he might need psychological help came after entering the military, where he became entangled in a dispute with two other soldiers. Mike remembered angrily telling his commanding officer, "I promise you if we go overseas, they [the two soldiers] are not coming back." Mike emphasized in counseling that he truly had homicidal intention, "I had intended to kill 'em, I never had any doubt in my mind. I never realized how deep my anger was. . . . When I realized that I really meant it, I had to find out how to control my anger, how to be totally in control at all times." Mike fears that he can lose his self-control, and he tries to prevent this possibility by exercising excessive self-control. He describes his self-control as "a device, a safety valve essential to my existence. It is a method of living in which you have to keep all your feelings inside." Mike equates his self-control to a traffic cop who "stays on duty."

Mike's need for control encroaches on his relationships with others. He took an overly controlling stance on his children's care, demanding that he must be their guardian all the time or not at all. Obviously, this is an unreasonable position for a father to take when the children's mother is a fit and loving parent. Mike's need for control would seem to overshadow the needs of others. In interpersonal relationships, he feels that the other party must compromise and conform to his opinions and behaviors.

Mike has difficulty in discussing his intimate feelings. He finds safety in intellectualizing. Like his father, he believes that the only way to communicate with people is on a nonemotional level. When discussing his feelings, Mike's voice rises, and he starts to stutter. Part of Mike's repression of feeling may have a cultural and familial element because African American men historically have had difficulty in expressing emotion.

CASE ANALYSIS
Conceptual Perspective

It appears that Mike's achievements throughout his life have not equaled his expectations. The many challenges in his life—touching interpersonal, physical, and professional issues—have engendered feelings of bitterness, frustration, and anger.

Racism has proved to be the greatest challenge in Mike's life. Although a subtle and unseen force, racism may have kept Mike from rapidly advancing in the military and workplace. Although he attempted to equip himself against it by attending a predominantly White college and absorbing the language and mannerisms of the majority culture, he was unsuccessful. The anger evident in his verbal and nonverbal expressions is most likely the result of a combination of the racism he has experienced and his hostility toward what he feels was a prejudicial culture that blocked his upward mobility.

Mike believed that had his father been born of a different race and in different social circumstances, he would have understood the value of skipping grades in school. Mike felt that his father's judgment put him at great disadvantage because, had he skipped two grades, as was recommended to his father, he would have been a senior in college at the time of the draft and therefore might have avoided it. Mike emphasized, "Had I volunteered, I would have gone in at an officer's level and might have continued in a military career." He considers racism and the miltiary draft as major life forces that undermined his professional development.

The dissolution of Mike's marriage and the disintegration of his family were significant sources of demoralization for him. Mike blames the breakup of his marriage on his wife's self-centeredness, but the truth may be that Mike may not have possessed the relationship skills necessary for a successful marriage. Mike exhibited ambivalent feelings toward women, and such mixed feelings may have stemmed from his relationship with his mother. Although Mike had a close and positive relationship with her, she died prematurely in a critical phase of his young adulthood. Her unexpected passing may have instilled in Mike a fear of abandonment by women. To prevent women from hurting him, as his mother had by dying, Mike keeps women at a distance or devalues them—just as he did with his wife. At the same time, Mike acquires many female friends, because at an unconscious level, he may wish to reexperience vicariously the positive relationship with his mother through his relationships with his female friends.

Although Mike has devised a means to control his aggressive impulses, in so doing he has become something of a "control freak." In the military, he recognized the severity of his impulse control challenge and devised a perfectionistic way to address it. The result seems to be severe repression of feeling, which he uses as a response to all the painful events and failures in his life. Mike's excessive efforts to maintain self-control have become a new challenge because they interfere with his relationships with others. However, his repression of negative feelings may have later proved to be an ally in moderating his response to discrimination in the workplace, making it a double-edged sword.

Mike has no meaningful support system. He considers himself "a loner," who keeps his friends at arm's length. His mother, who was his main emotional support, died early. He is estranged from his ex-wife. His father is old, and, by Mike's account, his brother requires his assistance and cannot serve as a source of support. The most meaningful friend in Mike's life was the male friend who died last year. Mike faces life virtually alone.

Existential Perspective

Mike's life has been riddled with loss: his mother, his marriage, his best friend, and now his vision. These losses have increased his sense of existential anxiety, owing to the fact that the metaphorical and physical deaths of loved ones, dreams, and bodily capacities have become a familiar reality to which he has grown sensitized. All persons suffer from a baseline level of existential anxiety because of the universal fear of death, but repeated losses in one's life heighten this anxiety by creating isolation and reminding one of one's own mortality. Mike's fixation on self-control may be partly his unrealistic attempt to feel some measure of control over the uncontrollable givens of life.

Mike craved meaning in his life. He derived some meaning from his work, but with his recent loss of vision, Mike found himself unemployed, which created an existential void and the need for him to find sources of meaning outside of his work to fill that devouring sense of emptiness and frustration. He appears currently "stuck" in the search for new sources of meaning in work, social relations, and his contributions to humanity as a whole. Mike shows no religious or spiritual outlet, which may contribute to his lack of meaning.

DSM–IV (APA, 1994) Perspective

Mike's loss of sight appears to be the major psychosocial stressor in his life that is of any diagnostic importance. His visual disability is coupled with an inadequate social support system and his belief that he is functioning within a discriminatory culture that impedes his economic advancement. His background as an African American man should be noted on Axis IV to recognize the cultural factors that are possibly contributing to his repression of feeling and anger toward society— both of which may contribute to his anxiety and depression.

Multiaxial Diagnosis

Axis I	Adjustment disorder with mixed anxiety and depressed mood—chronic (309.28)
Axis II	No diagnosis
Axis III	Chronic open angle glaucoma (365.9)
Axis IV	Victim of racial discrimination, contributing to anger; possible cultural inhibition from expressing emotion
Axis V	GAF = 65 (current), with moderate difficulty in social and occupational functioning

INTERVENTION STRATEGIES

Mike possesses a number of strengths that can be used in his rehabilitation and healing. He is intelligent and well educated and has ample experience in the business world. His willingness to take courses for the blind demonstrates that he partly realizes the gravity of his situation and his need to take adaptive measures. He has shown throughout his life a desire to improve himself, and even if he now appears hopeless and resigned to his situation, the seeds of self-improvement lie dormant inside, awaiting the encouragement of the counselor.

In working effectively with Mike, developing trust will be a critical issue, especially because the counselor is a White woman. The client has been hurt many times in life by women and what he believes to be a discriminatory White society. A White female counselor must expect distrust and anger initially in the counseling relationship but should remain unfazed by these demonstrations of emotion so as to prove to Mike that she can be trusted and is committed to his therapy.

Mike should be encouraged to find work and increase social contact as an immediate way to decrease his isolation. It may prove useful to explore his history of relationships with women so that patterns that created hurt and misunderstanding can be identified. This realization could help him learn to experience more enriching relationships with women. His history of racial discrimination is also a fertile area for exploration: Allowing Mike to discuss his unfair treatment may allow catharsis of his anger and help him to gain a realistic perspective on why he never realized his expectations in life. The release of anger often is a potent remedy for depression because this condition often is engendered by anger turned against the self.

The most important therapeutic issue, however, is to help Mike adapt to his blindness and assume a meaningful life. Blindness is a major life trauma whose proportions are so painful that many persons who are losing their sight must deny this eventuality to buffer the pain its realization would bring. Blindness is an eternal immersion in darkness. It conjures up our most primitive childhood fears of the dark.

DISCUSSION OF THE CASE

The conceptual, existential, and *DSM–IV* perspectives coexist when interpreting a client's behavior. One of the common threads that runs through the three is the interaction between Mike's physical disability and his emotional state. Mike's loss of vision was like a small tremor that revealed the fault lines in his social relationships, sense of purpose, and ability to find happiness. Before he lost his vision, Mike was a productive and hardworking individual, but he neglected to attend to the personal issues that were unsettling his life. Now he needs the friends and family from whom he distanced himself to provide his physical and emotional support. His blindness may present an opportunity for reconciliation and better human relationships with others.

Mike had faced discrimination in his life because of his race. Now he must be prepared to face discrimination once again, but this time because of his visual disability. There is no doubt that Mike is a strong person: He has never conceded to the challenges before him but has faced them courageously. However, his courage could be emboldened with the support of better human relationships. Discrimination has also filled Mike with a passionate anger. But it is a general principle of psychotherapy that the degree of a client's anger is proportionate to the positive energy available for change, if it is channeled properly. Mike must learn more adaptive responses to discrimination. With all his passion, he should eventually find greater happiness in life.

DISCUSSION QUESTIONS

1. What other sociological, psychological, and physical factors, other than those mentioned, may have contributed to the client's present state?

2. How might you encourage a client such as this one who represses emotion to express feelings more fully?

3. How can a counselor help this client to "let go" of some of the pain he has experienced in his life?

4. Discuss the relationship between the client's thoughts, feelings, and behaviors.

5. List three short-term goals and three long-term goals for this client.

6. List two techniques to increase the possibility of generalizing adaptive behavior outside of the counseling session.

7. How has the client contributed to his own feelings of existential isolation?

8. Using the *DSM–IV* perspective, what additional cultural considerations could be acknowledged?

9. What are some methods you, as a counselor, could use to determine the level of acculturation of this client?

10. What personal qualities could you, as a counselor, bring into a counseling relationship with this client that would improve the therapeutic alliance?

CHAPTER FIVE

Where Courage and Sexuality Meet: The Challenge of Being Gay

INTRODUCTION

Hermes is a gay Latino man. The very merging of the words gay and Latino seem a contradiction in terms. Latin male culture, at least in its popular stereotype, is perceived to be defined by machismo and hetero-sexual prowess. The idea of a gay Latino would be a new and monumental accommodation in an old and traditional Catholic culture, particularly in the mind of a client who finds himself in this situation. Hermes's homosexuality, an issue of greatest privacy, had intersected with the powerful cultural forces that had shaped his psychology, bringing him into conflict with himself.

Hermes left his native Caracas, Venezuela at the age of 23 with all his worldly possessions. In one pocket was a one-way plane ticket with the destination of Washington, DC; in the other was an angry letter from his mother, Rosa, written with the passion of a mother who wanted her son to renounce his "strange attraction" to men and stop embarrassing his prominent family. Hermes had the best of everything in a country that was stratified between rich and poor. His father was an esteemed lawyer whose name was proposed periodically to fill the position of justice of the nation's highest court. His mother was a proud and traditional homemaker who was devoted to the well-being of her family, particularly that of her youngest son, Hermes.

Hermes's quest to leave his family and home country was fueled by a profound desire to find expression of his true self—a self that he felt was bottled up and disguised in layers of deception. To be gay in a family and culture that does not sanction your sexuality is to live with a part of yourself invalidated. Because sexuality is almost invariably tied to the full reception and expression of love, Hermes felt the need to leave his privileged upbringing to find the love that his culture sadly denied him. He landed in Washington, DC, without a connection or a specific plan, but with the hope of finding the love he yearned for.

PRESENTING CHALLENGE

After living in the states for 11 months, Hermes's inner confusion joined with a disillusionment over what he found to be gay culture in Washington, DC. He realized that his quest to find identity and love was not as simple as a departure from Latin America. The United States was tolerant of homosexuality but not embracing of it. He found a safe enclave and friends in the Dupont Circle section of Washington, but even there, he was having difficulty finding himself. He asked a gay friend for advice and was referred to a branch of a mental health clinic specializing in gay issues. Realizing that the clinic may charge a fee for its services—unless he was diagnosed with HIV/AIDS or was indigent— he decided to arrive under the pretense of having HIV/AIDS.

Although Hermes was raised to be immaculately honest by an upright lawyer father, he felt that he had "HIV/AIDS of the soul." Although not physically stricken—and without the psychological mindedness to describe his problem—he thought that he was being partly honest in metaphorically comparing the extent of his despair with HIV/AIDS. He saw himself as an infected leper in a leper colony and wanted to free himself from the heavy stigma, self-loathing, and guilt he carried that seemed like a contagious viral presence in his body. For a while, he almost believed himself to be physically sick, as apathy, morbid rumination, and listlessness overcame him. His challenge was not a physical ailment, however, but the severe sadness that is attendant to not being able to love one's self as a gay man.

When the day of his appointment arrived, Hermes was greeted by a counselor he hardly expected. Her name was Angelica, and she too was from Latin America and was a lesbian. Hermes knew this almost immediately. Many gay people report that they have a "spiritual radar"—a sixth sense—that communicates without words a likeness and shared plight on first impression. Hermes knew that Angelica was a lesbian before she disclosed it as part of her introduction. His meeting of another gay Latin American individual "opened [his] soul"—as he put it—from which poured out his loneliness and confusion. He missed his family in which he was the youngest. In the United States, there was no family to nurture him or from whom to seek comfort, however rejecting his family later became.

Hermes also felt that his skills were not relevant in a foreign country. Without a green card, his honors degree in business administration and his creative marketing ideas were of no use to any company. He would not even get a job interview. His occupation as a part-time street vendor, cabdriver, and janitor–handyman was embarrassing coming from a family who employed two full-time housekeepers. Had he given up everything only to discover an absurd poverty with no greater insight into himself than before? A long pregnant pause ensued in the first counseling session between Hermes and Angelica.

CASE HISTORY

Cultural Background

Hermes came from a culture where the concept of *familismo* is strongly ingrained. The member of a traditional Latin American family is accustomed to being embedded in an extended family system that is composed not only of blood relatives but also of close friends who are given the status of quasi-family. The individualism that is popular in the United States is less pronounced in Latin America, where the family both directly and indirectly shapes the life course of each member. In the Latin American family, there is always a family member who has the status of an elder, from whom one usually solicits advice. To seek advice from a counselor may not be as rare or unusual as is commonly thought in the modern Latin American family, but it may be seen as a deficiency in the family in managing its affairs. Seeing Angelica was indeed a departure from tradition as great as being gay. Hermes constantly found himself at odds with his culture: The repeated clash of personal and cultural worldviews overwhelmed him with confusion and sadness.

Feeling the loss of his family, Hermes yearned to feel close to and bond with another human being. Ironically, the mixed messages his family gave him regarding his own sexuality caused him to fear intimacy. He believed that love and pain were intertwined because the models of his primary love relationships with his parents and siblings were associated with rejection. Every time Hermes began to get close to a gay lover or friend, he welled up with fear that the intimacy could lead to rejection. As his defense mechanism against rejection, he felt that he became "bitchy and sarcastic" and pushed the budding lover or confidant away. "No friendship" is better than a "friendship that could end in pain" was how Hermes rationalized his behavior. His thinking was black and white, but so too was the experience of his family: He was a gay man, and they rejected him.

Soothing Pain With Alcohol

In the Dupont Circle and Adams Morgan sections of Washington are a half dozen gay bars where Hermes frequents after finishing one of his miscellaneous jobs. Bar hopping is a means for Hermes to find companionship, however transient. He enjoys talking to strangers in bars who, in turn, are intrigued by his highbrow Spanish accent, naive curiosity regarding American culture, and particularly his youthful appearance, which some feel is prized in American bar culture. Hermes has met a few friends in bars and had one anonymous sexual encounter on an evening when he was feeling very lonely and had had "a little too much to drink." He realizes the dangers of HIV/AIDS and believes that he wore a condom during the brief sexual liaison, which occurred in the stranger's parked utility van.

Hermes is concerned that he has turned to alcohol to dull some of his pain. He was never a drinker before he came to the United States, but he found that alcohol can be a quick relaxant from the anxiety of his loneliness. It is also interesting that alcohol heightens Hermes's self-confidence and provides him with added bravado in approaching strangers in bars. When he has too much alcohol, however, he is reckless and foolhardy, and, at times, the alcohol will disinhibit his anger and give him permission to vent at his family, the universe, and the god who imbued him with a "strange attraction" to members of his own sex. Alcohol provides cathartic release of Hermes's anger, but the anger never seems to drain out and extinguish itself.

Although Hermes drank infrequently before coming to the United States, he and alcohol had a long and familiar history. Hermes's father, Enrique, frequently drank to unwind from his heavy responsibilities as a government lawyer. Like Hermes, when Enrique had too much to drink, he vented his frustrations openly, and family members were often the sounding board. Hermes remembers hiding when he sniffed the smell of a martini or of whiskey in his father's study: The odor was a signal to stay clear or receive the fury of his father's anguish for any peccadillo. The association between alcohol and his father's anger may have been why Hermes was uninterested in alcohol while growing up but later resorted to this dysfunctional coping mechanism that was modeled by his father.

Hermes's Estranged Sister

Hermes's older sister, Carmen, had moved to Peru to live with a boyfriend whom she met in her last year of college. There was a family rumor that Hermes's father, Enrique, had made sexual advances on his daughter during one of his drunken stupors. Hermes's mother would extinguish any discussion about the episode when a sibling would inquire, but Carmen became alienated from both her mother and father, leaving home at the age of 17 to live at the university and, on graduation, striking off to Peru to live with a boyfriend whom she had scarcely known for 2 months. Interestingly, she tried to make contact with Hermes by letter when he arrived in the United States. Hermes called her in Peru but found her to be reticent and detached, perhaps distrustful of him. He wondered why she wanted to reach him but became so aloof when he responded. In his heart, he knew the answer: She had been traumatized by their family as much as he had, but she was not ready to find support in their similar life histories.

Hermes worried about Carmen. He knew that her choice of men was never wise. She always seemed drawn to men who were charming and exciting but who were often emotionally abusive or unappreciative of her many wonderful qualities. Hermes had heard that the Peruvian boyfriend was an alcoholic like their father and had already cheated on Carmen. But Carmen tolerated the abuse with cool composure. She had been ingrained with the cultural value of *marianismo*, the belief that a woman's spiritual superiority over a man can enable her to endure any hardship that is inflicted by him. Carmen had seen *marianismo* practiced by her mother, who tolerated Enrique's drunken fits and aggressive sexual advances toward her.

Hermes's Father and Brother

When Hermes was 16, he tried to tell his father that he was gay. He had an idealistic fantasy that his very traditional Latin father would love him despite his sexual orientation. Enrique was perplexed by his son's ambiguous confession of "liking men" and perhaps "wishing to marry one." He became more confused than angered by this awkward discussion and simply assured his son that he would one day marry a beautiful woman and be very successful. He told Hermes that he felt that he was too young to be having sexual intercourse but wanted him to come to him when he had found a girlfriend. Enrique thought that Hermes was simply creating a diversion to talk about having intercourse with a girlfriend. Enrique thought of himself as a creative lawyer and that his son had simply learned from him to package the truth in a cunning disguise. Ironically, he was proud of his son's trickery but failed to realize that it was not a trick at all.

Enrique favored Hermes's older brother, Pablo, who was the quintessential son of an affluent lawyer. Handsome, charming, and bright, Pablo was also in the United States studying for an advanced master's degree in international law at Harvard University. The unequal feelings of affection expressed by Enrique created resentment in Hermes and some jealousy toward Pablo. Hermes knew that Pablo had an uglier side that his father did not wish to see. Although he still appeared to be superficially everything a son should be, internally, Pablo was morally flawed. He traveled in fast circles and burned up his father's money on fancy designer clothes, high-grade cocaine, and women. Although Pablo's relationship with Hermes was civil, Pablo was too preoccupied with chasing superficial pursuits to spend any time trying to connect with his brother or to understand his issues. Pablo called Hermes once to say that he would be in Washington briefly to meet a female friend in Georgetown, but Hermes was unable to catch up with him. Hermes's most successful communication with Pablo was through the latter's hotel answering machine.

In his unconscious mind, Hermes was glad to have missed his brother. It was his childhood attraction to his brother's sculptured and muscular body that led to the awakening of Hermes's homosexuality. To hang out with Pablo as an independent adult would feel awkward and even shameful if those feelings returned. Pablo was a very attractive man, but he was also Hermes's brother. Hermes was relieved to avoid incestuous feelings by not seeing Pablo; however, he bemoaned that he could not connect lovingly with his own brother, who would remain a stranger to him.

When Hermes turned 13, he discussed the sexual feelings toward his brother with a young male teacher. The conversations continued for months and turned into "movie dates" and "dinners." Finally, the teacher invited Hermes to his apartment, where there was some awkward sexual contact, particularly petting, that did not culminate in undress or sexual intercourse. The episode was very disturbing to Hermes, who never mentioned it to anyone, except Angelica. Hermes had no further sexual contact with the teacher, but he remembered the teacher constantly bumping into him in the hallways, admonishing him to "always keep our little secret." The memory of the teacher filled Hermes with a disquieting ambivalence: feeling revulsion at the exploitation by an adult but also learning about his sexual identity, if in a twisted manner.

Expressing His Homosexuality

Through his college years, Hermes began a chain of brief sexual encounters with men. His first encounter was with a man who had a wife and several children whom he would meet in a hotel in downtown Caracas. The men Hermes associated with were always older and often emotionally cold but successful. In a moment of reflection, Hermes acknowledged how similar these men were to his father: All were unloving, and Hermes had to work hard to elicit their affection. All his partners broke off the relationship after reaching a point of sexual boredom with Hermes and moved on to their next conquest. Hermes realized that these encounters had no love in them, only the trappings of love—the touching, the kissing, and the togetherness—but not the spirituality of love. It was for the possibility of this nobler emotion that Hermes wandered from lover to lover in vain, never realizing that the superficial relationships that he had developed would only be conducive to physical intimacy and nothing more.

By the end of Hermes's college years, his father and mother became aware of Hermes's homosexuality through both gossip and the disclosures of Pablo. Enrique wanted Hermes to enter a sanitarium or "never step foot again" in his house. Hermes's mother, Rosa, being obsessively conscious about her family's image, felt that there was less of a stigma in telling neighbors and friends that Hermes was a drug addict and was not responsible for his sleeping around with older men. She explained that the "drugs created a craving" that forced him to prostitute himself for money to feed his destructive habit. She avoided being seen with her own son but periodically sent him sizable sums of money so he could finish college and, consequently, would not further embarrass the family by becoming a vagrant. Hermes knew he had reached a point of no return: It was "America or bust."

CASE ANALYSIS

Conceptual Perspective

When considering the case of Hermes, one is struck by the clash of culture and biology. Hermes's homosexuality is evolving despite the prohibitions against homosexuality by his family and culture. Obviously, the biological force is the stronger of the two that cannot be escaped or rejected. It is a respected thesis in psychology that homosexuality is no more a choice than heterosexuality, and some research suggests that it may be genetically predetermined (Bayer, 1987; Hammer, 1993; Lavely, 1991). If one accepts the biological predetermination of a homosexual orientation, there is little that a gay man or lesbian can do in a culture that rejects homosexuality, except to reject the values of that culture.

Rejecting cultural values is not a simple or painless act. As we develop in a culture, its values exist not simply as academic propositions to be accepted or rejected but as intimate parts of our personality. Somewhere in Hermes's psychology is the self-hatred that was instilled by his family and culture for being a gay man. He cannot erase those messages and memories with the simple acknowledgment that homosexuality is natural and accepted by many cultures outside his own. The prohibition against homosexuality will always haunt him because it was instilled by the powerful influence of his culture, translated through his family, whose values will assume an irrational hold over him. When love is provided in a family for exhibiting a cultural behavior, or refraining from one, however illogical that behavior, it will become a part of the person's value system, not easily extinguished through logical reasoning or therapeutic confrontation. Declaring one's homosexuality would be at the expense of severing family and cultural "bonds of love," whose undoing is excruciatingly painful.

Angelica, Hermes's counselor, had her work cut out for her. Her first task was to convince Hermes that a gay lifestyle was as natural as a heterosexual one. In the first three sessions, she repeated this statement over and over again, but Hermes did not hear it. He acknowledged that he was a gay man but preferred to hold simultaneously the belief that "homosexuality is less than ideal." It was interesting that Angelica noticed that this intrapsychic conflict was even reflected in Hermes's choice of clothing. He constantly wore fancy pink and green silk and cotton shirts underneath a dark colored vest. Angelica observed, "Hermes, you want to be gay, but you don't want your sexuality to be known to anyone but yourself. How will you find support and companionship when no one knows what you are?"

Being deceptive concerning his sexuality was an art that Hermes had honed in his native country. The deeper problem was that he had deceived even himself about his sexuality. Hermes's sex life became a secretive avocation that was peripheral to what he deemed as his core identity: Like an alcoholic, Hermes was in denial. He continued to see himself as the upper-class Latin American who would one day have a successful career and family and perhaps return to his native Venezuela. He maintained this fantasy to protect himself from cognitive dissonance, or the intrapsychic conflict between the rejection of homosexuality by his native culture and its acceptance by his host culture. Inner conflict leads to pain, and pain was what Hermes wished to avoid at all costs, even if it meant resorting to the alcohol that he despised his own father for depending on.

Angelica was a very insightful therapist: She realized that Hermes required a more powerful intervention to break down his ineffective style of coping with his situation. It so happened that the clinic in which Angelica worked was running a gay support group that, although not intended for a multicultural population, was very multicultural in its composition. Although Angelica feared that Hermes would be hesitant to join such a group, she persuaded him to join. His initial response was "no," but Angelica devoted the next two sessions to convincing Hermes of the group's necessity. She realized that other gay men could challenge and support Hermes better than she could, irrespective of her own gay and Latin background. Angelica knew that a group was a powerful experience, but she also realized that she was taking a therapeutic risk by encouraging his participation against his own sense of readiness.

Hermes's first group meeting was a disaster. Although he felt that he was ready to announce his homosexuality to the world, he backed down and, oddly, felt repulsed by the comembers' own openness regarding their homosexuality. In a situation of stress, the old cultural messages replayed in his mind and served as a retreat against moving forward toward his true identity. He also believed irrationally that a group of fellow gay men would reject him, just as his family had rejected him, so that he had to reject them first. Hermes was silent in the group until one of the comembers, who was also Latin American, asked him to comment on his conflict with his male lover. Hermes retorted in a sarcastic tone, "I wouldn't know about that." The group angrily jumped on Hermes, calling him arrogant and a "closeted fag." He dropped out of the group that first evening but fortunately returned to working individually with Angelica.

After five more sessions with Angelica, Hermes felt confident that he could return to the group. It was interesting that he no longer wore his "black vest," his symbolic covering of his identity from others. Midway into the group's 2-hr session, Hermes opened up. At first, he commented on a comember's problem but then said a few words in response to the group leader about what had provoked him to rejoin the group. It was a liberating "six sentences" for Hermes, beginning with, "I wanted to learn how to accept myself, even if my family would never accept me." Hermes realized that the group's support had the power to supplant the negative messages of his family and culture, although a few such messages might linger forever and need to be challenged periodically in therapy.

Existential Perspective

In helping clients to find their sexual orientation, counselors often focus on issues of sexuality to the exclusion of issues of love. Although Hermes undoubtedly felt sexually attracted to other men, his choice of sexual partners did not reflect a healthy quest for love. In college, his sexual partners were rich, older men (like his father) who used him as a "sexual object" and later discarded him. It was easy to discern what Hermes gained from these relationships: the love and acceptance of his father expressed through men who resembled him. When Hermes came to Washington, he had an unplanned sexual contact with a partner whose name he did not even know. In a stressful, new environment, he seems to have regressed to the curious, teenage boy who had the secret sexual liaison with his teacher. He wanted to experiment with homosexual expression but could not accept having an open gay relationship with a loving partner.

Although counselor training programs often have succeeded in instilling an intellectual tolerance of homosexuality, many heterosexual counselors have conceded retaining an emotional rejection of it. Intellectually accepting individuals' sexual orientation, however, may not be sufficient to be a good counselor to them, especially if counselors reject their lifestyle emotionally. Counseling requires empathy, and this mindset is not possible when the counselor possesses a preexisting emotional barrier to the client. An intuitive and nonrejecting heterosexual counselor will realize that gay men and lesbians, as much as heterosexuals, require healthy, loving relationships. However, many heterosexual counselors may not see that Hermes's issue revolves around finding a healthy homosexual love relationship in which he feels validated and loved as a person, because they are so focused on the unsettling issue of sexual orientation.

Because Hermes is having homosexual liaisons, many heterosexual counselors may perceive him as developing a self-acceptance of his sexual orientation. But the truth may be that gay men cannot maturely accept their homosexuality by merely having sex with other men. Sexual intimacy is not a sign of mental health unless it becomes an expression of love in a caring relationship. Unfortunately, the popular media show us few examples of loving homosexual couples, so many heterosexuals assume that the normative homosexual experience reflects the wild and promiscuous portrayals of homosexuality that is prevalent in dramatic movies. However, the normative homosexual couple functions no differently than the normative heterosexual couple: Ideally, they will love each other exclusively and live together indefinitely. Of course, this is an ideal that is difficult to achieve for both heterosexuals and homosexuals in our modern culture where sexual infidelity, separation, and divorce are becoming commonplace.

The fact that the search for authentic love is a core issue for Hermes's siblings may substantiate that it is a core issue for him and point to its origin in his family's dynamics. Hermes's sister, Carmen, rashly moved in with a boyfriend she scarcely knew and tolerates his infidelity. Her behavior reveals a desperation for love and a poor sense of self-respect. Just as Carmen's father, Enrique, withheld his love from Hermes as a punishment for his homosexuality, he sullied his love toward her through his sexual abuse. Enrique broke the inviolable bonds of trust and love that exist between father and daughter, and, for this reason, his daughter has no model of mature love either from the relationship with him or from the marriage of her mother and father, in which there was spousal abuse. Pablo's womanizing and drug use, although more subtle, seem to reflect a superficial understanding of love. Neither Hermes nor his siblings learned how to love in their family, and there is usually no school outside the family that teaches love, except the counsel of an intuitive therapist (who often gets the client long after the sometimes irreversible damage has been done).

Hermes's use of alcohol may be a sign of a love problem, too. The pain he is trying to dull with alcohol, involving self-loathing and loneliness, is derived from a deficiency in love. It is fascinating that after leaving South America, he finds himself in one of the world's largest gay communities, but he still cannot find identity or happiness. Wherever he goes, or with whomever he associates, he still carries the emotional experience of his family in which love was not taught. He must learn how to love so that his sexuality will become the expression of that nobler emotion. At present, his sexuality is an affirmation of his attraction to men and a pleasurable release of sexual feelings, but identities and happiness are built out of more enduring feelings and relationships within the context of a supportive community.

By living "in the closet," Hermes most emphatically reveals his lack of self-love. Although there are dangers of rejection and discrimination in living an openly gay lifestyle, to not "come out of the closet" even among those like one's self, can only reflect shame and self-hatred. Surely, one must be prudent about where and when to reveal one's homosexuality, but to never reveal it is to live with a part of one's self denied and to forego the loving partner that could have been attracted had one's sexuality been explicit. Hermes must learn to love himself before the love of another is possible.

DSM–IV (APA, 1994) Perspective

In all honesty, the mental health community, like the rest of society, was not historically tolerant of homosexuality as an alternative sexual orientation. Until 1973, homosexuality was considered a mental illness, and various psychoanalytic and behavioral treatments were used to return gay men and lesbians to "normal" heterosexual behavior (Bayer, 1987). Even though homosexuality is now considered a normal form of sexual expression along the spectrum of human sexuality and is no longer even mentioned in diagnostic manuals, it would be disingenuous to state that all segments of the mental health community are in agreement with this viewpoint. Many politically conservative and religious mental health professionals, and even a few in the orthodox psychoanalytic schools, continue to believe that homosexuality is unnatural or neurotic. That reminder of social context is perhaps a necessary preface to the choice of compassionate and realistic diagnoses.

Hermes's therapist, Angelica, chose the least stigmatizing diagnosis of identity problem (which is considered in the *DSM–IV* as a "V-Code," or a problem in living). She considered adding substance abuse as a secondary diagnosis but felt that although Hermes's drinking was serious, it was not severe enough to warrant that label. She would keep his drinking problem in mind and encourage him to reduce his use of alcohol, although she believed that it would subside with the resolution of his issues. In deciding on the diagnosis of identity problem, Angelica was stating that Hermes was having difficulty accepting his sexual identity. She never liked labeling anyone, particularly gay men and lesbians having difficulty with their sexual orientation, because she realized that in a culture that stigmatizes homosexuality, every gay man or lesbian has an identity problem, at least at some point in his or her life.

Most gay men and lesbians with whom Angelica has worked have confided to her that they would never have chosen to be gay had they actually been given the choice. Every gay man or lesbian goes through an identity problem after acknowledging that they possess a sexual orientation that is in the minority. For some, this is a very serious internal conflict that can lead to depression and end in suicide. For this reason, identity problems must always be considered significant issues, even if they are simply classified as the nonserious V-Codes. Whereas the *DSM–IV* has a label for an identity problem, ironically it has none for Hermes's lack of self-love that seems to drive his quest for identity. Perhaps self-love should not be mentioned in the *DSM–IV*, because it is an unscientific term, but in not mentioning or conceptualizing this important feeling, we may be glossing over the essence of good mental health.

Multiaxial Diagnosis

Axis I	Identity problem (313.82)
Axis II	No diagnosis
Axis III	No diagnosis
Axis IV	Raised in a culture not accepting homosexuality
Axis V	GAF = 80 (current)

INTERVENTION STRATEGY

Angelica was very wise to refer Hermes for group counseling. Some counselors want to solve a client's issue on their own as a matter of vanity, but Angelica realized that placing Hermes in a group with others like himself was the best treatment. Although it was necessary to prepare Hermes for the group in individual treatment, there could have been no substitute for the group: Hermes needed to connect with those who shared his issue and to feel accepted by them. The group was a template for his learning to find companionship and love among those who openly and maturely accept their homosexuality.

It was interesting that Hermes initially rejected the group and its members' homosexuality. He wanted no part of it. Competing within his psychology were the two powerful forces of his sexuality and his cultural heritage. One had to be rejected to quell the identity conflict, and Hermes initially chose to reject his sexuality. This is not an unusual choice and, perhaps, reveals the power that culture has over behavior. But, eventually, the sexual urges returned, and Hermes needed to renegotiate which parts of his culture were congruent with his true self and which parts he needed to reject in order to live honestly with his sexual feelings. Although culture is powerful, it is not immutable, like one's sexuality, and it was the weaker link that could be broken so as to allow a new construction of identity.

It is important to respect the client's culture but not to treat it as sacrosanct. It is also important to empower the client with the ability to reject part of one's culture thoughtfully if he or she believes it to be injurious to the self. This is not to advocate a "cultural" or "moral" relativism but to emphasize that acculturation involves choices along the way. Hermes needed to reject his culture's prohibition against gay men and lesbians, and he needed to assimilate the tolerance of homosexuality found in America, out of mere psychological survival. Of course, this whole notion of "rejecting culture" and "differentiating good from bad cultural behaviors" enters the realm of philosophy. But counseling is, in essence, an applied philosophical exercise, where the ultimate judge of right or wrong, for better or worse, must be the client.

DISCUSSION OF THE CASE

Some student counselors and current professionals may passionately disagree with the treatment plan for Hermes outlined here. Hermes's treatment certainly can be conceptualized in different ways. A behaviorist may wish to focus on limiting his anonymous sexual contacts and drinking. A psychodynamically oriented counselor may wish to explore the early dysfunctional relationships with his parents that formed his behaviors. A cognitively oriented counselor may wish to focus on his negative self-talk and irrational beliefs regarding his sexuality. A biologically oriented counselor may even refer Hermes for antidepressant therapy by conceptualizing his lack of self-love and other symptoms as "clinical depression."

The difficulty with the field of counseling is that there is often no one right treatment plan for problems-in-living, although there are various "shades" of better approaches. Angelica allowed her "gut feelings" to lead her to believe that identity and acceptance were at the core of Hermes's issues. She felt that a group experience would be the most expeditious way to answer these concerns. In her individual sessions, she was primarily nondirective and supportive. She did allow Hermes to explore his past, but at his urging and not hers. Her treatment of Hermes became more "artistic" than "scientific," allowing intangible feelings to guide the therapy. Therapists often "live" in the realm of art—even though this may feel scary and unguided—because the "science" of psychotherapy cannot in formulaic terms provide the answer to life's every issue.

Perhaps Angelica's treatment was so effective because it was grounded in the simple humanism that lies at the heart of the counseling process. She truly empathized with Hermes and understood his issues. She allowed his issues to guide her treatment and did not impose a theoretical framework that was alien to his issues just because she enjoyed using that theory. Sometimes counseling is the simplest task in the world, if only counselors would listen to what their clients need, which more often than not involves the opportunity to love and be loved by other human beings (Glasser, 1965).

DISCUSSION QUESTIONS

1. Because Hermes's counselor was also gay, do you think that there was the possibility of her unconsciously confusing her own issues surrounding her sexuality with his?

2. Do you think that Hermes was appropriately referred for group over long-term individual treatment?

3. Do you agree with Hermes's diagnosis? Would you have labeled him as depressed?

4. Was self-love a valid construct to guide Hermes's treatment or was it too fuzzy and sentimental?

5. Should Angelica have tried to counsel Hermes to be heterosexual, if that's what he really wished to be?

6. Should HIV/AIDS education have been a part of the treatment plan for Hermes?

7. Would you feel comfortable counseling Hermes? Discussing gay sexual practices?

8. How would you help Hermes pick an appropriate boyfriend?

9. How much of a risk is there that a person having an identity problem may commit suicide? How would you assess Hermes's risk?

10. Do you think that homosexuals are the best counselors of other homosexuals? Do heterosexuals understand homosexuals sufficiently?

CHAPTER SIX

An Escape From Iran: The Challenge of Being Collectivistic in an Individualistic Culture

INTRODUCTION

In the American mind, Iran often conjures up images of Islamic revolutionaries burning the American flag, the siege of the U.S. embassy, and President Carter's failed rescue of the hostages. Although a distorted depiction of an ancient and proud culture, it is a critical part of Iran's history that cannot be ignored because it disrupted and traumatized the lives of thousands of its citizens. Harout is a 29-year-old Armenian man who was born and raised amidst Iran's political turmoil. Unwilling to tolerate its oppressive political climate and seeing no future living as an ethnic minority in Iran, he emigrated to the United States. His struggle to uphold his Armenian identity was the legacy of his ethnic group. They had lived for generations as a minority in a country where the overwhelming majority are Muslim.

Harout and his family were among the small percentage of non-Muslim minorities, including Zoroastrians and Jews, who were in Iran. The Armenian population of approximately 60,000 was concentrated in three major areas: Azerbaijan, Isfahan, and Tehran (Cottam, 1979). Many Armenians became alarmed at the overthrow of the Shah by Muslim fundamentalists in 1979 and believed that the new Iranian regime would no longer tolerate their religious freedom. They fled in droves. Harout's case depicts the plight of one emigrant seeking individual freedom while struggling to maintain connection to his family in an ancient Armenian tradition that cherishes filial piety (Ponterotto, Casas, Suzid, & Alexander, 1995).

Unfortunately, Harout did not find utopia in the United States. He emigrated from a society where his religion was in the minority to another where his complex mixture of Armenian ethnicity and Iranian nationality was in the minority. Now he finds himself caught between respecting the Armenian tradition of being the primary caretaker of his aging parents and pursuing his personal and educational development—a value that is highly regarded in American culture. Harout is split in his allegiance between the values of two cultures, although some of these individualistic values must have been part of the psychology that drew him to the United States.

Harout's counselor is a Latin American woman who is a few years his junior. Coming from an Islamic culture, Harout felt a little uncomfortable seeking assistance from a woman, no less one younger than himself, but her empathy and support were so soothing for Harout that the initial cultural discomfort decreased with each session and eventually was forgotten.

PRESENTING CHALLENGE

Harout lived with his parents, his eldest sister Osana, Osana's husband, and Harout's niece. The living situation became unbearable for Harout because of the strained relationship between his parents and his own resentment toward Osana and her husband. Harout believed that Osana did not give his parents the respect they deserved, nor did she attend to their medical or social needs. Harout explained that Osana is a hairdresser who works every day and only has 1 day off. "On her day off, all she does is sleep," Harout emphasized. "My sister works late and comes home tired. She claims that she doesn't have the energy to deal with our parents." Harout will not speak with Osana's husband, whom he described as obstinate and domineering, and who "thinks he's always right." To add to the intrafamilial strife, Harout was at wit's end with the couple's 16-year-old daughter, who is out of control and enjoys shocking adults with each new obscene word she learns from her friends at school.

In many Armenian families, it is the duty of the eldest son to be the primary caretaker of the parents when they become elderly. Harout is the youngest son, but because his brother Kervork still lives in Iran, and Osana and her husband have expressed their reluctance or apathy for the caretaker role, the responsibility has fallen on his shoulders. It is expected that Kevork will obtain his visa to come to the United States in 2 to 3 years. Even so, Harout did not rely on his brother's anticipated arrival to alter his plan to assume sole responsibility for his parents. Harout described his brother as being unreliable and unable to hold down a job for more than a year. Considering that Kervork would have to learn to speak English to secure a job that would earn enough money to take care of their parents, Harout felt that he would be required to be the caretaker of their parents. He was skeptical that Kervork would ever be able to assume a responsible role in his family. In fact, Harout was unequivocally critical of his brother's maturity, bemoaning, "How can you expect someone to feel responsible when he doesn't even understand the meaning of the word? . . . I feel like I am the only son in the family."

Harout's primary complaint was the resentment he felt toward his sister, Osana. He believed that she was a poor host to her parents, who have expressed the desire to move out, which is an unfortunate stance for a mother and father to take toward their daughter. Because Harout's parents relied solely on him for financial, medical, and emotional support, he was under tremendous pressure to live up to familial and cultural expectations that required him to care for them. His parents wished to join relatives in California, and Harout realized that he must accompany them, but at the price of leaving everything he has become familiar with over the years. The challenge that Harout faced was trying to uphold his cultural traditions while satisfying his newfound American individualism: He had to balance the individual need to finish his education with the family need to support his parents financially and emotionally.

Harout's decision to leave his girlfriend, Dalila, who lived in Washington, to care for his parents in California was a most severe expression of the primacy of family needs over the individual's. Although Harout cared very much for her, he felt that Dalila did not understand his responsibility to his parents. Dalila likewise felt resentful that Harout planned to leave without addressing the future of their relationship. With a gaspy, pained voice, Harout confessed, "I care about her, and it hurts me when I think about her suffering and that I was the reason for it." Harout believed that his fate had been sealed and that there was no hope for the relationship. His parents came first, over and above his own happiness.

CASE HISTORY

Family History

Harout was born last in a line of several children. His mother gave birth to him on July 12, 1967, in Tehran, Iran. His eldest sister, Osana, 43; his middle sister, Seta, 37; and his only brother Kervork, 33, were each born some years before. The family would be considered working class by most estimates. Harout's mother, 61, worked as a seamstress in a sewing factory; his father, 67, owned his own shoe store. The family has lived in Iran for three generations, beginning with the maternal and paternal grandparents, who were forced to leave Armenia to escape political persecution. Sadly, Harout never met his paternal grandfather, and he was very young when his paternal grandmother died of leukemia.

The family lived amicably for 13 years in a house that was built by Harout's paternal grandfather, father, and two uncles. However, an occasional conflict disrupted family life. Harout recalled a dispute that occurred between his eldest uncle and his father that elicited painful memories. When Harout's grandfather passed away, he left each of his sons money, and the eldest with ownership of the house. On his own father's death, Harout's father became ill and was bedridden for approximately 6 months. Harout's uncle, who agreed to oversee the shoe store during his brother's sickness, instead cheated him out of money made from sales and later refused to take a smaller portion of the inheritance to compensate for the theft. Harout's relationship with this uncle remains strained, and the resentment still lingers in Harout's memory as freshly as if the offense occurred yesterday.

At the present time, Harout's immediate family is dispersed between Iran and the United States. His sister, Seta, is married with three children and continues to reside in Iran, as does their single brother, Kevork. Seta is satisfied living in Iran, and, like those who are able to repress or deny the political persecution that surrounds them, she is oblivious to the state of affairs of her nation.

Religious History

The Armenian church is composed of three denominations: Apostolic, Protestant, and Catholic. Although Harout claimed that religion has not played a major role in his life, he held a formal membership in the Armenian Apostolic Church. While living in Iran, Harout and his family attended church only on major holidays, such as Christmas and Easter; however, living in the United States, Harout found it difficult to go to church because of his busy work schedule, which required him to work on Sundays. Unfortunately, he was unable to accompany his parents to church, even if he was so inclined. On those rare occasions when Harout did attend church with his parents, he worried that he might be publicly embarrassed because arguing inevitably arose when he and his parents were together, irrespective of the sanctity of the place.

Educational History

In Iran, as in other countries outside of the United States, students are required to choose a specific major as early as high school. Harout's major was electronics. Part of its required curriculum was to attend an electrical workshop 2 days a week to receive hands-on experience with wiring and electrical circuits, which he found to be very useful and interesting. Harout considered electricity a magical force, and he enjoyed learning how to harness and use its potential. Other classes included technical math, technical drawing, English, reading and writing in Farsi, and Islamic philosophy. When he arrived in the United States, Harout enrolled in English as a Second Language classes at a local community college in Washington, DC. When he felt that he was sufficiently fluent in English, Harout began taking courses to fulfill his major in computer information systems. Interestingly, not completely fluent in English, he took a basic course in Spanish so that he could converse with his Spanish-speaking classmates in their language.

Before coming to the United States, Harout had never seen a computer but quickly became interested in them when he realized the important role computers would play in the future. Harout plans to obtain a master's degree in computer science one day. He realizes that a good education will hasten his social and economic advancement, and he has seen the benefits of a good education at work with Iranian acquaintances who are prosperous dentists. Because of his high grade point average, Harout earned membership in Phi Theta Kappa, an honor society for community college students, and he plans to maintain his high level of scholarship.

Armenians in Iran

Despite the differences between Armenians and Iranians in religion, culture, and language, Armenians played an extremely important role in the evolution of Iranian government. Armenian intellectuals helped bring Western ideas to Iran and assisted in introducing many Iranian Muslims to secular thinking (Cottam, 1979). Both Armenian and Iranian intellectuals firmly believed in democracy and in resisting the influence of foreign powers, but the two sides later split into opposite camps, squashing the future of a liberal regime. For the Armenians, no greater enemy existed than Turkey, whom the Iranians befriended. In the Armenians' view, the Turks had perpetrated against their ethnic group one of the most atrocious genocides the world has seen (Cottam, 1979). If the murders of Armenians in Turkey were not enough, beginning in 1890, the Turks urged Iranian Kurds to massacre Christian villagers, both Armenian and Assyrian. Russian troops occupying Azerbaijan after 1909 frequently came to the assistance of the Armenian Christians. Thus, the Armenians gave strong support to Russia and, in 1914, staged a major pro-Russian demonstration in Tabflz. Iranian nationalists saw the Russians as "evil incarnate" and viewed the Armenian support of

Russia as treason. Many Armenians were killed by Iranian Muslims in retaliation (Cottam, 1979).

During the Revolution of 1979, Harout was a small child, unable to recall any of the discrimination that became rampant during those inflammatory times. He remembers playing with Muslim kids in the street and not feeling any different from them. However, after the Revolution, Harout recalled that Armenians were stopped at checkpoints in the street at night and body-searched for weapons. Tape recorders or cameras were not allowed in cars because they could serve as caches for ammunition or bombs. Because Armenians, unlike religious Muslims, consume alcohol, it was not unusual for them to be stopped and harrassed by police on the pretense of checking their alleged insobriety. Social parties also were not safe for Armenians because they feared police raids. "It happened to a friend of mine at a party," Harout recalled. "Everyone was dancing and all of a sudden, the lights went out, and there was a guy in a green uniform with a machine gun standing at the door; the gun's sights were aimed at the crowd."

Another area where Armenians felt the effects of the Revolution was in the school system. Before the Revolution, there were many Armenian schools where their own language and religion were taught. After the Revolution, boys and girls went to separate schools, and the hours for teaching the Armenian language were reduced. Moreover, because the government funded the schools, it began imposing its own curriculum by adding Islamic courses and hiring Muslim principals. A system of secular schools, with implicit tolerance for religious minorities, became the explicit proselytizer for Islam.

Coming to the United States

Harout's sister Osana was the first person to flee Iran. Along with her husband and young daughter, she first moved to Greece, where she lived for 2 years, and eventually made her way to the United States. Harout explained how her move affected his family: "We were very close. She lived in the neighborhood with us, and then, all of a sudden, she was gone. There was a big void in our hearts." Despite their close ties, Harout and his family did not keep in regular contact with Osana after she left. They communicated with her every 3 months, mostly by telephone and occasionally by letter.

Harout was the second member of his family to leave Iran. After receiving his high school diploma in 1985, Harout worked in Iran as an electrician and, eventually, opened his own electrical repair shop where he worked for 4 years. Harout decided to leave Iran to get away from its oppressive government and to pursue higher education in the United States. He began to save money and planned to leave in

August of 1990. However, it took an extra month before Harout could begin his journey. To escape, he received help from an international rescue coalition. Along with two other Armenians and two Iranians, Harout and the rest of the group were helped by guides to cross the Iranian border into Turkey. It took 4 days to pass the mountains and desert by foot and on horseback. Harout described his feelings during those 4 days: "It was scary. At one point, we could see the soldiers at the border. That was the worst part—crossing the border at night. But we knew once we made it past the border, everything would be all right."

As soon as they crossed the border, a smuggler was waiting with bus tickets to take them to Belgrad, Yugoslavia. They stayed there for 2 weeks, during which time they had their pictures taken, received Greek passports (one of the smugglers was Greek), and purchased train tickets to Vienna, Austria. Once they arrived in Vienna, the Greek smuggler collected the passports and returned to Iran. Harout called a friend who lived in Vienna and stayed with him for the weekend before entering a refugee camp. After filling out an application for the camp, Harout was accepted and was reluctantly separated from his Viennese friend, with whom he was recently reacquainted. The camps were at the site of antiquated military bases used during World War II.

"They put you with all nationalities, mostly Eastern Europeans—it wasn't a pleasant experience," Harout recalled. After living in the refugee camp for 3 weeks, Harout filled out some paperwork and moved to a rooming house that used to be a private home. There were two bathrooms for 10 rooms, which all the tenants living in the rooming house had to share. Harout took advantage of English classes that were offered there. Additionally, he requested political asylum in Austria and applied for a visa to the United States. "I wrote my case, got my friend to translate it, and sent it to the rescue coalition. They do the paperwork, send the case to the U.S. embassy, and complete the legal documents," Harout explained.

In March of 1991, Harout was called for an interview for political asylum in Vienna and was granted a visa to enter the United States. "I can't even describe how I felt at that moment! We had a party that night," he beamed with fond memory. He waited for his visa to arrive and, in June of 1991, flew to New York's Kennedy International Airport. Tolerating a flight delay and a long waiting period for the baggage to be reloaded to his connecting flight, Harout finally arrived at Washington National Airport, where he was reunited with his sister, Osana, and her family, whom he had not seen in 6 years. Harout remembered thinking to himself as he laid down to sleep that night, "Thank God! I made it to America!" The memory of the Capitol dome that he passed on the way back from the airport emerged as part of a serene mountain in his dreams.

Living in the United States

Harout described his first 3 months of living on the outskirts of Washington, DC, as "terribly lonely." He had recurring dreams of Iran and nightmares that some American official would send him back based on trumped up charges. His first impression of the United States was of sprawling "streets, row houses, and shopping malls." Harout said that he yearned for the activity of city life and often would drive to downtown Washington just to see the historic white buildings and the endless flow of people scurrying to important jobs and places of entertainment. Living in a suburban area increased Harout's sense of isolation even though it was free of the crime and congestion of the inner city and, in this respect, was easy to settle into.

To distract him from his loneliness and self-absorption, Harout focused his attention on learning to speak English. When he first arrived in the United States, he understood a few important English words. Although an avid television watcher in Iran, the only American television show he could understand was *Star Trek* because of the actors' good pronunciation. Mr. Spock, the show's famous Vulcan physician, spoke in a slow and methodical English drawl that was easy for the novice English speaker to interpret. At night, Harout left the radio on so his unconscious mind could "listen" to English. His desire to master the language of his new home was as fervent as his desire to succeed there.

It was around this time that problems arose between Harout and his brother-in-law. Harout recounted a conflict that developed when he attended a George Michael concert—the sexually provocative rock singer—within the first 3 months of his residence in the United States. A friend had informed Harout that George Michael would be performing at the U.S. Air Arena. With his limited English, Harout called to order tickets for himself and his friend. His brother-in-law advised him against going, saying that there was a lot of fighting and crime near the arena. Harout decided to go anyway and enjoyed his first American concert. Harout explained that Osana and her husband hardly ever go out to eat or for anything else. "All they do is work and come home. They don't see that city life is an important part of the American culture," he emphasized with sad resignation.

Harout's brother-in-law is self-employed as an electrician and asked Harout to work with him. "Everyone who comes to the United States goes through a kind of enslavement period where you don't know too much, and if someone helps you, you feel that you owe them something—and they take advantage of you," Harout explained. Harout was having financial difficulties while working with his brother-in-law because he wasn't getting paid very much and business was slow. To earn extra money, Harout resorted to reselling his prized computer textbooks after the completion of each community college semester. He decided to obtain another job altogether and found a well-paying part-time job delivering pizzas while continuing to attend the community college.

Harout began to achieve a livable income, if barely, and to acclimate to American life. By studying and working, he made friends and became more fluent in English. He also gave Osana money each month to help her with expenses. At the same time, his brother-in law's business started to pick up, and the brother-in-law asked Harout to return to working with him. Harout told his brother-in-law that he would be unable to do so because he had plenty of studying to keep him busy. From that point on, the relationship between Harout and his brother-in-law became icy. The brother-in-law felt betrayed by Harout's rebuffing him when he needed his help to manage the influx of new business.

Harout wanted to look for his own apartment because his parents expected to move in once they emigrated from Iran. However, Harout soon realized that he could not afford an apartment and decided to stay at Osana's home. In anticipation of his parents' arrival, Harout began working at an airport shuttle company to earn enough money to help Osana support their aging parents, both of whom arrived in 1993. Harout recalled thinking, "Before they came, I had a plan to leave the house and rent a room somewhere else, finish junior college, and then go to the university, but when my parents came, my plans were turned upside down." In contemplating why his educational goals were disrupted because of his parents, Harout confessed, "You have two people staring at you, and you have your goals to achieve. From one point of view, I'm glad they're here, not living in Iran with all those problems, but since they are here, I have to take care of them."

In the few years since Harout's parents arrived, they have all remained in Osana's home. However, as mentioned earlier, the challenges of living together brought the parents to the point of wanting to move to California, where there was a growing Armenian community and the chance of securing a bigger house in which they and Harout could live more comfortably. Harout received his associate's degree in computer information systems from the community college 3 months before his departure to California. Harout's plan was to work through the summer in order to make enough money for the move, leave in September, get a job in his field, and make enough money to maintain his parents in California. After working for a year, he planned to finish his last 2 years of college and then pursue "the American dream."

CASE ANALYSIS

Conceptual Perspective

Filial piety is a cultural concept that implies giving primary importance to the immediate and extended family (Ponterotto, et al., 1995). Filial piety involves this obligation even when individuals have established their own separate families (Lee & Richardson, 1991). Harout's strong sense of filial piety toward his parents was best exemplified when he disclosed, "In my culture, the kids always have to take care of the parents. My sisters got married, my brother is an unreliable person, so my parents always said, 'Oh, who's going to take care of us?' I told my mom when I was 8 or 9 years old that I was going to take care of them. So, it's my promise to them." Harout's promise was a matter of devotion and tradition.

Harout's filial piety clashed with his desire to acculturate into American society, with its individualism and declining emphasis on family loyalty. Harout's counselor assessed his level of acculturation by asking him to complete a cultural autobiography (see chapter 1). The counselor determined that in the years that Harout had been living in the United States, he had maintained a strong sense of his Armenian identity. As indicated in the autobiography, Harout maintains friendships mostly with Iranian Armenians, with the exception of a few members of other ethnic groups. It is interesting that Harout indicated that he does not have any Anglo acquaintances. Because Anglos make up the majority of the United States population, this indicates that Harout has not reached a high level of assimilation into the American culture. Many other factors indicate that this is true. The most obvious is Harout's strong commitment to filial piety, which is a common characteristic in the Armenian culture, but not in the American culture, in which this value is sadly, if truly, disappearing.

Additionally, Harout maintains his Armenian identity by reading Armenian literature, being involved in public actions for the well-being of the Armenian community, patronizing Armenian businesses, speaking only Armenian at home, and expressing that in the future, he would teach his children to speak Armenian. Harout, however, has learned to speak English fluently, has finished his associate's degree in computer information systems, and maintains a relationship with his non-Armenian girlfriend. Thus, he has adopted some of the necessary skills, such as language and a culturally relevant career direction, in order to assimilate into the American culture.

Existential Perspective

Although concepts of collectivism and individualism have been used widely by cultural theorists to explain the differences among societies, they have existential implications that often are ignored. Collectivism refers to societies in which individuals submit themselves to the interest of the group, which may be the family, community, work colleagues, or other affiliations that provide a sense of belonging for the person. It is a collectivistic society from which Harout comes, and it is through the eyes of this society that he views his world. On the other hand, individualism refers to societies in which the needs, desires, and aspirations of individuals take precedence over those of such groups as the family, work group, and the community at large. This is the typical orientation in the American culture.

The nature of our changing world where people are in constant flux from one nation to another impedes the tendency to hold rigid views regarding these two types of societies. People who are collectivistic in one country often become individualistic in another and vice versa, for various reasons (Fischer, 1965). The human organism is infinitely adaptable, but even changes in worldview come at the price of stress, transient confusion, and a chronic feeling of alienation from the society to which one assimilates if it possesses a different worldview. The movement from collectivism to individualism that Harout experienced was a huge paradigm shift that required the reconstruction of the meaning of his personal relationships and, in turn, the meaning of his life.

Harout had to modify his traditional, collectivistic perspective in order to assimilate and find meaning in American society. For example, when Harout decided not to return to working for his brother-in-law and instead maintained his studies and part-time job, he took an individualistic view in order to enhance his financial as well as his educational status. Had he maintained his collectivistic perspective—deferring dutifully to the best interest of family—Harout would have returned to working with his brother-in-law, but, as a result, he would have had to cut back on study time and may never have completed his degree program at the time he was forced to accompany his parents to California. He would have been a reed blown by the winds of his family dynamics, but he chose to resist in order to salvage his own dreams. He achieved a reasonable compromise, which may be the inevitable solution in most interpersonal conflicts.

DSM–IV (APA, 1994) Perspective

Harout does not possess psychopathology in the traditional sense. However, the DSM–IV provides the classification of adjustment disorder to specify problems-in-living that create significant distress. A counselor must ensure that this diagnosis will not stigmatize a client and is truly necessary to help the client. In forming a diagnosis of adjustment disorder, a counselor implicitly makes Axis IV a statement of the issues that must be resolved if adjustment is to be reestablished.

Multiaxial Diagnosis

Axis I	Adjustment disorder, unspecified (309.9)
Axis II	No diagnosis
Axis III	No diagnosis
Axis IV	Problems with primary support group, problems with social environment, occupational problems, economic problems, and housing problems
Axis V	GAF = 75 (current)

INTERVENTION STRATEGY

Effective cross-cultural counseling requires the assumption of multiple cultural perspectives and not simply the cultural viewpoint of the counselor. In discussing the following intervention strategies for Harout, the counselor has assumed both the emic (client's culture) and etic (host or universal culture) perspectives. With the emic perspective in mind, the counselor believed that Harout had a positive prognosis for the future because he recognizes that part of his identity and purpose is preserved by abiding to the Armenian value of filial piety. He has overcome many obstacles in remaining true to his family obligations. The problems his family faced in Iran with his father's brothers only add to Harout's strong sense of duty to live up to his promise to take care of his parents and shield them from further disappointment.

A culturally sensitive counselor should be aware that many cultures, such as the Armenian, find it difficult to discuss family problems with total strangers, even those assuming the role of professional helper. Harout's counselor initially recommended that Harout turn to a trusted friend or to his girlfriend to voice his concerns regarding his current situation. The counselor made this recommendation on the basis of their previous counseling session, in which Harout openly expressed his anger and resentment toward his sister, Osana, but was reluctant to vent his emotions fully or reveal basic information regarding his family members, including innocuous details, such as their first names and ages. The therapeutic alliance between counselor and client gradually grew stronger over the course of six sessions. By the last session, Harout was able to express his resentment toward Osana—his very last chance to achieve catharsis.

Harout wanted to tell Osana how he felt about her attitude toward their parents just as he had expressed it to his counselor. Harout decided that he would tell his sister Osana how he felt after he and his parents settled in California. Harout's counselor recommended that he follow through with his plan, but she persuaded him to consider speaking with Osana before moving so that any conflict could be resolved then so that distance would not add to the misunderstanding. Harout's counselor pointed out that both he and Osana were united in wanting better lives for their parents. Osana enabled them to come to live in the United States for a better life, and Harout is planning to move them to California for the same reason. Talking this through with Osana may relieve some of his burden, and he may find an unexpected ally in his sister.

From the etic perspective, Harout's financial dilemma may have been avoided had he planned his move better. He could have prepared more extensively for his career while in the Washington area before leaving for California. As he himself recognized, it was the family conflict that made him anxious to leave and that caused him to procrastinate about planning for the future. If his parents had been methodical in their plan to leave rather than reacting impulsively to family conflict, he too would have been more prepared to move with them.

Because Harout had not made any specific vocational plans on arriving in California, it was recommended that he seek career counseling there to learn how to prepare best for a career in his field. Another option was to consider returning to the Washington area after his parents were settled comfortably. He has more contacts in Washington and can easily find job opportunities in the information systems field, as indicated by the numerous job postings for computer specialists in *The Washington Post* and on the Internet. Harout might also consider a work–study program at a 4-year college where he might get experience in his field while completing his bachelor's degree and earning tuition reimbursement.

Harout does not necessarily need to be confined to the same living situation as his parents. Harout's fatalistic tendencies make him think that he does not have any alternative but to live with his parents. However, a possible source of income for his parents, as legal immigrants with green cards, is to receive social security benefits. Harout's counselor suggested that he look into this program because the financial help that his parents could receive from it would lessen Harout's financial pressures. This also might enable Harout to save money to afford his own apartment, thus freeing the three of them from the uncomfortable position of having to live together.

DISCUSSION OF THE CASE

The word *respect* was used by Harout several times when referring to his parents. He enunciated the word with a special depth and passion that elicited an awe in the listener as if a sacred message had been conveyed. Respect is the unquestioned authority of one's parents and the loyalty expected from their children that is learned early in life (Lee & Richardson, 1991). Respect includes deference for all elders and persons in authority. Harout was raised with this type of respect for his parents, and it was evident in his effort to make a better life for them by adhering to their wish to move to California, even if it diminished the quality of his own life.

The use of what existential philosophers called the I–Thou rapport—an honest and caring therapeutic alliance—enabled the counselor, whose cultural background is Latin American, to empathize with the issues of respect and filial piety. She was also raised with similar cultural expectations, and she shared openly with Harout that she too has had to make important compromises out of her obligation to her parents. Her life has not taken the direction she would have liked, but respecting the traditions of one's culture is not painless. Harout's counselor's honest self-disclosure was the most healing moment of his therapy, for there they both sat face-to-face realizing their vulnerability to forces that are greater than themselves and finding solace in discovering that they are not alone. Harout eventually found inner peace by respecting his parents' wishes. He fulfilled his obligations as a son that he realized gave his life special meaning.

DISCUSSION QUESTIONS

1. What role did filial piety and respect play in the therapeutic relationship?
2. What are the benefits of having a counselor and client from similar cultural backgrounds?
3. How might the historical experiences of Armenians affect their worldviews?
4. How does the concept of filial piety in Armenian culture differ from American familial relationships?
5. As a counselor, how might you deal with differences in values when working with an Armenian client?
6. What approach or approaches would you, as a counselor, take in specifically dealing with the communication barrier between the client and his sister?
7. How would you determine the therapeutic goals for this client?
8. Discuss what role the I–Thou relationship played between the client and counselor.

9. Why would a client reared in the Middle East be reluctant to self-disclose to a young, female counselor?

10. Do you agree with the counselor's assessment of the client's level of acculturation? Is the cultural autobiography a valid technique?

CHAPTER SEVEN

Running From the Past: The Challenge of Forgiving an Abusive Family

INTRODUCTION

Maria Elena did not have a positive view of mental health counseling. In fact, she made her hesitation very clear. Had Maria Elena, 39, been asked to engage immediately in a counselor–client relationship, she might have felt uncomfortable or even decided that therapy would not be helpful. In recognition of this reality, a creative counseling approach had to be developed. Maria Elena was asked to teach the counselor, a 26-year-old European American woman, about Mexican American culture. Maria Elena enthusiastically responded and seemed flattered. In addition, the traditional clinical setting did not seem appropriate. Therefore, therapy took place after hours at the client's office to provide a safe and comfortable environment in which Maria Elena could feel free to share. This began a counseling relationship that eventually developed into a deep rapport and interchange, but more important, the relationship lent itself to promoting positive change for the client.

PRESENTING CHALLENGES

The initial counseling session began with Maria Elena's perceptions of her family's Mexican American values, attitudes, and customs. Maria Elena expressed great interest in focusing on the difficult and strained relationships that existed in her family that had driven her from home years ago. She wished to explore these issues and how they created the complex psychology that had developed within her. Maria Elena was considering returning to the southwestern United States and was experiencing intense feelings of ambivalence concerning her return home. She wanted to examine the origin and meaning of these feelings. In addition, she was interested in discussing her troubled interpersonal relationships and concerns regarding her brother, who was suffering from full-blown AIDS and teetering between a debilitated life and death.

CASE HISTORY

Maria Elena was born in El Paso, Texas, and lived in its rural suburbs until she was 8 years old. Subsequently, her family moved to Tucson, Arizona. Maria Elena is the 6th of 10 children and has never been married. Her religious background is Catholic, but she does not practice her faith actively. Maria Elena is exploring meditation to help manage her anger and is reading about Buddhism as an alternative religion. She seems to be searching passionately for a source of transcendant meaning but has not yet found a comfortable spiritual outlet.

Until Maria Elena and her siblings entered public school, Spanish was the only language spoken in their home. The advent of public schooling influenced her family's use of English as well as its level of acculturation. On the recommendation of Maria Elena's teachers, she, her parents, and siblings tried to practice English in and around their home. The use of both languages engendered a broken form of each that she calls "Spanglish." In the third grade, Maria Elena was taken out of her Spanish-speaking classes and was abruptly pushed into an English-only class. She was challenged to overcome her "English language deficiency" and succeeded, but not without a struggle, both educationally and emotionally.

In 1996, Maria Elena received her bachelor's degree in elementary education and became the only member of her family to graduate from college. Only three of her siblings graduated from high school, although one received a general equivalency diploma and two completed some college courses but failed to complete their degrees. Maria Elena currently resides in Northern Virginia, works full time in Washington, DC, as an administrative secretary for the U.S. Department of Education, and has been living in the Washington metropolitan area for approximately 10 years.

Maria Elena's family has a long history of substance abuse. Her eight brothers and one sister, who range in age from 24 to 45, are alcoholics and drug abusers, except Mario, the first child, whose addiction never expanded beyond alcohol. Her father, who consumed hard liquor frequently, died in 1986 from alcoholism and its resultant damage to his liver and kidneys. Neither Maria Elena nor her mother consume alcohol, smoke cigarettes, or use drugs—as if to symbolize their distaste of their family's addictions. The second child, Reuban, committed suicide at age 35 in 1984 while high on drugs. It was his way of coping with the ending of his relationship with his girlfriend, whose rejection, ironically, was due to his drug abuse.

Maria Elena believed that at least four more of her siblings have seriously considered suicide. Three of her brothers have served time in prison for robbery, distribution of drugs, or spousal abuse. Alberto, 35, the eighth child, is gay and has full-blown AIDS. He resides in Colorado with his significant other, Chad. Since moving to the East Coast 10 years ago, Maria Elena has remained in touch with Robert, the third child, primarily through letter writing because he is serving a 20-year prison term for trafficking drugs; with Alberto, the sibling with whom she has always felt the closest; and most recently, with her mother through occasional telephone conversations.

Maria Elena had just turned 21 when her mother and father divorced in 1978 after a 30-year marriage that was riddled with physical and emotional abuse. Maria Elena's father was very abusive to her and her siblings, especially when he was intoxicated, which, sadly, was often. Retrospectively, she feels that her brothers experienced more severe physical abuse because her father would "punch and beat them up . . . [whereas] with me, he used to make one of my older brothers lay me across their lap and beat me with a belt while he watched." Although her brothers and sisters refrain from discussing their past abuse, Maria Elena expressed that they all had different perceptions of the beatings and some felt more abused than others. As children, they coped with the physical abuse through sarcasm. "One brother would playact a boxing match where my father and mother began in opposite corners. . . . Our enemy was our father," Maria Elena recalled. They would also play house and their "father" would come home and physically abuse their "mother."

At age 15, Alberto's homosexuality was revealed accidentally by a probation officer. He was forced "out of the closet" to the surprise of the family, who merely considered him slightly effeminate and nothing more. After his brothers discovered that he was gay, Alberto experienced a traumatic thrashing at their hands. Maria Elena's father instructed three of her brothers to "take care of it." One brother responded, "I will take care of him. . . . He will be a man tomorrow." Against Maria Elena's vehement protests, they forced Alberto outside in an attempt to "beat the homosexual out of him." Among the lower strata of Mexican American culture, homophobia is an accepted "norm," as expressed in the value of machismo, which seems to embody the very opposite of femininity and is characterized by excessive bravado and shying away from expressions of feeling or vulnerability.

From a young age, Maria Elena was socialized to assume the role of a traditional Hispanic woman. Throughout childhood and adolescence, Maria Elena was not allowed to play with other children and was required to remain indoors, tending to the family. However, her brothers were encouraged to go out and socialize with whomever they chose. She remembered her father as being "a fanatic about unchaperoned women in the streets. He wanted to control his women and made us stay at home." Her patriarchal grandmother, who was a very controlling and demanding figure, upheld and enforced the position of their father. She remembered not wanting to tell other children, even her cousins, that she was not allowed to go outside to play. Instead, to avoid embarrassment, she would say, "I do not have time to play"—a statement that was very truthful.

Beginning with towels and T-shirts to practice ironing at age 5, Maria Elena worked her way to ironing the family's clothing. "I was a little girl slave," she emphasized. She did substantial cleaning, washing, and tending to her brothers' meals and other needs. Often they would shout orders at her: "Hurry up! Get my food, hombre." Often, Maria Elena was called "hombre," or boy, because her grandfather could only relate to men and eccentrically refused to recognize that Maria Elena was female. He expected her to work in the fields and possess the same strength and endurance as her older brothers. In essence, Maria Elena was expected to maintain her feminine sensibilities while demonstrating a male capacity for work—a real catch-22 situation. Raised with mixed messages, she was berated in adolescence for not possessing the highly regarded *marianismo*—the Hispanic ideal of femininity. In the Mexican American culture, the oldest daughter must assume most of the family's responsibilities, and this expectation does not abate with time. "The curse of being the oldest daughter never escaped me . . . and I could never quite be the daughter my family admired," Maria Elena confided.

Maria Elena was very withdrawn as a child and could not relate to kids her own age in school. With a serious expression, she explained that by assuming most of the family's responsibilities, she played a parental role, which caused her to wonder continually, "Who was taking care of me?" Maria Elena continues to feel that there is a distance between others and herself, and she has few friends or acquaintances. She confided that she has had difficulties in establishing interpersonal relationships with men and has found that when she does "they start out okay but turn into one big mess."

Christina, Maria Elena's closest friend, recently ended their year-long relationship with the vague excuse "It is time for distance," even though they were inseparable companions. Maria Elena was very hurt by Christina's actions. Months later, she tried to return Christina's books through the mail, but they were not accepted. "Return to sender" was written in Christina's handwriting on the returned package. Maria Elena remembered their relationship with mixed emotions because Christina was a very angry person with an explosive temper. Maria Elena was always walking on eggshells around Christina, and, occasionally, she would "crack a shell" and "all hell would break loose."

Maria Elena recalled some of the first words Christina spoke to her: "The bitch in me will cut your heart out." Maria Elena nervously laughed when she mentioned this line and said, "Oh, she warned me all right." Maria Elena did not want to develop the same bitterness that Christina possessed. "She made me realize that I could become angry and unforgiving about the past. I learned a lot about myself through her. I always put other people's needs before my own. I want to be able now not to do that," she explained. Furthermore, Maria Elena disclosed that she, like Christina, had never been involved in a serious, romantic relationship. She announced that "trust, intimacy, and commitment are still very big challenges for me. I have perfected the art of not letting others in. . . . I have built a castle around my heart."

In Tucson, Maria Elena's brothers were very much exposed to the American culture. They were involved with sports, friends, current style of dress, and the popular group The Beatles. Maria Elena viewed the world from her "brothers' eyes." As a truck driver, Maria Elena's father was not home very much. She recalled his absence as being a good time in her life. However, her father later resigned his trucking job and became a roofer, making her situation increasingly more stressful. Maria Elena confided that "often my father would drink the rent money away." When this happened, the deep-seated collectivism of the Mexican American family was called on to pull everyone through the hard times. All the children would assist the family financially by obtaining odd jobs and paying the rent and other bills. To avoid eviction, which happened often, Maria Elena, then 14 years old, mowed lawns and delivered newspapers while her brothers worked in gas stations or convenience stores.

While Maria Elena was attending elementary school, her family moved five times because of eviction. Finally, her family ended up in the public housing projects and received public assistance. She remembered the children's room resembling an army barracks, with rows of beds and no privacy. Because her family's financial situation was bleak, Maria Elena clearly recalled her mother learning how to make meals stretch. However, through all of her family's hardships, Maria Elena did not realize how bad her situation was. She thought that "everyone's family was this way." It was not until she was older that she realized the extent of her family's poverty and dysfunction.

After 30 years of marriage, the physical and mental abuse inflicted by Maria Elena's father became unbearable for her mother. Against the very core of the family's Catholic beliefs, her father and mother divorced. Three years before the divorce, Maria Elena, on turning 19, had moved out of her parents' home. It was a momentous declaration of her disgust with her parents' relationship, but its symbolism may have been too little, too late. While working in an alcohol treatment center, Maria Elena enlisted the counseling skills of a coworker and together they convinced her mother to leave her father. Throwing knives and ranting maniacally, the abusive behavior of Maria Elena's father had escalated. Sensing the urgency of the situation, Maria Elena acted to safeguard her mother's life. She remarked in exasperation, "My mother still blames me for her getting a divorce . . . to say nothing of saving her life." Only recently has Maria Elena's mother come to appreciate her daughter's intervention.

Maria Elena often became angry with her mother because of the abuse and suffering she endured without protest. Her mother would respond, "It is God's will." Maria Elena would reply, "How can God's will be so cruel? He would not want us to suffer!" "In the Mexican culture, children should always have the utmost respect for their parents," Maria Elena explained. "You do not question authority under any circumstances. The culture views corporal punishment as a God-given right." Her mother would become very angry with Maria Elena and would remark, "*El diablo está en esta casa*" (The devil is in this house). The power struggle between Maria Elena and her mother was a constant battle in which the former would not relent. Her mother viewed Maria Elena as "stubborn and aggressive"—not the qualities of a "good" daughter or of a nice, Mexican American woman.

Ten years ago, Maria Elena moved to the Washington, DC, area to live with some friends for a couple of months. She secured a job in the federal government and decided to experience living in the area but always planned on moving back to the Southwest. Coming from a large Mexican American community, Maria Elena was shocked by the racism and discrimination she received from Anglo Americans. At the time, she lived in a predominantly White community and was "mistaken" for a maid on several occasions. Eventually, Maria Elena moved out of her friends' house and into a rented room in Northern Virginia.

Over the past 10 years, Maria Elena has been studying for her bachelor's degree in elementary education and working full time to support herself. She continually sent money home to help her family until 5 years ago, when she discovered that it was being diverted to buy alcohol and drugs. Maria Elena decided not to send any more money home and became the target of much anger from her siblings. In the Mexican American culture, family members always attempt to assist those back home, but Maria Elena defied this norm. After graduating from college, she allowed herself to accept $50 that was given to her by her mother. For Maria Elena, this was a significant gift because for once, her mother was revealing her pride in her daughter. Currently, Maria Elena hopes to pursue a master's degree in educational technology.

Maria Elena feels that she has become highly Americanized because she thinks, "Why is a bachelor's not enough? Anglo Americans always want more, more, more. I could make a decent living with a bachelor's. Why am I pushing for more?" Because she does not feel that she writes very well in English, Maria Elena is a bit worried about the graduate school application process, especially about writing admissions essays. Over the course of therapy, she devoted her extra time to improving her English vocabulary and grammar.

After Maria Elena felt that she could "open up," she began discussing her relationship with her AIDS-infected brother, Alberto, and the fear of his impending death. She had grave concerns that the person with whom she is the closest in the world was going to die. Maria Elena wanted very much to visit Alberto but was apprehensive. She did not know whether she could "handle seeing him." During the course of counseling, she decided to visit him in Colorado. Even though they are very close, they have only seen each other twice in 10 years. Maria Elena spent a significant amount of time talking about her fears and anxieties over seeing Alberto, possibly for the last time. The thought of losing the one stable relationship in her life was overwhelming for her. Yet she talked about the inner strength that will pull her through. In the recent past, perhaps as a result of Alberto's illness, Maria Elena decided to move back to the Southwest once she obtains her master's degree.

Maria Elena strongly wants to return to the Southwest to make amends with her family and reconnect with the Mexican culture. She misses the Mexican traditions and wishes to return to the heritage that defined her. "I am learning that I can still get what I want to advance my career while being true to my family and culture," she explained. Maria Elena believes that she "will never be able to cut her family off completely. As dysfunctional as they are, they try to help each other." She explained that her "brothers, in their own crazy way, loved me. I do not want to die angry." Maria Elena is trying to work through her anger while pondering, "Why do I have so many battles? I have to start letting go." She believes that her purpose in life, however counterintuitive, is to return to the Southwest to be involved in the family's problems—to make her family a part of her life again.

CASE ANALYSIS

Conceptual Perspective

Maria Elena is a highly acculturated woman who is trying to come to terms with her past so that she may live harmoniously in the present. However, as a counselor, it is important not to take Maria Elena's high level of acculturation for granted. It has become increasingly more important to Maria Elena to reach out and reconnect with her Mexican identity. To that end, the counselor will diagnose her from both the emic (client's culture) and etic (host or universal culture) perspectives. From an emic point of view, it is paramount that the counselor help Maria Elena work through her issues with a recognition of the Mexican culture's norms and values. In the Mexican culture, the family is of utmost importance, and Maria Elena would like to embrace it. Ignoring this perspective might cause misunderstanding and disconnection with the client.

It is also important to diagnose Maria Elena from an etic perspective because she has aligned herself with several of the values of the dominant culture. Maria Elena might possess a "bicultural" worldview in seeking to straddle both her heritage and some American values. On the basis of Maria Elena's case history, it appears that she is simultaneously seeking an understanding of ugly family memories while pursuing reunification and peace with her family. Moreover, her desire to return to the Southwest suggests that the emotional and physical scars endured in the past with her family members are less painful than her estrangement from them.

Counseling from an emic perspective includes the recognition of Maria Elena's *filial piety*. In moving to the East Coast of the United States, thereby leaving her family, Maria Elena experienced enormous feelings of guilt. In the Mexican culture, as in many other collectivistic societies, persons are expected to remain close to the family system. However, Maria Elena was a nonconformist and developed an individualistic attitude: "It is my life," she would repeat to herself in order to rationalize her worldview. Ten years later, her family continues to criticize her for leaving. Her mother's sister constantly says, "You deserted your mother," and other relatives have said, "You did a bad thing in leaving your mother." Over the years, Maria Elena has felt increasingly guilty for relocating to the East Coast and is developing plans to return to the Southwest.

Maria Elena might be a marginalized person, not fitting in anywhere. She recognizes that she has become too Americanized to be accepted in her culture. Maria Elena has received many criticisms from home, such as "Oh, you are so American, so aggressive," as evidence of her family's negative perceptions of her Americanized characteristics. She said that "there is a gulf between us now that cannot be bridged." At the same time, she is not accepted in the dominant culture in which she has found herself surrounded. The nonacceptance by those in her immediate environment may be partly beyond her control. Many Anglo Americans cannot understand or relate to her history or worldview, which is compounded by America's racial consciousness, where many simply relegate Maria Elena to second-class status by virtue of her dark skin. These social and interpersonal realities have fostered Maria Elena's inclination to remain alone and introverted. At the same time, she has not made any attempts to explore the Mexican American cultural enclaves of Washington, DC, or to connect with other Mexican Americans living in her Virginia neighborhood. Her living a sheltered existence and not having an active personal life are, in part, choices she makes so as to avoid the pain of personal rejection.

A touch of "woman's intuition" assisted the counselor in understanding Maria Elena's plight. Both the counselor and client were women who could understand intuitively life in a male-dominated world, as there are universal feelings shared by women, irrespective of their culture, race, or class. Although having this understanding is valuable, it may be of equal importance to comprehend the client's cultural experience. The ability to empathize with how it must have felt to be treated as a "Hispanic woman" who should know "her place" and serve men was important to the counseling relationship. When a counselor demonstrates cultural knowledge that is unexpected of a person of her cultural group, this is a powerful sign of empathy, whereas cultural ignorance causes distance and disconnection.

Existential Perspective

Maria Elena has struggled to come to terms with her brother's impending death from AIDS. Clearly, this caused substantial stress and worry for Maria Elena and made her confront her own death. At age 39, she realizes that half of her life has passed, and she is now evaluating how she wants to live the remaining half. She feels that she has made mistakes and has many regrets. An often frightening experience for many people is confronting their lack of personal growth, or underused potential, "as life begins to run out"—which is the basis of *existential anxiety*. The fear of one's own or a loved one's demise often is powerful enough to evoke a profound change that encourages living authentically. As evidenced by her desire to reconnect with family and culture, Maria Elena is using her existential anxiety as a catalyst to make the appropriate changes in her life—before there is no family left to reconnect with.

Maria Elena is also trying to work through the anger she has harbored from childhood. She confided, "I no longer want to continue being a bitter person." She realizes how much of her life has been spent being angry and does not want to continue expending the precious moments of life in such a negative disposition. Currently, Maria Elena is taking inventory of her emotional life and is hoping to let go of her anger and replace it with a love of family and life.

DSM–IV (APA,1994) Perspective

Like so many clients who enter therapy, Maria Elena has no specific mental illness but is grappling with the need to understand herself. The *DSM–IV* is not very good at providing a diagnostic category for those who are seeking self-understanding and positive growth, but the following is an attempt to label the problem without excessively pathologizing it.

Multiaxial Diagnosis

Axis I	Adjustment disorder, unspecified, chronic (309.9)
Axis II	No diagnosis
Axis III	No diagnosis

Axis IV	Problems with primary support group:
	    Health problems in family
	    Physical abuse
	Problems related to social environment:
	    Inadequate social support
	    Difficulty with acculturation

Axis V	GAF = 70 (current)

INTERVENTION STRATEGY

At the time Maria Elena terminated therapy to attend graduate school, her prognosis was very good. However, she faced several life challenges. She said, "The first 40 years you learn how to live, the next 40 you do live." Nearing age 40, she was tying up the loose ends by "learning how to live." Maria Elena reported that she had made peace with her father, who she used to refer to as her "old man." She realized that the past cannot be undone and that "he can no longer do anything to me." As for her mother, Maria Elena is letting her anger subside and is trying to establish a closer relationship with her. She is gaining more *respeto* (respect) for her mother and now accepts that her mother did the best she could. "She fed us. She clothed us. We never went hungry. She just could not leave her husband. She had the potential to be a lot more, but she had to suppress it because of the cultural prohibitions. That is what made me angry—her weakness in not standing up to him. But I have begun to forgive my mother, because I see that I am just as imperfect as she is," Maria Elena resolved.

"Letting go of anger" is a very positive process for Maria Elena. If it is continued, some of her guilt and "loss of culture" may lessen as she reconnects with the heritage at which she became so enraged. As for the counseling process, it is highly appropriate for Maria Elena to continue working on these reconciliations, primarily from an autoplastic, or self-determinative, perspective. Maria Elena has come to terms with her family's unwillingness to change, so she is left with the choice of changing the behaviors and feelings of her own that can be changed. Reconciliation with her family can only come from her, on her terms, and at her pace.

Regarding her bicultural identity, Maria Elena has accepted the reality of being a "blend of two cultures and of neither one." Devising a long-term plan to alleviate the cultural alienation when she moves to the Southwest is a wise compromise. After completing her graduate degree, Maria Elena intends to move to New Mexico. It has a rich Mexican American culture and is not far from Tucson. She said, "The distance will allow me to maintain my sanity while still being close enough to engage in occasional contact with my family." Maria Elena is "going back" to her family in small increments of geographical distance and is feeling that this move will help fill the void of being "cultureless." She will be able to partake in true fiestas and Mexican holidays. Maria Elena stated that her "purpose in life is to go back to the Southwest to be a part of my family problems and to make them a part of me. . . . I can do this. I can go back and give what has been given to me. If I help one niece or nephew, we break another link in the chain."

Maria Elena and her mother finally flew to Colorado to visit Alberto. Maria Elena successfully worked through many of the anxieties that surrounded visiting her dying brother. However, Maria Elena will continue to adjust to his debilitating virus and eventual death. Maria Elena should continue working on her inability to establish close relationships with men. Understanding her dynamics with her father and male siblings will be the springboard in tackling intimacy issues. Once her past feelings are worked through, she might be able to explore how she envisions herself in a future intimate relationship and continue to experiment with intimacy by dating or simply pursuing male friendships. This is a topic that is very hard for Maria Elena to discuss and certainly will have to be explored at her pace. It is hard to move forward with enthusiasm when the past remains a bitter memory.

Recently, Maria Elena began participating in activities around the Washington area that are culturally focused. At the onset, she found an authentic Mexican restaurant. She said with a smile, "I had forgotten how good Mexican food can be. It took me right back to my childhood. I really missed that." It was recommended that Maria Elena continue exposing herself to both the Mexican American community and the Anglo American community. On the whole, Maria Elena has a very good prognosis. Becoming bicultural may be a healthy accommodation when neither culture can completely serve her needs or aspirations. Biculturalism might be a creative compromise to cultural conflict.

DISCUSSION OF THE CASE

Maria Elena required a different approach than traditional therapy. She needed to feel safe within a comfortable environment before she could disclose her intimate feelings and thoughts. As many cross-cultural clients have an intrinsic distrust of mental health professionals, it is imperative that clinicians be flexible in their delivery of services. In this case, meeting with the client at her place of work or, at times, conducting the session sitting in the park, helped facilitate the building of rapport. Furthermore, the counselor's assumption of a student's role in learning about the Hispanic culture while the client assumed a teacher's role was extremely beneficial and an effective means to help the client to self-disclose. In addition, it is important that therapists exercise patience and spend ample time building rapport. These novel roles in therapy allowed the counselor and the client to meet on an equal plane, thus creating a therapeutic relationship that resembled a good friendship rather than an impersonal professional–client exchange.

One of the most important aspects of this case is acculturation. Acculturation cannot be taken for granted and must be assessed constantly with the new information the client presents. When meeting and listening to Maria Elena, it seemed that she was very acculturated, as evidenced by her drive for professional success and her belief in the equality of women in all settings. However, in delving deeper and hearing of her desire to return to the Southwest, it seemed necessary to reexamine her level of acculturation. For example, she very much desired to be a part of her family system but not so enmeshed that she had to relinquish the values and customs of the American culture she needs to solidify her identity as an independent woman.

Where does this leave Maria Elena in terms of biculturalism? Perhaps there can be a happy medium between being a traditional Mexican woman and a feminist, and Maria Elena can negotiate it creatively. Returning home is a transition that might have to be addressed from an autoplastic point of view. This means that Maria Elena will be required to adjust to her family and home, but her family members cannot be expected to adjust to her as easily, because she has been exposed to a multitude of experiences and ideas that they have not. Nor can Maria Elena expect to return to the same place she left, because life will have changed the people there as well. Although adjustment will require effort on Maria Elena's part, in the end, her challenges might be satisfactorily overcome and, perhaps, she can return at least to something that resembles home— or maybe something better, because she sees the world in a different light. Her life plan, like most life plans, must be a compromise—a midpoint between what is possible and what cannot be changed.

DISCUSSION QUESTIONS

1. Compare the conceptual, the existential, and the *DSM-IV* perspectives with respect to Maria Elena. How are they similar and how do they differ?

2. Although existential psychotherapy does not subscribe to a multitude of techniques, how would you raise existential issues in a counseling interview?

3. Excluding the manner in which the author describes building rapport with a cross-cultural client, what other non-traditional avenues would you pursue?

4. If you were the therapist whom Maria Elena consulted about preparing her move to the Southwest, what family issues would you focus on to prepare her for the transition? Would you recommend that she visit for an extended period of time before relocating permanently?

5. Take a moment to ponder what living an authentic life means. What changes could you make in your own life to live authentically?

6. Does the *DSM-IV* diagnosis accurately describe the issues Maria Elena is facing? If not, how could the *DSM* be revamped to incorporate your ideas?

7. What, if any, limitations does the client have in dealing with her problems?

8. How could you assist the client in dealing with her brother's illness? How could you help her confront his death?

9. How would you help the client with her intimacy issues?

10. What, if anything, would you have done differently with Maria Elena?

CHAPTER EIGHT

Revered in One Culture, Ignored in Another: The Challenge of Being Culturally Invisible

INTRODUCTION

Mika is a 27-year-old Japanese woman who came to the United States as an international student to pursue graduate studies. Mika has struggled to be recognized and valued in American society the way she was in her native Japan, where she came from a prominent family. There, her recognition and favorable treatment were automatic to her social status. However, now Mika lives in a state of invisibility, which is not physical, but psychological. Members of the dominant American culture cannot attribute to her any special importance; in such a setting, Mika finds it difficult to value her own uniqueness.

Mika's counselor is also from a foreign culture. She is a married woman of Egyptian heritage but who was raised and educated predominantly in the United States. She is a very highly skilled therapist who radiates a spontaneous love and caring that puts Mika immediately at ease.

PRESENTING CHALLENGE

Mika's usually serene face was filled with anguish as she described her issues. Her difficulty in adjusting to American society had become a source of inner turmoil as she attempted to discover her own identity in a foreign culture that offered her little direction. She described her major issues succinctly and with little show of emotion in her very soft and deferential voice. She claimed that she felt as though she didn't belong in American society: She felt unaccepted by Americans, particularly her classmates and peers; she struggled with graduate school and her career choice to become a psychologist; and she confessed to her intellectual intimidation by the formidable language barrier presented to a Japanese speaker by English.

CASE HISTORY

Family History

Mika was born on March 15, 1965, in Tokyo, Japan. When Mika sought counseling, she was a graduate student in a counseling psychology program at a major university on the East Coast. Mika is the daughter of a high-ranking political official in Japan; her father's position is comparable with a congressman or senator in this country. Thus, she comes from an affluent, political family and grew up enjoying the privileges of status and money. Mika's mother, as a politician's wife, spent most of her time with her husband, aiding him in his political duties. Consequently, Mika and her brother, who is 31 years old, were raised primarily by their paternal grandmother. Mika said that they were much closer to their grandmother than they were to either of their parents. The grandmother died 3 years ago, which was a great shock to Mika.

Although Mika and her brother had the best of material possessions, they missed having a "normal" family life that included their parents available at home, family dinners, and family vacations. Mika expressed much resentment toward her parents for what she perceived as uncaring treatment and emotional neglect. She felt envious of her friends whose parents were home and there for them, both physically and emotionally. The unavailability of her parents caused Mika to feel a sense of emotional detachment from them as she became older.

Mika's home life was very atypical of Japanese families. Her mother was very work-oriented rather than focused on being an ideal parent; thus, Mika grew up sensing an aloofness from her mother. Although Japanese mothers often are not overly affectionate and tend to refrain from making overt statements of love, there is still the presence of the mother and much physical nurturance. Thus, Mika expressed that her family life did not fit the typical Japanese pattern.

In Japanese culture, there are almost always two parents, and they are very involved in their children's lives, especially in school. Mika angrily recalled that her father only attended one parent–teacher day at school and that it was not a very pleasant experience. She recounted that all the other parents admired her father and treated him with extra deference because of his political position, but that special treatment only emphasized the fact that her father was different. Mika said, "Everyone bowed to my father so much more than they did to anyone else." She continued, "I didn't like the fact that he was a politician because it reminded me that my father belonged to the public and not to me." Mika never really talked to her father because he was never home. He was always absent during the day and was busy with business dinners and political meetings in the evening.

When Mika spoke about her mother, she described a lack of closeness. Mika claimed that her mother avoided her considerably as she got older, because during her period of adolescent rebelliousness, Mika began to express some of her anger in open confrontations with her mother. In Japanese culture, anger and even asserting one's self with parents is highly unacceptable. Thus, Mika's mother was extremely uncomfortable with this behavior and reacted by avoiding Mika, which only angered Mika more. Mika disclosed, "It made me so angry that she wouldn't even talk to me about it; I felt as if she didn't care." Mika's anger was compounded with guilt, because in expressing the anger, she was violating a cultural taboo. As she grew older, Mika tried to let go of some of the anger, realizing that it was self-destructive and only alienated her mother further.

Mika adopted the philosophy that family is paramount. She came to believe that it is essential to "forgive and forget" the hurts that are inflicted by one's family. Mika continues to struggle with her anger, but she has learned to "compartmentalize" it—to push it out of daily awareness and slowly let it go. She decided to do this after an incident with her mother that occurred during a visit to Japan after being in the United States for 1 year. Prompted by ideas learned from her American course work in psychology, Mika recounted that she confronted her mother about the emotional neglect and cold parenting that she and her brother received. This time, instead of avoidance, her mother broke down in tears and took all of the blame. However, all she could tell Mika was that one day she would have her own children and only then would she truly understand. Since that incident, Mika has tried to let go. She has started to see that her mother did care, but she was constrained by her obligations to her ambitious husband.

Religious History

Mika and her family are Buddhists. Mika's family is somewhat religious, but mainly in a ritualistic way. They observe important traditions, such as visiting dead relatives at the cemetery at designated times during the year. On occasion, Mika will have the priest pray for her. Buddhism is a way of life that preaches humility, being free of material things, and seeking salvation through saving others. The other major belief is in reincarnation. Reincarnation depends on one's good deeds and behaviors in the current life. For example, if one was a good person, one may be reincarnated into a person with good fortune and a happy life. On the other hand, people who are judged as not having been good are punished by being reincarnated as a pig, or some other lowly animal. Mika said that she and her family believe in all the tenets of the religion, even though their practice of it is more ritualistic than reflecting the Buddhist ideals of humility and nonmaterialism.

Educational History

In Japan, schooling is extremely competitive, and not everyone has the chance to go to the school of their choice. Even as early as elementary school, an entrance exam is required of all students. Usually, students will apply to many schools in the hope that they will pass at least one of the entrance exams and be able to receive a good education. This extreme competition makes education a tremendous source of anxiety and pressure for both children and parents. At each phase of schooling—elementary, secondary, and college—one must try to gain admission to a "good school," thus the pressure continues throughout one's academic career.

Mika was one of the fortunate students. She was admitted to a good college and received a bachelor's degree in psychology. However, she explained that she had applied to seven schools and was lucky that she passed the entrance exam for one school—the school she eventually attended. Mika explained that the process is extremely frustrating and that one must work very hard. However, regardless of how hard one tries, there are no guarantees, and there is much uncertainty. Mika described the pressure as being so intense that many students give up and look for menial work; others become depressed, even suicidal, when they have failed completely to gain acceptance to a favored school. The bitter reality of this situation is that in Japan education is critical if one is to succeed. Thus, to settle for a menial job means that one resigns one's self to reaping minimal success, both financially and in terms of social stature.

Mika explained that Japanese students learn early that failure is an inevitable part of the educational process. They also learn that the key to success is persistence. Everyone inevitably fails numerous times, so it is a concept with which they are well acquainted. The concept of failure came up in the interview because Mika had failed to gain admission to some of the doctoral programs in psychology to which she applied.

At the time that Mika was receiving counseling, she was finishing her master's degree in counseling psychology. Graduate school was challenging for Mika because of the language barrier. Despite this fact, she maintained a relatively high grade point average of 3.30. Coincidentally, during her own counseling, Mika was in the internship phase of her graduate program and had started to counsel clients. This had become a tremendous source of anxiety for her in light of a realization that she had recently made concerning her ability to counsel. Mika had decided that the language barrier was too great for her to counsel effectively; she felt that she did not have what she perceived as the necessary talent to "read people." Thus, she began thinking that she should pursue a doctorate in social psychology—a field that would not require her to work one-on-one with clients. Although she expressed sadness about this realization, she felt that one must know one's own limitations and accept them.

Support Systems

Mika has many Japanese friends and two American friends. Both of Mika's American friends are African American. She said that she feels more comfortable with other minorities. She believes that it is difficult to make American friends because of the language barrier. She often feels that people do not want to take the time to understand her because she speaks slowly and with a heavy accent. In counseling, Mika often expressed feeling frustrated; therefore, she does not try as much as she should to interact with Americans. Mika believes that if she had more interpersonal contact with them, she would become more acculturated and better adjusted to American society.

Adjustment in the United States

Mika came to the United States approximately 3 years ago to do graduate work in counseling. She spent the 1st year studying English and then started her master's program 2 years thereafter. Mika is still struggling with English, but she is fortunate because she does not have to struggle financially. Her parents are wealthy and completely support her stay and studies in the United States. Mika confided, "I'm really spoiled." Her struggles are more interpersonal, social, and academic than financial or material.

Mika described herself as "very independent." She has no trouble finding her way around and is not intimidated by her physical, foreign surroundings. She theorized that her independence comes from growing up without much direction from or dependence on her parents. However, what intimidates Mika and causes her much anxiety is people's treatment of her. She feels that Americans generally are not tolerant or accepting of foreigners. Mika said, "Even in a restaurant when I am ordering food, the people are abrupt and rude because they cannot understand me, but they don't even try to listen; it seems they see a foreign face and hear an accent and automatically act as if I am bothering them." This has been extremely trying for Mika, who takes these reactions personally.

In addition, Mika felt that classmates either patronized or ignored her, especially when they were in groups. Mika said, "It's okay one-on-one, but when they are in a group, I feel like a stranger and so left out." These kinds of interactions with others have made her withdraw, slowing down her acculturation and assimilation into American society. She realized that it also has implications for her language ability; the less she interacts with Americans, the longer it will take to improve her English. Mika talked about her self-imposed isolation, attributing it to her feelings of rejection and low self-esteem. Mika contended that her abysmally low self-esteem is a direct effect of the alienation she feels in American society.

CASE ANALYSIS

Conceptual Perspective

To understand any human being meaningfully, one must acknowledge that every individual exists within a cultural context. The problem is determining in which culture a person is placing him- or herself. Typically, in the field of cross-cultural counseling, counselors have used the "groups approach," which classifies the behaviors of people by their ethnic group in a stereotypical fashion. Although culture appears to be a seamless construct, it is really more like an onion, with numerous layers of class and subculture as one "peels" into its defining core. Thus, by predicting the behaviors of an individual by looking exclusively at the cultural group to which he or she is arbitrarily assigned is to exclude the intersecting factors of socioeconomic status and subculture.

The "cumulative culture" of the individual is not a sum total of parts but rather a special mixture. Thus, to limit one's self to understanding a client in terms of one or several layers of culture may result in a biased, incomplete, and stereotypical understanding of the individual. Although culture certainly affects individuals, it is important to realize that individuals affect culture, and the dynamics of how the individual's unique personality, upbringing, and free will manifest themselves illustrate how, in many respects, each individual may be a unique culture in microcosm.

Mika's family did not fit the typical mold of Japanese families. In many respects, the socioeconomic subculture to which Mika belonged influenced her and her family's life in very significant ways. Her father's position and her mother's involvement with her father's political career made them atypical of Japanese families, thereby creating a set of difficulties that is not faced ordinarily by other Japanese families. Furthermore, Mika's confrontation with her mother about the insensitive parenting that she received is not typical of Japanese children who are socialized to believe that challenging or expressing anger toward one's parents is a cultural taboo.

Although a groups approach can be useful to gain a general understanding of the values, norms, and mores of an ethic group, it can result in blinding the counselor to the individual differences among people. Even in homogeneous societies such as Japan, individuals are not clones, cut from a mold that produces genetically and socially identical human beings. The conceptual approach allows the counselor to understand the individual more fully "within the culture" versus through the groups approach, which results in understanding the individual through the poorly refracted lens of the cultural stereotype. In this vein, Mika was clearly a blend of her culture and the unique family circumstances under which she was raised, which in a sense made her as much like the child of an American congressman as that of a traditional Japanese father.

Existential Perspective

"Man is what he chooses to be" can be considered a first principle of existentialism (Sartre, 1957). What is interesting is that one of the fundamental beliefs of counseling is the ability of each individual to grow, change, and heal if one resolves to do so. Existentialism emphasizes the responsibility of individuals to shape their own destiny. Similarly, counseling is designed to help clients to change and restructure the course of their lives and is based on the premise that every individual, however impossible the circumstances may appear, can actively effect meaningful change in their life. In short, counseling's goals of responsibility and empowerment are consistent with existential thought; our profession may be an indirect product of this philosophical school as refashioned and simplified by counseling theorists.

In describing the existential counseling relationship, van Kaam (1962) argued that clients are best understood from their own subjective description of their universe. This is also consistent with the conceptual approach that was discussed earlier that emphasized the importance of understanding the individual by considering all of the dimensions of his or her culture and unique life experiences. In describing the special nature of the existential encounter between counselor and client, Arbuckle (1975) wrote, "Existential–humanistic counseling is an intimate and very real human experience between two human beings, one of whom has not yet experienced his inner self as much as the other. But both individuals are equal in their humanness and their sharing of each other" (p. 116).

Just as Arbuckle described, the key to success in working with Mika was the deep rapport—the meeting of equals—that was forged between herself and the counselor. This connection was especially critical in Mika's case because she was extremely withdrawn when she started counseling. She was feeling invisible in American culture, which led to a state of existential isolation that seemed to exacerbate her sadness and was coupled with an ongoing "cultural anxiety" stemming from her insecurity among those who were culturally unlike herself. Her inability to connect with others was becoming increasingly more pervasive in her life, and it was the connection with a counselor that she needed to help her come out of her physical, existential, and cultural isolation. This human linkage was an important reconnection with the American culture because her counselor symbolized the people from whom she felt alienated.

Mika's counselor did not use a fancy intervention. A safe, patient, therapeutic environment was created in which Mika felt comfortable enough to bond and share with a counselor who was culturally unlike herself. Mika opened up and began to talk about her intimate feelings and struggles and amazingly found that her ability to communicate in English was much better than she thought. Initially in the counseling interview, Mika expressed repeatedly that she was not sure that she could disclose her issues because of her limited English, so she was surprised when she found herself articulating them fluidly and profusely.

Mika realized that it was not so much that her English was weak, as it was that her anxiety was high. It was this emotional state that had greatly inhibited her ability to speak. She also realized that if her anxiety was inhibiting her ability to speak to the point of diminishing her sense of social competence, then the anxiety probably was clouding her ability to judge her competence in other areas. It is important to remember that Mika's presenting problems were low self-esteem and sadness. Her newfound ability to disclose emotion demonstrated the power of the I–Thou rapport in fostering an environment in which the client can feel safe enough to find the courage to be authentic in the face of a culturally different counselor. It is only when one is truly authentic that one can reach the root of one's feelings and perceptions.

DSM–IV (APA, 1994) Perspective

In assessing Mika from a diagnostic perspective, it appeared that she had an adjustment disorder with mixed anxiety and depressed mood (chronic low-grade anxiety and depression). This diagnosis is really a mild one, but it emphasizes that anxiety and depression, although stemming from various cultural and existential issues, can become sources of distress in themselves.

Multiaxial Diagnosis

Axis I	Adjustment disorder with mixed anxiety and depressed mood (309.28)
Axis II	No diagnosis
Axis III	No diagnosis
Axis IV	Psychosocial stressors: residence in new country or foreign culture; problems with school and career choice; problems with the English language
Axis V	GAF = 70 (current)

INTERVENTION STRATEGY

Mika's treatment may require multiple levels of intervention. First, Mika may benefit from an activity that would involve her interacting with Americans in a safe, nonacademic environment. One idea might be joining a YMCA, social club, or other organization devoted to a hobby or activity that interests her. Another idea might be to do some volunteer work, especially because finances are not a problem. Volunteer work would provide Mika with a chance to interact with Americans in an amicable and noncompetitive environment.

Second, Mika might benefit from joining a support group for international students. In a support group, Mika would have an opportunity to share her concerns with other students who are struggling with some of the same issues. This activity might broaden her perspective because the group would not only consist of Japanese students but also students from a wide array of nationalities. In addition, the group would be conducted in English, thereby providing her with a safe environment in which to practice her English. When she sees other students struggling with some of the very same issues, it might enable her to see that she is not alone. In the group, Mika may experience the social adequacy that she was unable to experience in the outside world and thereby prove that, under favorable circumstances, she can be very socially adequate.

Third, Mika may wish to experiment with counseling Japanese clients in their own language. Counseling in Japanese would be a good way to test her assumption that she does not have the necessary talent to "read people" that has made her consider leaving the counseling profession. Such an experiment might help her to make a sound decision with respect to changing her career—a decision based in clear thinking and not the impulsivity that anxiety can engender. Mika needs to delve more extensively into the reasons why she is leaving the counseling profession before she makes a final decision. Considering that Mika came to the United States with the intention of becoming a psychologist, this issue is one that needs to be examined carefully.

DISCUSSION OF THE CASE

Mika suffered from cultural anxiety, slow acculturation, depression, and low self-esteem. Her cultural anxiety resulted from her being in a foreign environment and feeling unable to integrate herself into it. Mika's cultural anxiety manifested itself in her tendency to withdraw and to avoid interacting with Americans as much as possible. Fearing rejection, Mika preferred exercising avoidance so as to reduce her anxiety. Her cultural anxiety also manifested itself by her sticking close to her Japanese friends while being somewhat apprehensive about trying to cultivate relationships with Americans. The fact that her two American friends are African American indicates that Mika is very hesitant to interact with White Americans, who she perceives as representing members of the dominant culture. Mika is better able to identify with African Americans, who understand firsthand what it means to be viewed with prejudice and treated as culturally invisible or insignificant.

As a result of her cultural anxiety and subsequent withdrawal, Mika experienced difficulty in becoming acculturated to American society. The less interaction she had, the less opportunity she had to learn and adopt the norms of a new environment. The lack of acculturation was reflected in her ongoing struggle with the English language. Mika realizes that her English could be better if she were practicing it more; however, her anxiety has made her apprehensive to interact with Americans. One issue has fed on the other.

Mika's feelings of incompetence resulted in her decision to change her career plans from being a counselor to being a researcher in the field of social psychology. Mika believes that it is not just the language barrier but also her inability to "read people" that has resulted in this decision. However, her overall lack of self-esteem may have affected her decision to change her career plans. Although it may be possible that she is accurate in her self-appraisal that she would be an ineffective counselor, her low self-esteem may be clouding the accuracy of that decision.

A deeper explanation for Mika's negative emotions and issues may be that she came from a well-to-do family in which she automatically enjoyed status and respect. In Japanese culture, she had a prestigious identity; in America, she felt invisible. The contrast between the two cultural identities was as stark as that between fame and anonymity. The invisible man or woman cannot be loved—which is what all men and women ultimately crave—because love requires the constant awareness that one is valued through the admiring eyes of others.

DISCUSSION QUESTIONS

1. Compare and contrast the conceptual versus the groups approach in the case of Mika. Would an integration of the two be best, or is the conceptual approach adequate to understand and correctly assess Mika's situation?

2. If you could create your own *DSM-IV* diagnosis that would most accurately describe Mika's condition (considering the cultural issues), what would it be called? Is the *DSM-IV* adequate in its scope with respect to multicultural considerations?

3. Given the case history, and examples of analyses through various perspectives, what other ways could you have approached this case?

4. Identify some of Mika's strengths and explore how, as a therapist, you could use those strengths to help Mika resolve her issues.

5. Discuss how Mika's socioeconomic status and her family life growing up may have affected the way she negotiated her environment when she came to the United States.

6. Differentiate cultural anxiety from anxiety in either the existential or pathological sense.

7. Is it possible for one to be culturally invisible in one's own culture?

8. Do you you think that Mika's conclusion that she would be a poor counselor is accurate or tainted by her cultural anxiety?

9. Why do you think Mika feels more comfortable among African Americans, even though those she associates with are from a lower socioeconomic level than she?

10. Can we be sure that Mika's anxiety is due to her unfamiliar cultural surroundings or rather a lack of self-confidence that she derived from her uninvolved family, or both?

CHAPTER NINE

The Anguish of a Beautiful Woman: The Challenge of Living at the Crossroads of Two Cultures

INTRODUCTION

With long, wavy, black hair with auburn highlights, Catherine could be a leading model in any fashion circuit. The gently chiseled features of her face revealed a beauty that belied the inner conflict that emerged as her counselor delved into her past. Catherine revealed a number of issues in her life that she needed to discuss with a nonfamily member. Catherine felt trapped at the intersections of two cultures, Latin and American, which were pressuring her to take opposite courses in life. Her struggle to find the right path brought her into counseling to explore her cultural identity and whom she would eventually fall in love with and marry.

Her counselor was a very genuine and compassionate woman who was raised in a close-knit Italian family from New York. She was involved in a wonderful relationship with a loving fiancé—the kind of relationship that Catherine yearned for herself. If Catherine wanted honest answers and support, she had found the right counselor, because her counselor liked to get to the bottom of issues and not become bogged down with insignificant details that could prolong the process of counseling and lead to frustration for the client.

PRESENTING CHALLENGE

Catherine is 26 years old and is a first-generation American. Her parents, half-brother, and half-sister were born in Ecuador. More than 30 years ago, Catherine's father was the first family member to immigrate to the United States. A year later, Catherine's mother and her paternal uncle, aunt, and grandmother immigrated. Catherine said that her father wanted to come to the United States because of the old cliché that "America is the land of opportunity." Catherine emphasized that her "family was struggling financially and emotionally in Ecuador. For them, Ecuador was tied to a lot of bad memories." This was one of the main reasons she felt that her family does not often return to visit.

Catherine's main issue was "the desire to reach an equal balance between the two cultures" that define her identity. She described herself as "bicultural" in the following proportions: 60% of her identifies with the American culture, and the remaining 40% identifies with the Latino culture. Although she is very happy to have been born and to live in the United States, she has a great desire to learn more about the Ecuadoran way of life. Catherine compared herself with her cousins, who are approximately the same age as she and who were born and raised in Ecuador before coming to the United States. She observed that her cousins are able to handle themselves with ease in both the Latin and American cultures. She said, "My cousins know who they are culturally and have a better understanding of which values are Ecuadoran and which are American, whereas I am unable to separate my Ecuadoran heritage, which was taught to me by my parents, from my experiences living and growing up in American society."

To understand Catherine's inner world, her counselor asked her to amplify her insightful disclosure "I cannot place cultural boundaries around my ideas and values." As an example, Catherine shared an experience during a game of Trivial Pursuit in which a question dealt with nursery rhymes. Catherine told the group the rhymes that she knew and grew up with. However, she said that "everyone was just looking at me dumbfounded and then someone asked me if I'd ever heard of Mother Goose. I realized that I must have been reciting Ecuadoran rhymes that not everyone in the group was familiar with. I tend to blend my two cultural backgrounds together and sometimes assume that the things I know are part of the American culture."

Recently, one of Catherine's cousins, who is a lifelong resident of Ecuador, visited her for a week. He told Catherine that she speaks Spanish with an American accent. Catherine feels that when she is at a party or a gathering with Latin people, she stands out as "the gringa," meaning "the American" in Spanish. She said, "Latinos can tell that I was born here because of how I dress and how I speak. I sometimes say a word wrong in Spanish or I hesitate to think about what I am trying to say and that immediately clues them in that I was not born in Ecuador." It also frustrated Catherine not to be able to participate in all conversations with other Ecuadorans her age. She mentioned, "Sometimes my cousins or friends will start talking about certain songs or particular stories or events going on in Ecuador right now, and I just listen and can't voice an opinion because I am unfamiliar with these topics."

Catherine mentioned to her mother recently that she regretted not spending a significant amount of time in Ecuador when she was growing up. She tried to explain to her mother the interest she has in truly developing an understanding of the Ecuadoran way of life. She said,

> My mother and I got into a big fight over this. I think my mother is in a difficult position, and she feels she can't win with whatever decision she makes in regard to this matter. When my mother first came to America, she could not afford to bring my half-brother and half-sister with her. They stayed with my maternal grandmother for 3 years in Ecuador. My grandmother was a very strict and serious woman, and I am sure it was no picnic for my brother and sister to live with her. My mother still feels a sense of guilt about the 3-year family separation and cannot understand why I would want to be separated from her and my dad in order to live in Ecuador. My mother thought that I was trying to lay a guilt trip on her for not allowing me to spend some time with my cousins, who live in Ecuador, while growing up.

Ideally, Catherine would like to visit Ecuador and spend some time in Quito, the capital of Ecuador, where several of her relatives live. She feels that this is one of the ways that will enable her to become more "equicultural," or, as Catherine says, "more fifty-fifty." However, she feels that she must first learn to discuss her desire to go to Ecuador rationally with her mother, without having her mother develop a sense of guilt or a feeling of loss that Catherine would be leaving her for a period of time. Catherine would not consider traveling to Ecuador without her mother's permission.

As illustrated by the case information, Catherine discussed the serious pressures that the Latin culture places on women to find a suitable husband by a certain age. Catherine said, "When my uncle who lives in Ecuador calls my dad, he asks my dad how am I doing. When my dad tells him about my master's work, my uncle listens politely, expresses how proud he is of me, then switches the subject, as he does in all of his phone conversations to the question of when am I getting married."

She expressed that "in the Latin culture, a woman has not lived her life to the fullest until she has married and raised a family." Catherine said, "I do not want to get married to have a family just to say I have done these things. Perhaps I am more Americanized in my way of thinking about marriage, for I feel I need to wait until I have found the right person." Catherine's family takes an active role in expressing their feelings about whom she should date. Catherine stated, "My parents do not pressure me to date only Latinos, but I feel that they would prefer it." Catherine is now thoughtfully considering the cultural background she desires in her future husband.

CASE HISTORY

Family History

Catherine was born and raised in Virginia to a middle-class Latin family. Catherine said, "The family unit plays a large role in the Latin culture. In America, when you think of the central family unit, you are referring to one's parents and siblings. However, for Latinos, the family unit means parents, grandparents, siblings, aunts and uncles, and first, second, and even third cousins." As she continued sharing her perceptions concerning the family, Catherine announced, "I cannot understand why Americans who live so close to their cousins never visit them. . . . To me that is a foreign concept, since I am so close to all my cousins."

Catherine's parents grew up in Quito, the capital of Ecuador. While growing up, her parents' families were fairly poor. By starting family businesses in Ecuador and then moving to the United States, her parents' generation began to change their economic status. On the coast of Ecuador in Guayaquil, Catherine has a paternal uncle who owns a gasoline station. She referred to him as her "rich uncle." Recalling her visit to Ecuador more than 15 years ago, Catherine explained that there are big differences between Quito and the coastal city of Guayaquil. Quito is surrounded by mountains and palm trees; it resembles the terrain of California. The temperature in Quito is springlike, never getting too hot. In Guayaquil, it is always hot and steamy. Catherine believes that the temperature affects the behavior of the people who live in these two cities. People in Quito are more conservative and reserved as compared with the relaxed atmosphere seen on the Ecuadoran coast. She observed, "This is even true right here in Washington, DC. People's attitudes and moods change for the better when it gets warmer out."

Catherine's mother grew up in a very strict and disciplined home and was not allowed out of the house by herself. Reflecting on her mother's life, Catherine expressed that "it must have been like living in prison." Catherine's maternal grandmother was responsible for her mother's strict upbringing and lack of freedom. Catherine said that her grandmother

> was never allowed to be a child. While growing up she accompanied her dad, who was considered a medicine man, on his rounds throughout the town. My grandmother helped her father deliver babies and take care of the sick. This is why I think she was such a serious lady. My grandmother had several children, my mother being the youngest. She had my mother at age 44, which was considered quite old to have a child.

Catherine's maternal grandmother believed in the home remedies that were passed down from generation to generation. Catherine explained that

> such remedies are very popular in South America. . . . If you have a stomachache, you are given a certain kind of tea to drink. I know of a few other remedies, but I am not sure if they are from the Latin or American culture. This is where I get confused by blending the cultures together. However, when I had a fever growing up, my mother dipped a towel in vinegar and put it on my forehead. This quickly reduced my fever. To cure a sore throat or a cough, my mom would boil some milk together with some raisins: It alleviates the pain, and the raisins make the milk taste very good and sweet. Also rubbing cocoa butter on a person's chest helps to relieve a sore chest that results from a bad cough.

Catherine asked the counselor if any of these home remedies sounded familiar to her. The counselor replied that she "had not heard of them before, but that [she] would try them the next time [she] got sick."

Catherine's mother was married once before in Ecuador and had two children, a boy and a girl. Her first husband passed away, and she later married Catherine's father. Catherine's parents met each other while working at the front desk of a hotel in Ecuador. Later, Catherine's father met an American at this hotel who offered him a job at a social club in Washington, DC. In 1962, Catherine's father immigrated to America to pursue the employment opportunity. He has been working for this club for more than 30 years, first as an accountant and now at the management level. A year after Catherine's father immigrated to America, her mother joined him there. Within 2 months of her arrival, Catherine's mother, hoping to fulfill a lifelong dream, attended a beauty school and later opened her own salon at a retirement home.

When Catherine's parents first came to the United States, Catherine's half-brother and half-sister remained in Ecuador with their maternal grandmother. Two years after Catherine's parents immigrated, they sent for the daughter. Because of financial concerns, they were unable initially to bring both children. Catherine's half-brother came to the United States 2 years after his sister. According to Catherine, the temporary family separation caused a great deal of guilt for her mother. She felt responsible for not being around to raise her children during those years.

Catherine has a paternal uncle who lives in Virginia. He immigrated to the United States 2 years after his brother but for a different reason. He was escaping Ecuador for his mental health. His wife left him and his five children. The uncle was "devastated and left to recover from his shock." He never talked about his wife leaving him and refused to talk to his children about it. He left his children with his mother and sister in Ecuador. When he was financially stable in the United States, he sent for his children, his sister, and his mother. Catherine's uncle later remarried a Chilean woman he met in Washington. Catherine said,

> My Chilean aunt raised my uncle's five children, and they also had a daughter together named Julia. On the whole, my five cousins turned out okay, even though they have been unable to talk over their feelings about their biological mother. My cousin, Luis, was 2 years old when his mother left him. Today, he stutters, which, as you know, is a psychologically based problem. My uncle and my five cousins have never gone back to Ecuador; and, in fact, these five cousins of mine do not speak Spanish well. This has to do with their negative feelings toward Ecuador and their sense of abandonment by their mother.

Personal History

Catherine grew up in a predominantly Anglo American community in Virginia. She said, "I did not want to stand out or be different. So I tried to fit in with everyone else in my neighborhood by speaking English without an accent. But I knew I was different because my parents were more protective of me than my friends' parents were of them." Catherine's parents ingrained in her the Latin tradition of respect and honor of one's parents and elders. Catherine abided by this tradition and expressed the view that her obedience was out of "a combination of respect and fear of [her] parents." Catherine mentioned, "You don't see that kind of respect in the American culture. You can go on the metro and you will see teenagers cussing in front of older people. I would never talk really loud or, God forbid, cuss in front of an older person. I do not even have to know them; it is just a sign of respect."

In the American culture, Catherine explained that "you are raised to be independent, whereas in the Latin culture, dependence on the family is considered a great thing. Not one of the women in my family was submissive. Yet, in the Latin family, everyone knows his place." Sharing her thoughts further, she said, "The father is the provider and has the last word in all family matters while the mother's major role is to raise the children, prepare meals, and clean. This is true even today. A woman can work outside the home, since it is hard to run a household without two incomes, as long as she maintains her household duties. She is expected to do all of this without ever complaining."

In addition to respecting one's parents, a child needs to be aware of his or her actions. "For one's actions directly reflect upon the parents," Catherine remarked. "When I grew up, if I did something stupid or foolish, my dad would be embarrassed for himself, not for me. My bad behavior would hurt the family honor. This tradition is found in the Indian, Asian, and Middle Eastern cultures as well. This could be why I can relate to people from these cultures more easily than the type of Anglo American people I grew up with," she continued. Catherine and her parents had disagreements when she was in high school. She saw that she had different values from her friends, and that her friends were given more freedom by their parents to do whatever they wanted without having a curfew. She said, "It was hard for me to accept such differences, but I think I avoided a lot of problems by not dating much in high school."

In 1991, a year after Catherine graduated from college, she began dating a Latin American whom she met while working at a temporary position at her father's office. She said, "The biggest struggle I have ever had with my parents was over this guy. In the Latin culture, class difference and the color of one's skin are big issues. The lighter your skin color the better, since it means that you have more Spanish blood." The person Catherine dated was from Guatemala and had dark-colored skin. She explained that it "might sound stuck up, but the South Americans look down on Central Americans." Her parents were "in an uproar" that she was dating this young man. Catherine fell in love with him and could not understand why her parents disliked him. Her dad was "so disappointed" in her for not respecting her parents' wishes. He even threatened to quit his job because he felt that he would lose his reputation and honor at work.

Catherine tried to explain to her father that most of his colleagues at work were American and "could care less" whom his daughter was dating. Catherine said, "There was no reasoning with him. He felt his honor was tarnished, and there was nothing I could say. I knew my dad was disappointed in me, and when that happened, I felt horrible."

The rest of Catherine's family also became involved with her personal life. Accordingly, Catherine's paternal aunt inquired why she was trying to embarrass her father and disregard his wishes. Even her cousins intervened by talking to other Latin people, who they knew worked at Catherine's father's office, to find out more information about Catherine's boyfriend. Catherine disclosed that she "resented her parents because of how they felt about my boyfriend and there was no way I could reason with either of them." As a result, she decided to move out of their house. Subsequently, she lived with her half-sister and, thereafter, with one of her cousins. She said, "My cousin and my sister were very supportive of me throughout this time. This was a classic example of how everyone in the family comes together and goes out on a limb to help make things better."

Catherine was frustrated with her parents' interference with her relationship. She felt that it was difficult to follow the Latin traditions of honor and obedience of her parents. Catherine explained, "I felt that if I were part of an American family, the whole family would not have intervened like mine had. In fact, American parents might say go ahead and maintain this relationship with your boyfriend, after all, it's your life and you need to make your own mistakes. You will have to deal with the consequences."

Catherine concluded that she had to break off this relationship, not because her parents were unhappy, but because all the controversy was making her unhappy. Catherine explained,

> This was one of the worst times in my life. All the family tension and stress made me physically sick. The constant pressure weakened my defenses and it took a long time to build up my strength. Breaking up with him was a good experience for me. I learned to make better judgments about what it means to form a good relationship with someone. I think I am now capable of ending a relationship when it is necessary. Another important thing is that I proved to my family that I could stand up to defend myself.

Catherine's father can be quite strict. Catherine explained that

> even though he can go overboard and drive me crazy sometimes, he still is a lot better than his brothers. My cousin Isabel's father will not allow her out of his house after 10 o'clock at night. I think this is a little crazy since Isabel is 23 years old. Isabel likes being at home, and she never dates. I know her parents would be devastated if she ever moved away from home. Her parents want her to get married, yet they do not seem to realize the process she needs to go through in order to find the right person. This truly gets me down, but I am very thankful that my parents are not as bad as that.

Educational History

Catherine was the only person in her family to go away to college. Most of her cousins went to college in order to "make something of themselves." However, while going to school, they all lived at home with their parents. Catherine told her counselor that in the Latino culture, children, regardless of sex, live at home with their parents until they get married. It is also not unusual for a married couple to live with their parents in an extension of the family's home

When Catherine left home to attend college, her paternal uncles questioned her father. They felt that Catherine's behavior was incongruent with traditions and a sign of weakening parental authority. Most of Catherine's cousins who either live in Ecuador or in the United States have never left home. Catherine's paternal aunt also reprimanded Catherine. Catherine recalled, "My aunt tried to make me feel guilty for leaving home. She told me that my parents were going to be alone because I was not going to be around. I told my aunt that they were going to be fine. They had the rest of the family to rely on." Catherine refused to follow the traditions of her culture. She said, "It is a reality that I must leave home to get an education." Catherine felt, "My family views me as the one who has broken a few family rules."

Catherine graduated in 1990 from Virginia Wesleyan College in Norfolk, Virginia, where she majored in mass communications. She enjoyed her studies there and was an excellent student. Catherine loved to read books, exploring an extensive range of subject matter. While attending college, she had the opportunity to travel to Los Angeles to visit several television and movie studios while investigating and developing a more in-depth comprehension of the entertainment and production fields. She said that this was a very exciting time in her life, and she was even able to attend a seminar given by David Geffen, a leader in the entertainment industry.

In college, Catherine became friends with a girl from Peru and one from Quito, Ecuador. Catherine said,

> We were known as the Spanish girls on campus. The school was predominantly White. I quickly learned that I was different from the other American students. I truly did not recognize this as much in high school. I think this was because at the end of the day, everyone goes to his own home. In college, it is a more intimate environment and you see how people live and what they are really like. My roommate in college was American, and I will never forget the screaming matches she had on the phone with her parents. I was shocked, and I knew I was not like that because of the tradi-

tional values my parents raised me with. My two Latino friends in college were a lot like me in this respect. I learned a great deal about myself by going away from home. I had a better understanding of the upbringing that my parents gave me. I know now why it was important for me to hold a fork properly and to speak politely on the telephone. I embrace these differences that I have from my American counterparts for it has made me understand who I am. College was an awakening for me.

Through her college experience, Catherine realized that she had developed a strong sense of self. She observed,

I learned to stand up for myself and express my feelings and ideas. I became confident in my abilities. I had accomplished a lot by going away to school and learned how to cook, make decisions, and live away from my family in a dormitory. In the process, I think I became a stronger person. In high school, my parents basically made a lot of decisions for me, and I went along with them. When I graduated from college, my family was expecting me to remain the same. But I had changed, and I am not sure they were prepared for that.

While in college, Catherine dated an American boy named Mark. Catherine's parents met Mark and "fell in love with him." During a spring break from school, Mark asked Catherine to accompany him to Florida to visit his parents. This was an issue for Catherine's family. She claimed that "this would not have been a big thing for an American family, but because we were not married, my family did not approve." After assuring her parents that Mark's parents would also be in their presence in Florida, she was granted permission to travel with her boyfriend.

Currently, Catherine is enrolled in a master's program in rehabilitation counseling at a university in Washington, DC. She has achieved academic excellence in her program and is a member of the department's honor society. Catherine's sister graduated with her master's degree in community counseling from the same university 12 years earlier. Catherine admired the type of work her sister performed as a probations officer in the District of Columbia court system. Catherine said, "Although being a counselor might be emotionally hard, it is the best type of work for me because I will be able to help people directly. I chose rehabilitation counseling because I liked the specialized nature of the field and wanted to help people overcome the physical problems which have such a negative impact on their lives."

Catherine believes that her parents are very proud of her accomplishments. She said,

My parents understand how much counseling is valued in America. However, I am not sure that they would ever go for it themselves. The Latin culture does not view counseling in a positive light. Instead, Latinos are afraid of it. Traditionally, if a family member has a problem, he or she should turn to his family for advice and comfort. As a Latino, you are taught not to reveal your problems and concerns to a stranger. The most difficult Latin American client would probably be a male. Most Latino males affect a "macho" attitude, which means that they would feel that they do not need help and certainly do not need to confide their true feelings to a counselor.

However, Catherine believes that her generation views counseling quite differently. Many see it as beneficial and not an embarrassing process. Catherine claimed, "My family probably could use a little counseling. Especially my uncle whose wife left him and his children. He still cannot talk about this problem even today, and I know his children would really like to talk with him about it."

Relevant Work History

In Catherine's senior year in college, she had an internship at a cable television station in Virginia. A year later, the television station hired her full time. At the station, she had the opportunity to learn computer graphics, which was a real challenge for her. She said, "I just kept saying to myself if I could learn this, I would feel really good about myself. This was the one thing I did accomplish all on my own and that I am most proud of." However, she did not like the position's low salary and lack of benefits or health insurance. In discussing the job further, Catherine said, "The worst part by far was that I had to tape city council meetings that could go on for 7 to 8 hours. I would not be able to go home sometimes until 2 in the morning. This is the aspect of communications that I did not like."

After college, Catherine experienced a period in which she felt that she wanted "to save the world." She felt that the media were responsible for "negatively influencing people and politics, and that was not what [she] wanted to be associated with." She concluded that the communications field is a "dog-eat-dog world," so she decided to leave it and begin to seek other types of employment. However, she had a difficult time finding work in the District of Columbia. To satisfy her financial needs, she began working temporarily as a receptionist for her father at the social club. Although she was not interested in this type of work, she was happy to have a job and to feel productive again. She said, "I really got into a slump after I left the communications field. I missed college, my friends, and my boyfriend."

After 9 months of temporary work, Catherine obtained employment in the audiovisual department of the medical library associated with the university she attended. After receiving a promotion a year later, she began working at the reference desk of the library. Catherine has worked there for 3 years now, and the library gives her tuition benefits in order to attain her master's degree in rehabilitation counseling. She feels that her work in the library is more suited to her than her prior job because in the library she interacts with people all day. She assists medical students, nurses, and doctors to find the material they need at the library and supervises two undergraduate students who work for her. Catherine finds that this arrangement of working in the day and taking classes in the evening to get her master's degree is very satisfying at this time of her life.

Religious History

Catherine expressed that religion is a strong component in a Latin American's life; approximately 98% of the culture is Catholic. She said,

Religion is a foundation that trickles down to everything else. A person is taught to respect and love God and abide by His rules. Everyone wears a cross around his or her neck to symbolize what a large part in one's life religion plays. Catholics in America do not celebrate religious holidays with the same intensity that they do in Ecuador. In Ecuador, my parents have told me, religious holidays are a big event and people have all kinds of parties. Everyone in the community participates and celebrates the day together. I would love to be there for a holy day to experience that.

Including herself and her father, approximately 50% of Catherine's family is Catholic. However, her mother, paternal grandmother, aunt, and uncle are Seventh-Day Adventists. Catherine mentioned, "This part of my family converted about 12 years ago. The practices associated with this religion forbid smoking, dancing, drinking alcohol, and wearing makeup. However, the members are a very friendly and warm religious group, unlike what you find in the Catholic church today." She wished that her family enjoyed dancing as much as she does. Catherine asserted that "when I get married, my uncle will probably leave the room when the music starts because he strictly follows his religion."

A Catholic priest helped Catherine's mother deal with Catherine's decision to go away to college. He explained that this was a good opportunity that Catherine should not pass up. Religion has played an important role in Catherine's life. A year after college, Catherine and her father were in a serious car accident. Their car was demolished, and an intoxicated motorcyclist who hit it died. Catherine confided, "It was a miracle that we were not killed. This accident made me take a good look at my life. I feel that I do not have ultimate control over my life, but that God does. He plans our lives, and my life is up to Him. From that point on, I felt more daring and more assertive about what I wanted out of life, especially since I saw how life can be taken away from you in an instant."

Current Situation

Tomás, an Ecuadoran cousin of Catherine's, came to the United States to spend a week with her. During his visit, she spoke Spanish most of the time and tried to learn as much as possible about Ecuador from him. She said,

> Tomás and I had a great time together and now I really miss him. It is interesting to see America through his eyes. Tomás told me that he thinks my cousin, Pedro, who is the son of my paternal uncle whose wife left him, rejects the Latino culture. He feels this is true because Pedro grew up not speaking Spanish; going to school in Louisville, Kentucky; and then marrying an American. As we spent more time together, I became aware of how my cousin perceived me. I do try to keep the ties to the Latino culture through telling family stories, cooking traditional foods, and following Latino values. However, as Tomás sees it, I am very Americanized and speak Spanish with an American accent.

Catherine said, "I am envious of my cousin Isabel, who grew up in Ecuador and now lives in Virginia. She truly knows who she is and when she says she is a Latin American, she knows what that really means." Catherine sometimes feels uncomfortable in situations where she is with a group of Latin Americans and they are talking about particular stories, songs, or events that are going on right now in Ecuador. She sighed, "I just cannot relate to or participate in these conversations, and it makes me feel like I am missing out on a big part of who I am."

Catherine compared her life with that of her cousin, Tomás. She said,

> I am happy to be living in America where one's rights are protected by law, and people follow the law. But in Ecuador, for people to survive, they sometimes cannot follow the law and must do dishonorable things. In America, people pay their taxes every April; if they don't, they will have to deal with the IRS. However, in Ecuador, most people work their way around taxes by cheating. I know only the basic things about Ecuador; if you were to ask me anything specific, I probably would draw a blank. I just want the opportunity to learn firsthand and to be able to communicate this desire to my mother.

Catherine is very concerned about who she will eventually marry. She said, "My other cousins escaped from living at home with their parents by getting married. The great thing about having a lot of cousins is that you can see the mistakes they made and learn from them. Many of my cousins' marriages have ended in divorce. I know my parents want me to get married, but I think they understand I cannot marry just anyone. That would only cause trouble."

Catherine wants her husband to understand and respect the Latin culture because her culture is important to her. She told the counselor that she "likes Latino men because of their machismo. It is this trait that guides men to treat women with respect and courteousness. A Latino male grows up learning to open doors for women and to treat a female like a lady. They revere their mothers, and this influences how they interact with women." On the other hand, Catherine hopes that her husband will be somewhat Americanized in order to help "do the dishes, cook, and clean. Most importantly, though, I am looking for a man to consider me an equal partner in our relationship by valuing my opinions and decisions."

CASE ANALYSIS

Conceptual Perspective

An accurate diagnosis of Catherine must recognize her culture and its significance in her life. The counselor's first impression of Catherine, which later proved to be false, was that she appeared to be very Americanized and seemed to identify with many of the customs and habits of the majority culture. Catherine dressed, spoke, and even acted like an American. On the surface, it appeared that both the counselor and Catherine subscribed to the same set of values and ideas. However, after closer investigation, it became evident that Latin values, beliefs, and attitudes played a significant role in Catherine's cultural identity.

Catherine was raised in the Latin tradition of honoring and obeying her parents and elders. This value is referred to as *respeto*, or respect, where a child learns while growing up not to question parental authority (Lee, 1997). The respect and honor given to one's parents also may be an aspect of the value of filial piety, which is an integral part of the Latin culture, where one holds the interests and needs of the family unit over those of the individual member. Catherine was aware that her actions directly reflected on her parents' honor, as she explicitly discovered when she defied their wishes and dated a man from Guatemala.

Catherine has a strong desire to spend time in Ecuador to learn about her heritage. However, her mother's "feelings of guilt" and recurring sense of loss from when she left her children in Ecuador prevent

Catherine from making this move. Even though Catherine feels that her family views her as "the one who has broken a few family rules," she would not intentionally disobey her parents' wishes or cause them any dishonor. Therefore, she will not go to Ecuador if she cannot receive her mother's approval.

The role of a woman in the Latin culture can best be described by the concept of *marianismo*. This concept considers the ideal woman as one who is selfless and self-sacrificing. When Catherine told her mother about her frustrations with not having "spent time in Ecuador as a child," like her siblings and cousins, it is possible that her behavior indirectly might have caused her mother to feel a sense of failure and dishonor. By not giving Catherine this cultural experience as a youngster, her mother might feel that Catherine is accusing her of not being a good mother, which is the essential role of a woman in the Latin culture. If such an accusation is interpreted by Catherine's mother as a criticism, this could cause great feelings of guilt. This may be the reason why Catherine's mother would prefer not to talk about the matter.

If Catherine's counselor took an etic perspective—that is, the perspective of the host culture—the counselor might accuse Catherine of not being assertive enough in communicating to her mother her strong desire to visit Ecuador. This perspective may be "culturally inappropriate" and may cause misunderstanding in the therapeutic relationship. To counsel Catherine properly, the counselor must understand and treat with respect the role of filial piety. The emic perspective—that is, the cultural perspective of the client—takes into account the roles that filial piety, *marianismo*, and acculturation play in Catherine's family and enables the counselor to see Catherine's dilemma from her point of view. In diagnosing the problem from an emic perspective, the counselor helped Catherine develop a clearer understanding of her situation with her mother.

Catherine described herself as "bicultural," believing that 60% of her identity is defined by the majority culture. Closely tied to this concept of cultural identity is the process of acculturation. Because Catherine is a first-generation American, she has a higher level of acculturation, or identification, with the attitudes and lifestyles of mainstream America than do her parents, uncles, and aunts. As Lee (1997) mentioned, differences in the level of acculturation between parents and children can exacerbate intergenerational differences. Catherine might have attained a high level of acculturation due to several factors. The first is her achievement of a high school and college education within a predominantly Anglo American setting. A second factor may be Catherine's perception that she was never "discriminated against" because of her background and believes she enjoys the honorary status of "Anglo American."

Catherine wanted to identify the cultural origins of her beliefs, values, and attitudes rather than allow them to exist as an indistinct mosaic. She felt that by becoming more in touch with her Ecuadoran culture, she would be able to accomplish this goal. Catherine does not want to be bicultural but equicultural. She wants both of her identifying cultures to be represented equally in her life. While growing up, she wanted to blend the values of her high school, family, and neighborhood. She did not want to "stick out." However, Catherine now believes that her Latin side has been compromised in the process. From an etic perspective, the counselor might simply dismiss Catherine's "cultural identity crisis" because she appears to be so well adjusted and integrated in the majority culture. Taking an emic view, however, strongly suggests that Catherine is searching for deeper self-understanding through her cultural identity.

Existential Perspective

Viktor Frankl was convinced that what inspires a person most deeply is the search for meaning (Missinne & Wilcox, 1981). Through Catherine's desire to explore her cultural identity, she was ultimately trying to discover the meaning of her life. Frankl felt that human beings are confronted with the challenge of creating meaningful lives for themselves. Catherine's current work experience at the library and her devotion to her master's course work provided meaning in her life. Catherine was also very close to her family, which included her parents, grandmother, uncles, aunt, and cousins; her relationship with them was another source of meaning. Catherine understood the great value and importance of being able to give and receive love from one's family, who often are one's truest friends in the world.

Without a cultural identity, Catherine felt "unanchored in life." As Frankl pointed out, "Motivation can come only from having a purpose and meaning in life" (Crimbaugh, 1975, p. 23). Since her car accident, Catherine has had a more "philosophical outlook" on life. She feels that the ultimate control of her life is "in the hands of God." Therefore, she explained that she might as well live whatever time she has to the fullest. Religion has offered Catherine a type of "unconditional faith," or a secure anchoring in an absolute value system (Crimbaugh, 1975). Catherine is trying to develop an understanding of how her Catholic values provide meaning for her. She might gain greater insight after pursuing a comprehensive investigation of the religious beliefs in Ecuadoran culture.

Closely linked to Catherine's desire to learn more about her cultural identity is her search to understand the qualities she values and needs in a future husband. In this aspect of her life, she is "stuck" in her development because she has not made any decisions about her choice of a mate and might not do so until she establishes a more definitive vision of her own cultural identity. In other words, she cannot select a husband who will "suit" her until she discovers who she is and what she requires in a life's mate.

Catherine has observed during numerous family gatherings the way her cousins and their American spouses interact with each other. She told her counselor that the American spouses always disparage the Latin family members for being "too emotional." She does not like the way her American cousins make fun of Latin Americans. In this respect, Catherine feels that she needs to find a man who can appreciate the Latin culture. Catherine does not want to isolate herself from the Latin culture, and she feels that by marrying an American, this might happen. She remembered what her cousin Tomás told her about their cousin Pedro. She does not want anyone to think that she wants to break her ties with her Latin heritage. However, Catherine is in a real quandary because she feels that she is very "Americanized." She needs to consider this aspect of her identity when defining herself and when she looks for her future husband.

DSM–IV (APA, 1994) Perspective

In conceptualizing the difficulty that Catherine is experiencing with her mother from a *DSM–IV* perspective, her diagnosis might reflect a parent–child relational problem (V61.20) or an identity problem (313.82). However, it must be emphasized that Catherine is very well-adjusted and not mentally ill. Her *DSM–IV* diagnosis is simply a means of description required by the medical model perspective. Having conflicts or misunderstandings with others or searching for one's identity is not a sign of psychopathology but a normal part of life.

Multiaxial Diagnosis

Axis I	Parent–child relational problem (V61.20) Identity problem (313.82)
Axis II	No diagnosis
Axis III	No diagnosis
Axis IV	No diagnosis
Axis V	GAF = 75 (current)

INTERVENTION STRATEGIES

Catherine appears to be very committed to her exploration of her cultural identity. She honors and respects her parents, yet is determined and assertive enough to find a way to address her concerns with them.

If Catherine were to continue in counseling, an existential approach may be very beneficial in focusing on her need to find an identity and meaning in her life that respects the traditions of both the American and Latin cultures.

The therapeutic rapport between Catherine and her counselor was of great value. It appeared that Catherine's prior association with her counselor as a classmate in graduate school put her at ease throughout the counseling sessions. In addition, Catherine was able to trust her counselor quickly because she knew her personally before she engaged in a professional–client relationship with her. Catherine's counselor was not a friend but a person who was known to her previously as being kind and reputable. The construct of personalism, or *personalismo* in Spanish, was evident in the initiation and maintenance of the therapeutic relationship. Given her Latin heritage, Catherine would have been unlikely to solicit the assistance of an absolute stranger—however stellar the credentials or reputation—but would have felt more comfortable with someone who was part of her informal system of acquaintances.

Personalismo requires relationships to be mutual in their personal sharing. Catherine wanted to know about her counselor's family and religious upbringing—which most traditionally trained counselors might refuse to provide—but this seemingly irrelevant information was necessary for her counselor to disclose in order to maintain the therapeutic relationship. Catherine learned that her counselor was getting married in the summer, and she even had the chance to meet the counselor's fiancé. In providing counseling to persons like Catherine, counselors must be willing to open up and share their family values and personal beliefs. If the counselor plays a "blank slate"—the model provided by Freud's Victorian notion of the doctor–patient relationship—this will likely seem too cold and distant for many Latin clients, who expect equal disclosure in personal relationships.

Catherine's prognosis is very positive and was, truthfully, never in doubt. She is highly motivated to learn more about her Ecuadoran cultural background. In the past, she has demonstrated a commitment to self-improvement and to not following sheepishly the wishes of her family when they seemed "misguided" or "irrational." Despite the reservations of her parents, she left home to attend college and traveled to Florida with her boyfriend when she felt that it was in the interest of developing the relationship. She has the strength of character to defy her parents' prohibition against her traveling to Ecuador to explore her cultural identity. Should Catherine abort this plan, she might deny herself the chance to ultimately discover and clarify her cultural identity—and this would ironically be because she is attempting to honor the values of the culture she wishes to understand better.

When Catherine was considering leaving home to attend college, her mother shared her concerns about Catherine's behavior with their priest. Pastoral counseling might be an effective strategy in assisting Catherine and her mother in working through their differences. Assisting Catherine in developing a more open dialogue with her mother might aid her mother's recognition that Catherine respects her and is not challenging her performance as a good mother. With the help of her mother's priest, in the familiar and safe environment of the church, open communication between Catherine and her mother might occur.

It might be beneficial if Catherine's family played an integral part in her counseling experience. The family unit, in the Latin culture, gives an individual emotional support and identity. Accordingly, it seems appropriate to involve Catherine's family in counseling and to encourage them to understand her desire to explore her Ecuadoran heritage.

There are several additional ways Catherine can learn more about her cultural background. Although an ideal way would be for her to visit Ecuador, currently, this is not a feasible option. Because Catherine enjoys reading and has access to the university library, this may be a good place for her to start her quest for knowledge. Recently, Catherine's university began providing Internet access to graduate students. Catherine could use the Internet to access information as well as to participate in discussion groups pertaining to the Latin culture. She also can be connected to a computer network based in Quito, Ecuador. This linkup could potentially provide her with some interesting Latino contacts and computer pen pals.

Because Catherine enjoys interacting with others, she could take an autoplastic, or self-determining, approach by becoming involved in activities and clubs at her graduate school or in her community that involve learning about the Latin culture. This strategy might be an excellent avenue for her to meet other Latin Americans who share similar experiences and needs, as well as Latinos who are living temporarily in the United States. Such interactions with others from a similar background could provide Catherine with the opportunity to learn about current values, traditions, and beliefs that are associated with the Latin culture. From her studies in counseling, Catherine understands the value of interacting with others and applying to herself what she has learned from these experiences.

When Catherine has developed a more integrated picture of her own cultural identity, she might be better able to choose a suitable husband. Catherine may need to confront her fears and anxieties about finding a husband and possibly being rejected by her family. A counselor may need to help Catherine to clarify her values and recognize that her family will not ostracize her if she goes against their wishes. Several of her family members have not married into Latino families, yet they are still considered valuable members of the family. Similarly, as Catherine clarifies her cultural identity, no matter whom she marries, her identity will remain intact and serve as a guiding force in negotiating her life's challenges.

Free and open exchange of experiences and ideas with members of her ethnic group might provide new avenues of communication for Catherine that might lead to greater self-awareness. Identifying her issues in counseling has helped her to understand what she must do to surmount her life's challenges and grow. Catherine has already made a great deal of progress over a short period of time. Catherine's curiosity, intelligence, and desire to explore her Ecuadoran culture will eventually help her to overcome her cultural identity crisis.

DISCUSSION OF THE CASE

Rapport is a key component in any cross-cultural relationship. Because the counselor and Catherine were both members of the same university community, they had an opportunity to interact with each other before establishing a counseling relationship. Catherine observed that problems and concerns within her own family were only discussed among family members and not among strangers. Although the counselor was not a family member, Catherine was able to bridge this gap because of the various commonalities she shared with the counselor. Having some rapport before the counseling interview enabled the therapeutic alliance to be established with greater ease. Although it may seem unconventional to establish prior rapport (or prerapport) with a client, it had merit in this case. The culturally different client may be uncertain about entering into a counseling relationship and may feel more at ease with a counselor whom he or she is at least vaguely acquainted with through the same religious, academic, or social circles.

In addition to prior rapport, her counselor's self-disclosure dramatically facilitated the counseling relationship. Catherine was eager to know more about her counselor and asked her various personal questions. Many counselors are aware of the power of self-disclosure at the appropriate time within a counseling session. In addition, when self-disclosure is used, it usually is succinct and does not detract from what the client is expressing or feeling. However, with a culturally different client, such as Catherine, the counselor had to put aside what was considered an appropriate counselor self-disclosure for an American client and instead view the counseling experience from the client's perspective.

Within the first session, the counselor expressed to Catherine some of her own goals and values; this type of self-disclosure was used throughout the counseling interview when appropriate. It may be difficult to quantify what the right amount of self-disclosure is without establishing a dual relationship in which the counselor intermittently assumes the role of client. However, the existential view of the I–Thou counseling relationship allows self-disclosure to be a more natural and genuine part of the counseling process rather than a technique. In fact, mutual self-disclosures surrounding spirituality were vital to the therapeutic relationship. Catherine identified with the Catholic religion and felt that her fate was in the hands of a higher being and, therefore, wanted to live her life to the fullest. She was open and honest about her religious feelings, as her spirituality gave her life meaning. The counselor, who was also Catholic, could identify with many of the same beliefs and openly shared her own conception of spirituality with the client.

Catherine's family played a large role in her life. Therefore, to help the client appropriately, the counselor had to understand the concept of *respeto*. It was important to consider Catherine's family reactions and feelings when addressing her cultural identity concern. Initially, Catherine did not understand why her mother would not give her permission to go to Ecuador. However, after analyzing this situation from an emic point of view, Catherine was able to understand the motive behind her mother's prohibition, which was couched in her mother's sense that she did not want Catherine to be far away from her as her children who were left behind in Ecuador had been. Nor did Catherine's mother wish to feel responsible for Catherine's difficulty in finding a cultural identity and, thus, feel like a "bad parent." The different degrees of acculturation between Catherine and her mother were evident in this case. Specifically, Catherine, who is more Americanized, wanted to live in Ecuador for a period of time to develop her own identity, whereas Catherine's mother, who was still Ecuadoran in cultural identity, could not appreciate the fact that her daughter was not like her and possessed a different cultural identity.

Catherine wished to assume the perhaps mythical state of equiculturalism. However, in accomplishing this goal, she might find it necessary to begin evaluating and determining the Ecuadoran cultural beliefs she values and wishes to practice. For instance, the idea of *marianismo*, or the ideal woman, was not a value she wished to uphold. She felt that she had an Americanized view of marriage and her gender role. If she wants to develop her Latin American identity, it may be necessary for Catherine to realize that she may need to be satisfied with less than an exclusively Latino identity. There is no psychological principle that requires one to conform completely to a single vision of culture. It may be true that those who can creatively fashion a cultural identity that rejects the incongruent aspects of their culture while internalizing the congruent may be the healthiest of all.

DISCUSSION QUESTIONS

1. The concept of prior rapport is discussed in this case. How do you feel about establishing a prior rapport with a client? What are the advantages and disadvantages of this approach and how would this influence your decision?

2. Catherine wanted to learn more about the Ecuadoran culture and wanted to discuss this with her counselor. If you were this client's counselor and you did not feel knowledgeable about the beliefs, values, and culture of Ecuador, what would you do about this? For instance, would you refer this client to someone more competent in this area, or would you try to learn more about the culture yourself?

3. The client in this case was 26 years old. She sought her parents' approval before making a decision about going to live for a period of time in Ecuador in order to become more equicultural. If you were counseling this client, how would you interpret her seeking parental approval? How would you work with this client regarding this issue in order to achieve an effective outcome? Does *respeto* play a role in this situation?

4. Spirituality and religion were important concepts discussed in this case. The client was Catholic and openly discussed her beliefs. If you were working with a similar client, what role would spirituality play in your sessions? If spirituality is important to the client and you do not share the same beliefs as the client, how would this influence your level of comfort when working with this issue?

5. Why is it important to analyze a case from both the emic and etic perspectives when working with a culturally different client?

6. An autoplastic approach was discussed in this case. In what context was it used and how can you apply it to other counseling situations?

7. What concepts from the existential perspective did you learn from this case and how could you apply them to your own counseling work?

8. On the basis of the information provided in this case study, what diagnosis would you give this client? Is it possible to make a diagnosis of this client without taking into account the concepts of *respeto*, spirituality, *marianismo*, and acculturation? Why or why not?

9. Why was it important to consider this client's parents when generating interventions and recommendations?

10. Would it be appropriate to apply the cross-cultural concepts (*respeto*, spirituality, *marianismo*, and acculturation) that were discussed in this case to another Latina?

CHAPTER TEN

An Accidental Murderer: The Challenge of Finding Meaning in the Death of a Stranger

INTRODUCTION AND PRESENTING CHALLENGE

While other 26-year-olds were enjoying the benefits of youth and good health, Marco was admitted to an inpatient psychiatric unit after making a critical existential decision: He was going to kill himself. Marco had become very depressed after being involved in an automobile accident that resulted in the death of an off-duty sheriff. Before the accident, he apparently had consumed several beers with friends. As a result, he was charged with driving under the influence of alcohol, which is a felony offense in his jurisdiction. Within 24 hr of being admitted to the unit, feeling overwrought with guilt and sadness, Marco made an unsuccessful suicide attempt. He probably would have succumbed had it not been for the quick response of a psychiatric technician who found him hanging from a shower head in the bathroom and quickly untangled his neck from a makeshift rope composed of his hospital garments and the shower curtain.

As the result of the technician's heroics and quick thinking, Marco was resuscitated and placed under 24-hr suicide watch. Once his vital signs were stabilized and a regimen of antianxiety and antidepressant medications was prescribed, an order was written for referral to psychotherapy. Unfortunately, after his mental health counselor conducted an initial assessment of Marco and scheduled one session with him, a warrant was issued for his arrest because of the vehicular homicide, and he subsequently was transferred to a correctional unit located at a nearby psychiatric hospital. Fourteen days later, after being screened and classified by the state department of corrections, weekly sessions were initiated with Marco.

CASE HISTORY

Marco is single; his parents separated when he was 8 years old. His mother, who is unemployed, presently lives in Colombia, where Marco was born. Marco's father is employed as a short-order cook and has lived in Chicago for the past 18 years. The client's siblings consist of an older brother, who lives in Chicago, and his twin brother and a younger sister, who both live in Colombia. Marco confided that his "twin brother suffered from frequent bouts of illnesses and [his] mother slept a lot—always seeming depressed."

Marco received very little financial or emotional support from either parent during his childhood and adult life. Although Marco's mother's siblings were financially well-off, she did not benefit directly from their economic success. In fact, Marco recalls that as a young child he and his siblings were sent to work in the residences of these relatives and labored under conditions that he described as servile. "We were not allowed to eat in the formal dining areas and were never invited there for family gatherings or festive celebrations," he recalled. Marco's childhood was very unhappy, and he remembers that his mother took him to see a psychiatrist on several occasions because of his frequent complaints of headaches. He recalled that the only treatment he received was being placed on medication, but he was unsure of what he was being treated for.

After several weeks in counseling, Marco confided that he had been sexually assaulted by a cousin who was several years older than he. This incestuous relationship began at the age of 7 and continued until the age of 15. No other members of Marco's family were aware of this incident, and the cousin has not had any further contact with Marco in the 11 years since Marco threatened to disclose this information to family members. The counselor decided not to report the matter to the authorities, as is required by law, because the abuse occurred in another country. At the age of 15, Marco's father invited him to come to Chicago to live with him and his older brother. Despite Marco's ambivalence about leaving his mother, twin brother, and younger sister, he felt that the move to the United States would offer him more opportunities, including finishing high school and getting a well-paying job in the thriving U.S. economy.

After moving to the United States to join his older brother and father, Marco discovered that his father had three children out of wedlock and was living in a common-law relationship with a woman in Chicago. After this initial shock, his transition to American life went rather smoothly. His brother helped him with his schoolwork—when the former was not pursuing girls or playing basketball—and Marco was able to improve his speaking facility in English. However, in the classroom, he found it necessary to memorize much of his teachers' lessons because he had difficulty quickly comprehending the material presented to him in English.

Over the next year, Marco claimed that a friction developed between him and his father. It was during this period that Marco discovered that his father had an addiction to alcohol and cocaine and that some of his relatives were street-side dealers and kingpins in the city's drug trade. This discovery made Marco feel very uncomfortable because criminal values were so contrary to his upbringing in South America. He felt that his father was very strict with him and did not express as much love and support as his stepbrothers and stepsisters did. He also felt guilty that his mother had no knowledge that her husband had started another family. Marco's father maintained this shield of secrecy by denying Marco and his brother frequent contact with the family in South America.

Despite Marco's language difficulties, his teachers promoted him because he did not cause any discipline problems. However, Marco felt that he had been denied an education because they did not care whether he had learned anything. Because of his photographic memory, Marco was able to increase his vocabulary in English and devoted a significant amount of time to reading comic books and the biographies of baseball and soccer stars. He was involved in the gymnastics program where he attended high school. Within a short period of time, Marco made several friends on the gymnastics team and became a key member who was selected to compete in a city-wide competition. However, a couple of weeks before the competition, Marco was ambushed in a street brawl in his neighborhood, where he was struck with a baseball bat across his hip and suffered a serious fracture. Consequently, he was unable to enter the gymnastics competition. It was during this period that he decided to join the 82nd Street Homeboys, a violent street gang and drug-trafficking organization, as a means to protect himself. Marco observed, "This was probably a major turning point in my life. I was really very good in gymnastics and was thinking about attending a college where I could get on a team. But I had to think about survival in the streets, and joining a gang was my only guarantee that nobody would mess with me."

Shortly after his release from the hospital for the hip injury, Marco had an argument with his father over the latter's drunkenness and, consequently, decided to run away. With some help from his brother, as he phrased it, "I was able to survive on the streets, but it was difficult. At times, I had to sleep in vacant, dilapidated buildings. I tried to stay in school, but I had to work, and finally I had to drop out to take care of myself." Just as he was beginning to prove himself as an able gymnast, Marco devolved into a homeless street urchin. He was bound to get hurt, but his new stepmother, herself disgusted with the drunkenness and criminal behavior of her common-law husband, searched for Marco and convinced him to rejoin the family with the promise that she had a plan to improve their lives.

Marco gradually established a close relationship with his stepmother as well as his stepsiblings. Because of the untimely death of her 6-year old daughter and her disenchantment with her husband's lifestyle and his relatives' involvement in drug trafficking, Marco's stepmother made the diffcult decision to separate from Marco's father and relocate her family to Central Florida. Realizing that his father was neither dependable nor honorable, and not wanting to have any contact with his drug-trafficking cousins, Marco decided to follow his stepmother to Florida. It was during this time that his stepmother encouraged him to take a trip to South America to learn more about his native culture. Because of her multicultural background (French Canadian, Native American, and Italian), she wanted to expose him to his heritage and arranged to travel with him to meet the spiritual healers and medicine men of his village in Colombia. During the visit, Marco devoted his energies to studying the rituals and healing ceremonies of his people. This indoctrination into spiritualism included participating in sweat lodges both in South America and in the United States.

Until the time of Marco's admission to the psychiatric unit, he had been employed as a driver for a refuse company. Three years ago, the truck he was driving was involved in a serious collision and he suffered extensive physical injuries for which he received a workers' compensation settlement. For a short period, this provided sufficient income for him to meet his financial obligations. He was able to purchase two homes, one for himself and another for his stepmother. He now finds himself in financial difficulty as a result of his limited educational background and lack of vocational skills. In terms of his social constellation, Marco is presently living alone. With the exception of a couple of friends whom he socializes with on occasion, he spends most of his leisure time with his stepmother and stepbrother, who live next door to him, and a good portion by himself.

Marco's suicidal ideation was motivated by his sense of guilt and low self-worth as the result of causing the death of the other driver in the automobile accident. He discussed wanting to take his own life because he was responsible for taking the life of another human being. Marco believes that his present life circumstances dictate that he should be isolated from society for the pain and suffering that he caused the survivors of the victim of the automobile accident and his own family. He sees himself as an outcast who must be banished forever from the company of good people.

CASE ANALYSIS

Conceptual Perspective

Marco became adequately acculturated to American society while continuing to affiliate with various cultural practices from his native South America. At the age of 15, Marco began attending an English-speaking school, despite his limited fluency in English, where he adapted reasonably well to the social and emotional pressures of a culturally different environment. Marco was able to overcome his language handicap by relying on his photographic memory to recall information on tests, even though he had difficulty in providing oral and written responses to questions in class. However, at home, the flexibility and savvy that served him well at school were absent. Instead of adeptly evading his father during his drunken spells, Marco turned these into points of contention that he could not win. He felt compelled to leave home prematurely as a means of distancing himself from his father's irresponsible behavior. But, ironically, it would seem that Marco internalized his father's use of alcohol as an escape from reality, and it was this behavior that contributed to the fatal traffic accident.

Marco had limited exposure to the full spectrum of values that exist in American culture and, sadly, saw the seamier side that is highlighted in the international press and local media. Initially, he relied on his father to help him understand his new culture, but he found himself caught between the values of his native South America and those of a decadent, drug-oriented subculture of American society whose values his father favored. Marco found it difficult to respect his father because of his heavy drinking and use of cocaine. Marco interpreted his father's behavior as a repudiation of the Latin values of family solidarity, ethnic identification, and religious faith that he maintained as the central pillar of his own identity.

Another stressor for Marco was that he had to depend on his unreliable older brother for assistance in dealing with the demands of schooling (interpreting classroom instructions and tests) and negotiating interpersonal communications with English-speaking peers and family members. In addition, Marco's level of stress was exacerbated by his father's efforts to discourage him from maintaining a close relationship with his mother and twin brother in South America. He also had to accept the fact that his father was living in a common-law relationship with another woman and had betrayed his mother.

Marco's deep commitment to maintaining his cultural identity was reflected in his return to his native village in South America to be trained by the elders to become a spiritual healer and adviser. His passionate interest in the traditions of his culture was encouraged by his step-mother, who impressed on him that in the absence of a responsible paternal role model, he had a responsibility to commit his life to up-holding the values of his community and be a source of nurturance and support for others. Interestingly, the stepmother became his source of guidance and support. During the period of his psychiatric hospitaliza-tion, he felt especially helpless and under a great deal of pressure in not being able to provide for his stepmother and younger stepbrother. He also felt the need to compensate in some way for the loss of life that occurred as a result of the automobile accident. He resolved to repay his debt to society by offering his life to help others.

When Marco became depressed and expressed suicidal ideation, he consulted his stepmother before seeking the advice of a mental health professional. Some Hispanics believe that a mental disorder, or *enfermedad mental,* is less severe than being insane or *estar loco* (Dana, 1993). In the first case, the person suffers from a *crisis nerviosa* or *atague de nerviosa*—essentially, a nervous breakdown. In the second case, the client shows a complete loss of control or withdrawal from reality or the company of others (e.g., schizophrenia and major depression), re-quiring hospitalization. In such situations, some Latin Americans who perceive themselves as having an *enfermedad mental* seek help from friends, relatives, and healers rather than from mental health profes-sionals. When a family member brings his or her Latin relative to a clinic, that family member may consider the client *estar loco* in the sense that he or she is seriously disturbed.

An integral part of the counseling process was to encourage Marco to become involved in the spiritual practices of his native culture so as to counter his fatalistic worldview—that his life had to be sacrificed to compensate for the person who was killed. In the treatment of a fatalis-tic client, it would be appropriate to encourage the client to become involved in spiritual or religious activities that emphasize a "redemptive philosophy," if that were his or her inclination, to minimize the nega-tive impact of fatalism. In addition, in the course of counseling Marco, the counselor's sharing of personal information facilitated Marco's own ventilation of the confidential issues that contributed to his overwhelm-ing depression. Exchanging Spanish greetings at the outset of each ses-sion (¡Hola! ¿Qué pasa? ¿Cómo estás?), while seemingly a superficial gesture, served to demonstrate the counselor's sincerity in wishing to relate to Marco.

In the early stages of counseling with Marco, the nature of the counseling process was explored with him to minimize any anxiety regarding self-disclosure. With some multicultural clients, it may be necessary to explain the counseling process carefully, with frequent use of such techniques as paraphrasing and summarization. Some studies indicate that immigrants who were provided with information about the course of psychotherapy, appropriate client and counselor behaviors, and an explanation of typical problems encountered in counseling completed more sessions than a control group and tended to disclose more than those clients who were not given role instruction regarding the counseling process (Lambert & Lambert, 1984).

Marco's stepmother was involved actively in his psychotherapy from the outset. In clients from family-oriented cultures, psychotherapy works best with the involvement of family members, who may have been mobilized to prompt the client's entering therapy and may be required to support his or her continuation. The counselor's ability to self-disclose helped to strengthen the therapeutic alliance that seemed to hinge on the value of personalism—the mutual sharing of personal information between counselor and client—that Marco required to feel comfortable in the therapeutic relationship. Marco's trust in his counselor seemed to increase as the former revealed small, if important, tidbits of his own personal struggles with depression.

Existential Perspective

The counselor with an existential orientation would approach Marco with the view that he has the capacity to expand his possibilities for better living. Until Marco was capable of reframing his current crisis of "killing another human being," suicidal ideation dominated his conscious thoughts and motives. The fatalistic tenets of his religious and folk beliefs prevented him from freeing himself of the "deterministic shackles" that seemed almost to reflect Hammarabi's code of "an eye for an eye." Conveying to Marco that he does not have to pay "with his life" for an accident that he did not intend—but instead can be the architect of his future—was an important way to mediate the effects of his fatalism. His fatalism created a rigid belief system that contributed to his depression and inability to see any other option, except to commit suicide.

The existential counselor would clarify for Marco that he can expect to experience some degree of anxiety, aloneness, guilt, and even despair as a natural consequence of his actions. After all, his drinking indirectly contributed to the death of another human being, for which he must assume some responsibility. Some guilt may build Marco's conscience, but too much guilt can be self-destructive. Marco could learn that in spite of the tragedy that has befallen him, his guilt can be redirected to serve a valuable function, if it spurs him to use his untapped potential and prompts the development of his conscience. Marco might learn to accept that he may at times feel intensely guilt-ridden and alone in his incarceration, but he does not have to condemn himself to a life of self-inflicted isolation to punish and separate himself from the "good people," because all human beings have made mistakes and live daily with the residue of guilt from past actions that cannot be undone.

Marco's recurring suicidal ideation should be viewed as symbolizing his own anguish, which can be phrased to him as questions. Does he feel that his own decency has expired with the man he accidentally killed? Has he resigned himself to living needlessly in dejection instead of affirming life? After probing the dark abyss of Marco's painful emotions, the existential counselor would search for the meaning that could guide Marco out of his darkness. Is there any reason for him to want to continue living? What can he do to find a sense of purpose that will make him feel more significant and alive? These themes could be foci in challenging Marco's sense of hopelessness. The existential counselor's function would not be to tell Marco what his particular meaning in life should be but to point out that he can discover meaning even in suffering. Human suffering can be turned into human achievement by the stand an individual takes in the face of it (Frankl, 1978).

DSM–IV (APA, 1994) Perspective

Marco's conflicting fears of losing the support of others because of his fatal actions cause him to experience periods of sadness and a pervasive disharmony of mood. This core issue is compounded by the preexisting social and familial problems in his life, which do not disappear into the background because a more severe issue has emerged; instead, they need to be noted on Axis IV and addressed therapeutically to ensure a comprehensive treatment.

Multiaxial Diagnosis

Axis I	Major depressive disorder, single episode, severe (296.23)
Axis II	No diagnosis
Axis III	Chest and back injuries
Axis IV	Incarceration; social isolation Economic hardship; family discord
Axis V	GAF = 41 (current)

INTERVENTION STRATEGY

Marco is introverted and passive, so treatment efforts are best directed toward countering his tendency to withdraw psychologically. It would be advisable to ameliorate his state of depression by rapidly beginning supportive psychotherapy and, if necessary, providing medication. However, Marco must be encouraged to seek social support, which in itself is a powerful mood elevator. Therefore, the counselor should ensure continuation of some social activity to prevent Marco from becoming isolated and retreating into morbid rumination and guilt.

Efforts to facilitate Marco's social interest must proceed in a slow, step-by-step manner, so that he is not pushed beyond comfortable limits. Careful and well-reasoned "cognitive reframing" may help Marco to adopt a more precise and focused style of thinking—that is, Marco must learn that negative events can be reinterpreted for their "lesson" for future living. It is also essential that the counselor be alert to the spheres of life in which Marco possesses emotional attachments and encourage him to undertake activities that are consonant with these tendencies, such as spiritual and religious activities or sports, because these implicitly give him reasons, albeit small individually, for living.

The counselor should conceptualize Marco's problems in a manner that is consistent with his belief system and culture (S. Sue & Zane, 1987). It also is recommended that family counseling be considered as the first therapeutic approach with clients, such as Marco, who are from collectivistic cultures and are not highly acculturated to the individualism of American society. Paniague (1994) believed that many Hispanics prefer a family-oriented therapy because it reflects the emphasis they place on the centrality of the family in orienting their life. In addition, many Hispanics expect *personalismo*, or personalism—the mutual exchange of confidential information between counselor and client—in the therapeutic relationship.

DISCUSSION OF THE CASE

Counselors should give central prominence to the therapeutic relationship. The quality of this person-to-person encounter is the stimulus for positive change. Existential counselors believe that the basic attitudes they hold toward the client as well as their own personal characteristics of honesty, integrity, and courage are the most powerful assets they have to offer. The therapeutic relationship is seen as a shared journey. Buber's (1964) conception of the I–Thou relationship implies that clients should be viewed as persons in the process of change, not as fixed entities, and that through empathy, counselors enter the world of the client and experience their reality as if it were their own.

Jourard (1964) urged counselors to invite the client's authenticity through their own authentic and self-disclosing behavior. Counselors should work toward a relationship of I–Thou, one in which their spontaneous self-disclosure fosters growth and authenticity in the client. If counselors keep themselves hidden during the therapeutic session, or if they engage in the same inauthentic behaviors that generated symptoms in the client, the client will remain guarded and persist in his or her inauthentic ways. In other words, existential counselors model healthy behavior through their own behaviors. They never advise, "Do as I say, not as I do," but "Do as I try to do."

The *DSM–IV* must be used cautiously in diagnosing clients from different cultures and socioeconomic groups. Although the *DSM–IV* provides Axis IV to note cultural factors that may contribute to the client's diagnosis, the challenge is to minimize the probability of counselors overdiagnosing culturally different clients. Helms (1992) argued that these clients are likely to be assessed informally as more deviant from the White majority cultural value system, more likely to score as severely disturbed on assessment instruments, and more likely to receive inaccurate diagnoses that are reflective of more severe psychopathology than their majority-group counterparts. The diagnosis of a multicultural client must be made with care or else the mental health system merely adds an unfair label to an already unjust existence.

DISCUSSION QUESTIONS

1. What is the significance of *personalismo* in counseling Latin American clients?

2. How should the counselor address the issue of personalism during the first session in a multicultural counseling situation?

3. What are the implications of different levels of acculturation among family members in terms of counseling an intergenerational immigrant family?

4. Should all Latin American clients be assumed to be collectivisitic?

5. What is the difference between cultural intuition and acculturation?

6. How can fatalism (*fatalismo*) affect the goals of counseling?

7. Family therapy is recommended as the first approach with some Latin American clients. Discuss the efficacy of this approach.

8. How does the existential approach facilitate the multicultural counseling process?

9. What are some limitations of traditional assessment of racial and ethnic minority students?

10. How can Axis IV of the *DSM-IV* be used to identify psychosocial and environmental problems of a cultural nature for multicultural counseling?

CHAPTER ELEVEN

A Tribal Chief Comes to America: The Challenge of Being Bound by the Laws of Two Cultures

INTRODUCTION

When many Americans think of an African, they picture a primitive tribesman with spear in hand, resplendent with a lion-skin loincloth, who lives in a grass hut and communicates with bongo drums. When one meets Eze, a Nigerian of his country's upper class, his modernity and technological sophistication shatter this distorted stereotype. Eze came to the United States with his wife and four children to complete a doctoral degree in engineering. After entering the United States, he began experiencing many imposing cultural problems—interpersonal, financial, legal, educational, and psychological—that affected him and his family, particularly his children.

In his native country of Nigeria, Eze's childhood was structured around strict values and traditions that his own children would never experience in the United States. Eze completed his elementary education in a missionary school that was run by the Assembly of God. He was strongly influenced by the fundamental Christian teachings and biblically based morality of the school. Eze continued his formal education at a strict, British-style boarding school; in his home, he was versed in the centuries-old cultural traditions of his tribal group that clearly demarcated the roles of father, mother, and children.

These early experiences had an enormous impact on Eze's later spousal and parental roles and behaviors. Contrary to the model of the egalitarian American father, he learned that the Nigerian father is a benevolent dictator whose opinions and authority supersede all others'. This would include the American social services agencies, child protective service workers, public school officials, psychiatrists, psychologists, and other helpers who sought to impose their sense of cultural propriety on a Nigerian father and his family.

PRESENTING CHALLENGES

Eze was ordered by the Family Court of this jurisdiction to participate in counseling as part of a judgment against him for physically abusing his daughter, Mo. A charge for sexually abusing his daughter, Ada, was dropped because of insufficient evidence. In the intake session, Eze did not indicate a presenting problem in the usual sense. He simply stated that "I just want the child protective services to leave me and my family alone." Eze indeed loved his daughters, Mo and Ada, but his "strict and unusual" means of managing them was puzzling to American social workers and school officials.

Using the traditional methods of discipline of his culture, Eze had shaved off his daughter Mo's hair to punish her for having premarital sex with a half-cousin. Although to American sensibilities, the punishment appeared abusive or, at least, severe, to a Nigerian father, it was a method of discipline that had been used for centuries to control the libido of adolescent girls. For Eze, the loss of hair, which would serve as a deterrent to the attention of boys, was a less severe consequence than the teenage pregnancy of his daughter. However, the final arbiter of this matter, an American woman jurist, who was an ardent feminist and one-time civil rights activist, adjudged Eze as a child abuser and ordered him to receive psychological counseling to help him to become a better parent.

This case is based on facts that were developed from a series of interviews conducted with Eze and his wife; Mrs. Monroe, the vice principal of his daughters' elementary school; Mrs. Hallmark, Ada's teacher; Mary Kent, a case worker with child protective services; Alana Allegro, a psychiatric social worker at the hospital where Ada was treated; and Mo and Ada. Additional case information was ascertained from an African American counselor, who was assigned to Eze before the trial by child protective services, to help him learn culturally appropriate methods of disciplining his children. This counselor, who was a nationally respected expert in cross-cultural counseling, would serve as Eze's therapist and, later, become his only advocate.

CASE HISTORY

Eze is a Nigerian descendant of the Ibo ethnic group. When the Civil War erupted in Nigeria, he was forced to discontinue his education and leave school for 2 years. But this long absence seemed only to increase his motivation; he consecutively earned a string of degrees, receiving a Nigerian Certificate of Education in mathematics and physics from the University of Thadan in 1977, a bachelor's of engineering in civil engineering from the University of Pittsburgh in 1982, and a master's of science in mineral and energy engineering at West Virginia University in 1987. Eze is now a candidate for a PhD in operations research at the American University. During the 10 years he has been in the United States working on these degrees, he has held various academic assistantships to help him meet his expenses.

The employment history of Eze includes the following positions: vice principal at the public high school in Ekpoma, Nigeria; assistant marketing administrator at the Nigerian National Petroleum Company, Lagos, Nigeria; research assistant at West Virginia University, Morgantown, West Virginia; teaching assistant at West Virginia University; and graduate assistant in the Department of Operations Research, School of Engineering and Applied Science at American University. After completing his PhD, he is planning to return home to his native country of Nigeria with his family. However, he indicates that his family problems distract him from his studies. Reflecting on his life, Eze stated, "I am an individual who is trying very hard to achieve [his] educational goals and who, at the same time, loves [his] family and is trying to stay with [his] family. As a result of the high moral standards my society has implanted in me, I have become a strict father for my children."

As Eze continued to share his self-perceptions concerning his character, he stated, "I am a responsible man who has never been in trouble with the law." In fact, he is a leader, a person who is looked up to. In describing his self-image, he indicated that "I am president of the Ofias, about 3,000 members of my ethnic group living in the Washington, DC, metropolitan area and chief of my tribe back home, which numbers over 3,000 people." In executing his role as chief of his people, he is obliged to uphold their age-old traditions. One of the most prized traditions of his ethnic group is being a strong family man who controls his wife and children. In the experiential world of Eze, the control of his family is a major stressor for him. Laboriously managing two jobs and attending graduate school has been very challenging for him while carrying out the roles demanded by tradition.

Eze married his wife Orie when she was approximately 17 or 18. Before his union with Orie, he had two children from a previous relationship. Following and adhering to tribal customs, Orie became the mother of Eze's children, Ada and Mo, on their marriage. According to tribal customs, Eze is expected to discipline his wife as he does his children. He and the elders from his extended family are responsible for his wife's socialization into the group. Unlike Eze, Orie has very little formal education, less than a high school diploma.

When asked to be specific about what was creating stress in his life, Eze responded, "The only stress I have is the department of social services. . . . Somebody used to be around every week for this or that." Explaining how he was holding up under the stress, he said, "I am getting used to it, and I study mostly to relieve myself of stress, but I can only distract myself so much." Eze's financial situation is an added source of discomfort, which is hard for him to forget. With an annual income of merely $12,000, he commented that "the food stamps are a saving grace. The fact that the children are getting one meal a day at school is a tremendous assistance, too." Even with these forms of assistance, he is still struggling, because he has to pay $875 a month for rent. After bemoaning the condition of his car, Eze disclosed that "I don't know what I'll do if my old car breaks down, because I would then be unable to take my wife to work or get to school or work."

Aside from the mundane concerns of life, Eze worries mostly about the Americanization of his children and the interference of outsiders with his family. He was adamant about "searching for a way to put [his] children in a good boarding school to shelter them from the negative influences of American society." He was convinced that nobody cares about his children as much as he does. His caring is verified by the vice principal and a teacher at his children's school, who both acknowledged that Eze has always shown great concern for his children. However, Eze does not deny that he can be a strict father. He said, "I give guidelines. In other words, I do not let my children go out when I am not home. And I am insistent on certain things that in this society other parents can just overlook. For example, Mo wants to visit her boyfriend, whom I have never met. I will not let her do that."

Eze indicated that his teenage children may not understand or like the discipline that he is trying to provide for them, but he is sure they will understand when they are older. Eze really wants to send all of his children to a boarding school because of his inability to devote the time he desires to his family's upbringing. "My wife works and I work. As a parent, I have a moral obligation to direct my children to go where they ought to go. . . . Nobody else can or should do that for me," he explained.

Eze has received nothing but high praise from his undergraduate professors at the University of Pittsburgh. One of his professors said that he consistently performed well in both his "academic pursuits and personal life." He was rated in the top 10% in intelligence, originality and creativity, motivation and perseverance toward goals, maturity, ability to work independently, administrative and managerial potential, and overall potential for graduate work. His mathematics professor rated him in the top 10% in motivation and perseverance toward goals and maturity and in the top 20% or superior on intelligence, originality and creativity, ability to work independently, and overall potential for graduate study. Another professor rated him in the same manner. His mathematics professor added that "Eze is very personable and works well in a group."

Eze's Daughter Ada

Ada was a rambunctious girl of 11 who was the terror of her generally peaceful suburban elementary school. Being a very concerned and loving father, Eze followed the advice of the elementary school and consulted a child psychiatrist regarding Ada's behavior. However, the psychiatrist rendered a shocking diagnosis that left Eze "mind-boggled." Although the psychiatrist ruled out the possibility of neurological problems with Ada, he diagnosed her as having an "unspecified psychotic disorder," with dissociative episodes that are characteristic of either post-traumatic stress disorder or dissociative identity disorder (formerly multiple personality disorder). Ada was also reported deficient in speech and cognitive function and as showing inappropriate emotional responses for her age level. Her psychiatric evaluation form indicated "inappropriate laughter and hearing voices of women . . . out of control behavior . . . possibly stemming from traumatic physical or sexual abuse."

When the psychiatrist met with Ada's father, he described Ada as being currently "in touch with reality" but functioning at a below-average level of intelligence (65 on the Wechsler Intelligence Scale for Children—Revised [WISC–R] IQ Scale). In discussing her IQ with her father, the psychiatrist tried to soften the implication that Ada may be mentally retarded by interjecting that "the low score may be partly due to English being her second language." He emphasized that "the chances of Ada's having true clinical multiple personality disorder are very slim . . . but she has had some dissociative episodes." He indicated that the neuroleptic medication that he prescribed for Ada controls symptoms such as aggressive behavior and some psychotic behaviors, such as hearing voices, so Eze would not witness these symptoms unless Ada went off the medication.

Eze found the psychiatrist's diagnosis of his daughter ludicrious at best but also disturbing. He did not believe that Ada had episodic changes in personality. In expressing his disagreement with the psychiatrist's diagnosis, he angrily implored, "If my daughter has a double personality, then her teachers and friends would witness it at school. And we would also witness that, but this has not happened. It happened when she went to the hospital for an inpatient evaluation. For 1 week, she was not allowed to see any of her family members. She was taken there against her free will."

The psychiatrist indicated, "In the testing situation, Ada's IQ is variable, suggesting that an emotional problem impedes the accurate appraisal of her intelligence." This was an opinion that Ada's teacher, Mrs. Hallmark, echoed. Mrs. Hallmark said that "with Ada, anything is possible." Once Ada hid in the art closet and refused to come out. Her mother came to school to try to get her out, but she still refused to move. Mrs. Hallmark observed that Ada is moody, engages in child talk with her "finger in her mouth," and can be belligerent. Mrs. Hallmark pointed out that "Ada is usually thrown off when there is any change in routine." A note in the school service record reads, "The school is very concerned about sexual abuse between Ada and her father," but it did not specify why such an allegation was made or what evidence there was to support it, except the wild speculation of school officials that Ada's wiggling of her buttocks and hips to get attention was a possible indication of sexual molestation.

The school's allegation of sexual abuse was devastating for Eze. He pointed out that pedophilia is an abomination in his culture. He perceived the speculation to be an attempt to besmear his reputation, although he is not denying that his daughter acts out in school and can be difficult to manage. "She does not have any friends in her community, and there is no indication that she has any at school," Eze observed. "She is not crazy but angry that no one will be her friend." If Ada has no friends, the school officials think that Eze is to blame because he does not allow his children to go out unless he goes out with them. "I don't let them go out on their own, especially in this country. Back home, Ada had a chance to play with her relatives in the family compound, but here she is denied significant peer contacts in the neighborhood or at school because I am afraid of all the negative influences. . . . She might just get into trouble."

Eze queried the hospital's psychiatrist about why Ada could function adequately in a regular classroom for many years if she were truly mentally retarded and why such a diagnosis was never rendered before. The psychiatrist indicated to him that Ada has "serious emotional problems," but he acknowledged that she may be very intelligent and may have been "playing dumb" to fool her teachers and the hospital staff. If this were the case, Eze expressed grave concerns that his daughter was nevertheless classified as mentally retarded in the hospital records.

Eze felt that he was being "hassled by the system" in a conspiratorial fashion. In expressing his concerns, he said, "I have filed a complaint to the administrator of the hospital because I see a lot of inconsistencies in Ada's assessment." Without a definitive appraisal of his daughter's condition, Eze stated that the psychiatrist nevertheless made the radical proposal that Ada should be placed in a "group home" for about a year. Eze pondered with great anger, "Why? Is it because she has terrible parents?" In the doctor's conversation with Eze, he said that "even the best families cannot provide what a group home can." He pointed out that the group home can provide "routine and structure" for Ada. He also indicated that "her real need is to be involved with other people to provide her with what she hasn't experienced . . . in the type of family setting that now exists." In plain English, the psychiatrist was diplomatically calling Ada's living situation "dysfunctional." He further explained that "she's going to need some intensive psychotherapy . . . 3 or 4 times a week. Then she will need to be reevaluated."

The Psychotherapy of Eze

In providing an evaluation of Eze for the court, his counselor collected data on his daughter Ada from her elementary school. Ada's vice principal, Mrs. Monroe, and her teacher, Mrs. Hallmark, were both interviewed. They both reported what led up to Mrs. Monroe's call to the police on the day Ada "was emotionally out of control." The vice principal said she called "the dad immediately after I called 911. . . . I explained to him that I had called 911. I asked Ada if she wanted to talk with her father. She refused."

Recalling his experience with the school officials after the incident, Eze stated that they did not tell him what his daughter had done. He was also unsuccessful in obtaining any information from the police officers who answered the 911 call. In his conversation with one officer, Eze asked him if he would come to his home to explain his daughter's behavior. "The officer flatly said no, and he stated in an authoritarian voice that he was taking Ada to Rosewood—a state psychiatric facility." Eze believed that the officer had thought he was "some Black, ghetto father" rather than a tribal chief and doctoral candidate.

Recognizing that cultural differences may be a factor in Ada's behavior, Mrs. Monroe said that "Ada worked with a Black teacher as a helper, because I felt that the teacher would present an excellent role model for her." At the same time, the vice principal declared that "we run a pretty tight ship here . . . and just don't allow kids to run amok." It would seem that the school wasn't as much trying to understand Ada as to control her. In fact, Mrs. Monroe was very reluctant to respond when asked whether Ada's classmates befriended her or whether they teased her and treated her as an outcast in her predominantly White school. She also was asked whether Eze's son had any friends at school, and she was unable to say.

Eze does not feel fairly treated by his daughter's school officials. He believed that some White parents were concerned about his daughter's being at school there. "I think that the school had my daughter hospitalized to appease the parents of the other children." On his returning of Ada to school, Eze appeared very hurt after hearing that her peers teased and chased her through the schoolyard, calling her a "cuckoo bird," because she had been in a mental institution.

Evaluators of Ada

Mrs. Hallmark indicated that "Ada's behaviors are frequently immature or belligerent. Ada will suck her thumb and will continue to do so when other students question her about it." She further observed that "in the classroom, Ada's peers appear to tolerate her behavior." With an air of secrecy, Mrs. Hallmark disclosed that she "was instructed not to confront Ada about her behavior, and that [she] and the school administrators have developed a contingency plan in the event of an aggressive outburst." Mrs Hallmark believed that "Ada's social and emotional problems are having a negative effect on the learning processes of herself and the class."

Ms. Cox, a school social worker, administered to Ada the Vineland Social Maturity Scale (Doll, 1953). She scored an adaptive behavior composite standard score of 65, which "is considered in the low range with mild deficits." Ms. Cox also called attention to the child's move from West Virginia to Washington, DC, and finally to Montgomery Park in suburban Maryland, where she enrolled in elementary school. The school psychologist, Ms. Mallet, administered to Ada several tests, including the WISC–R. She reported a Full Scale IQ of 69 for the child, which matched the appraisal of the hospital. However, she did not qualify the score's validity with the disclaimer that Ada uses English as a second language.

Eze's Reaction

Ada had emotional and cognitive difficulties, but this did not justify the mistreatment of her father. Eze's experience in the United States was very different from his treatment in the communal and social worlds of Nigeria. His sense of control over his family was diminishing as outside agencies interfered with his customary and traditional ways of living.

Eze was witnessing his life, in particular his reigning control over his daughter's existence, being taken over by governmental agencies and nonfamily members who thought they knew better and brandished what he considered to be an unnecessary arrogance.

The disheartening results of the psychological testing and the recommendation to hospitalize Ada adversely affected Eze. Additionally, the remedial educational experiences sought for his daughter Ada did not materialize. In fact, he received very little information and cooperation from educational officials and her teachers, who secretly believed that he played some role in her disturbance as a sexual or physical molester—which often is the last explanation for childhood misbehavior of the Freudian-influenced American psychological establishment when none other can be offered. The behaviors of his daughter's teachers and vice principal were devoid of any benevolence and were, in fact, condemnatory. The experiential world of Eze was becoming inundated with anxiety, as he was being made the "evil bogeyman" who had tarnished his own daughter's life.

Eze's Wife

Orie is several years younger than Eze. As is the custom in his ethnic group, girls are usually very young when they marry. However, they do not move in with their husband until they reach puberty. It is the expectation that the husband will discipline his wife as he does his children. Eze married Orie when she was approximately 17 or 18. At age 28, she is the mother of four children. As custom prevails, she is also the mother of her husband's children from previous marriages or relationships. That is, Orie is considered to be the mother of his daughters, Ada and Mo. When children are brought into their father's extended family, their biological mother is no longer a consideration in their lives. Few exceptions are made to this practice, which seems highly insensitive and unnatural by American standards.

Orie has a severe stuttering challenge: It is difficult for her to express her thoughts easily. It was suggested to Eze that she could obtain speech therapy for her condition. He was very receptive to the suggestion and wanted to know more about that possibility. Despite her disability, Orie is a hard-working woman who aspires to obtain a high school diploma. Eze is encouraging her to take high school classes and earn a degree in practical nursing. The future plans of his wife are exciting to him. In fact, Eze proudly announced that "Orie will be a nurse when we return home. Nurses are badly needed in Nigeria and therefore have high status in the community." Mrs. Okon shared the same level of pride as she talked enthusiastically about her working on a practical nursing degree, which she hopes to earn over the next year.

Eze's Daughter Mo

When Eze was asked about Mo's biological mother, he reported that, although she did not finish high school, she came from a good family. Mo, who is now 15, came to the United States when she was 10 years old. At the time, Mo was given the WISC–R. The psychologist who administered the test indicated that her Verbal score was unavailable because of language difficulty, her Performance score was 86 (low average), and her Full Scale IQ was probably around 90. Three years later, Mrs. Dorfman, principal of Mo's middle school, wrote Eze to inform him that Mo had earned a place on the honor roll for the past quarter with a quality point average of 3.29. Eze indicated that both of his daughters were very good in math. In a bewildered manner, he said that he did not know whether it is "a genetic factor or some kind of environmental factor."

In discussing Mo's behavior, Eze pointed out that she wants to "have her own way. She would like to be the boss." In reviewing her behavior of a month earlier, he said that she was belligerent toward his wife. He declared that the belligerence increased when she established a relationship with the social workers in the department of social services, who he thought had turned Mo against her family with all their "feminist talk." Mo would call her mother and talk "nasty to her" after the "20-something social workers" encouraged Mo to "express her feelings" and "not allow herself to be coerced into assuming the traditional role of a Nigerian woman."

When Eze was asked about his daughter's personality, he described her as being assertive and as a person who likes to assume leadership roles among her peers. As he continued to share his perceptions regarding Mo, Eze stated that she is rebellious against the system. This includes social workers who come to his home to talk to her. "Once an older White social worker came to the house to talk, and Mo was very rude to her," he remembered.

Eze indicated that when Mo was a student in the Montgomery Park school system, "I smacked her, and she went to school and reported the incident, and that's when it all started." Mo had grown into a wild young woman. In fact, Eze reported that his son had seen Mo having sexual intercourse on a sofa. Mo also had confided in Ada that she had a sexual experience but told her not to tell anyone. Eze said that he discovered that it was his young half-cousin who was having sex with his daughter. He called his "nephew," who confirmed it, saying that the half-cousin had "done it only once."

In sharing his customs about sexuality and marriage within his ethnic group, Eze stated that if a young girl becomes sexually active before marriage, tradition requires that the parent shave off her hair as a disciplinary measure. He had consulted with his mother, who advised him to carry out the requirement. At first, he was reluctant to do it, but after reading a book on the subject, *Tribes of the Niger Delta: Their Religions and Customs* (Talbot, 1967), he decided to follow his mother's advice. In reviewing the book, the custom of shaving off an adolescent woman's hair after having premarital sex was recommended as an effective deterrent to further sexual misconduct: "It is the greatest disgrace for a woman to have her hair shaved off; save only in mourning" (Talbot, 1967, p. 214).

Eze expressed regret that the social workers interfered with his form of discipline. He said, "My discipline creates an understanding that there are consequences for actions. Mo thinks she can do whatever she wants because the social workers will protect her from my discipline." Recalling the statements of the social workers, he said that "they had gone so far as to say that Mo is at risk of physical abuse and that they are taking her away." Eze angrily implored, "Mo was at risk of becoming a teenage mother, but the social workers didn't seem to care about that."

Eze pledged that "if I can regain control of my family, I will put Mo in a boarding school either in this country or back home." If Eze's mother comes to the United States, he thinks that it might be a good idea for Mo to go back home with her. Back home, his daughter would not be belligerent toward his mother. His daughter would not run away from home in Nigeria, as has happened five times here. The community would not support the kind of individualism that "running away" from the family implies.

Eze's Son Umani

In sharing his feelings concerning his son, Eze expressed enormous pride. Sadly, Eze's son has only one friend in the neighborhood, who is a White neighbor about his age. As proud as Eze is of his son, he alleged that "he was slapped with a yardstick by a teacher." Mrs. Monroe, the vice principal at Seabrook Elementary School, indicated that "we have had consultation with the dad." She said that "on the test administered to Umani, the boy shows that he has the ability to do grade-level work. And the boy's father agreed to read to his son." When asked about the boy's behavior at school, she said that "he acts out, sometimes to the extent that he hurts others. He did hit the teacher at one time, and the teacher reacted to protect herself, although I would not have recommended that she grab a yardstick to deflect the child's blows during a tantrum."

Eze's Mother

Eze's mother is a very important figure in his life. His father is deceased. In Nigeria, elders are repositories of wisdom. During the period that Eze was becoming troubled over his daughter Mo's sexual behavior, he called his mother frequently. She advised him to take decisive action by nipping the problem in the bud. He respects his mother's view of his daughter because they have shared much time together. Subsequently, Mo feels very close to her grandmother. His mother also had admonished him for raising his children in a manner that did not inculcate the cultural values and traditions of their ethnic group.

Until Eze was convinced that Mo was sexually active, he resisted his mother's advice. In becoming receptive to his mother's wisdom and advice, Eze eagerly anticipates and talks of her coming to the United States to help him rear his children. However, she is very reluctant to travel here because she does not speak English. When speaking of his mother, Eze smiles broadly and talks about sending all of his children back to Nigeria with her if she comes to the United States. He perceives that his mother is the only person who can help him "look after [his] family."

Eze's Neighborhood

Eze was attracted to his residential neighborhood because it reminded him of the enclave where he used to live back home. He reminisced that "there, everybody in the compound knows everybody else. Children are running and playing together. The elders keep a watchful eye over them and help to discipline them. Young wives prepare meals under the supervision of older and wiser women. All of the adults in the neighborhood help to socialize children." Where he and his family now live, his neighbors barely speak to them. With the single exception of his son, who has a playmate, his other children have none. His residential manager has told him that she wishes he and his family would move out. With all the comings and goings of the police and social workers, Eze's neighbors are complaining about their presence. The hostile stares of his neighbors are very discomforting for a man who is accustomed to being admired and respected as a tribal chief.

Social Services and Eze's Family

Although the department of social services' case report was extensive in its workers' naturalistic observations of Eze's family, it would be easiest to survey their goals and objectives for Eze's family, which are very revealing of the social workers' low opinion of the family's level of functioning:

1. To have Eze obtain a mental health evaluation;
2. To have Eze follow recommended treatment;
3. To have the family involved in family counseling;

4. To have the family involved in parenting skills training;
5. To have Eze enroll in a men's violence program;
6. To have Mo and Ada undergo therapy for sexual abuse;
7. To have both Ada and Umani tested for educational special needs;
8. To attempt to contact the children's natural mother in Nigeria, possibly with the assistance of the Nigerian embassy, in order to ensure her involvement, if desired, in this case;
9. To follow up with the West Virginia Social Services to determine whether other child abuse allegations had been filed; and
10. To assist the family with other resources for which they may be eligible, such as family assistance.

It is not clear to what extent the social workers consulted with Eze in forming these objectives. According to Eze, "They asked me my name and what I do. They've asked me nothing else about myself." They did not talk to him about his Christian values or about the traditions of his ethnic group. In providing information about his experience with social services, Eze stated, "I think they are not interested in the positive aspects of my life." He feels that they are only "committed to breaking up the family . . . to taking my children away from me."

In a frustrated tone, Eze said that he had always thought of the social services system as a "last salvation or safety net," but he does not see people in the system playing that role. He alleged, "They give you an order, and if you refuse, then they say, 'All right, we are going to take you to court.'" Whenever attempting to discipline his children, he is told by the social workers that he has to work out a compromise with them. Ironically, Eze indicated that he had filed his own abuse complaint against Mary Kent, one of the social workers who had accused him of abuse, for forcing his daughter into a room and twisting her foot to make her sit still. The following day, he said that he spoke with Mrs. Holland, the social work supervisor, about the incident but was "brushed off with a lot of bureaucratic talk. . . . It was really a lot of bullshit."

Eze sees himself being treated unfairly in others ways. He indicated that he wanted the rest of his children to see Ada in the psychiatric facility where she was being housed, but was refused. The primary nurse tried to delay their visit by requiring him to sign some type of release form and having them wait for almost 2 hr. After he signed the form, the attending psychiatrist denied his request because the unit social worker, who had to brief the staff on the "sexual abuse concerns," was on vacation

Eze believes that the department of social services' concern with getting in touch with Mo and Ada's biological mother is unreasonable. In his country, all children belong to the father and his family. There is only one mother—the woman to whom the father is married. The concept of stepmother does not exist in his ethnic group. He is concerned that the social workers' talk to the girls about Orie being their stepmother undermines her relationship with them. He reported that Ms. Kent, one of the social workers, said she wanted to get in touch with the girls' biological mother "to find out if [Eze was] actually their father." Eze considers her behavior insulting because he had to present evidence of family relationships when he applied for a visa at the American embassy in Nigeria.

Eze is particularly disturbed by the social workers' sending a big package of documents "back home to the children's natural mother, saying that the children are under an order of emergency protective custody." In his culture, natural mothers understand that they are not to interfere or meddle with the father's upbringing of his children. In the social work file, a case note was recorded that "Ada and Mo's natural mother has an interest in her children and would want to know what is happening to them." According to Eze, Ms. Kent imparted to him that it is the county's law that she "has to get in touch with the other parent." Eze continued to express concern over this matter. He said, "You don't keep telling the child that she's a stepchild." He is concerned that "all this stepmother talk" is harming all his children and splitting his family apart.

CASE ANALYSIS

A Conceptual Perspective

Eze now finds himself in a grossly unfamiliar world. He has brought his family from his native Nigeria to the United States, where he is facing many cultural differences in family customs and traditions, parenting practices, neighbor and community relations, and his children's education—not to mention the absence of extended family members, the loss of control over his family through the imposition of outsiders, and climatic and environmental differences. In his present situation, those who are representing the social agencies, helping professions, and public education—the purported "good guys"—are presenting arduous challenges to his balance and sanity. Eze's life is being overwhelmed by "culture shock."

In developing an objective understanding of Eze's life, it is most appropriate to explore his native culture. As a Nigerian man, father, and husband, Eze is simply a progeny of his culture, whose customs consciously and unconsciously pervade his existence. Tradition has it, within the tribal group of Eze, that a husband is assumed to be the head of the household (Nwadiora, 1996). Executing his paternal responsibilities is a customary and expected way of life for him. However, this way of behaving in his new environment, the United States, is confronted with intense opposition. The actions of the social workers, school officials, and mental health experts and the hospitalization of his daughter, Ada, are creating ongoing distress for him in usurping his paternal prerogative.

Acculturating his family to American society was not Eze's intent. He came to the United States to acquire an education, at which point he will return to Nigeria. He chose to create a culturally encapsulated environment for his family, and in so doing, he rejects the attitudes and values of the host culture regarding parental behaviors. Instead of earning respect for efforts to preserve his traditions, he finds outsiders questioning, interfering, and imposing their values and attitudes on him. Their intrusion symbolizes the imposition by force of an alien culture. As the patriarch of his family, he is expected to maintain complete control over it. Yet his paternal responsibilities and controls were seemingly being undermined by outsiders.

As the case information shows, Eze sought and desired for his family a residential environment in the United States that resembled that of his native country of Nigeria. He looked for a residential neighborhood that reinforced the familiar interpersonal world of his ethnic group. Instead, he found himself and his family surrounded by cold and unloving persons. He did not experience the cooperative and cohesive bonds among the adults or elders in his new American community that existed in Nigeria. With the exception of his son having one playmate in the neighborhood, his daughters did not have any playmates or friends. Experiencing the unwelcoming stares of neighbors, and the negative pronouncements of his residential manager urging them to move, provoked great shame in Eze's life. Nwadiora (1996) confirmed that "a major source of stress for Nigerian families in the United States is acculturative stress that results from attempting to live in two worlds" (p. 137).

Should Eze and his family change their traditional ways to assimilate into their new environment? Or should those in their new world change or open up to accommodate them? Conceptually, this might represent the old struggle between autoplasty and alloplasty, the changing of Eze versus the changing of persons in his community. From the actions and behaviors of others, Eze perceived that his position as the leader of his family was being disrespected. The social workers, school officials, psychiatrist, residential manager, and neighbors made no attempt to establish any meaningful channel of communication with him nor respected his judgment. In his ethnic group and culture, this form of behavior would be alien and abhorrent. These perceived culture clashes created an ongoing state of anxiety for Eze. In his American community, he became a nonentity.

The cultural world to which Eze is accustomed consists of cooperative groups, immediate and extended family, social and interpersonal collaborations, and meaningful affiliations. In his Nigerian culture, there exists an ardent sense of community within his tribal group. His ethnic group's cultural norms and mores generate a sense of belonging for its people. However, as evidenced by the case information, his American community vastly contrasts to that of his native home of Nigeria. Conceptually, his ethnic group's community is represented by collectivistic behaviors, deeds, activities, and the like, whereas his American community is characterized by a cold individualism. He is futilely attempting to live as a collectivist in a very individualistic world.

To develop an understanding of Eze's world, the etiology of his behavior must be examined fully. As demonstrated by the case information, Eze is a disciplinarian—a strong family man who needs to control his wife and children. The traditions of his Nigerian heritage undergirded his development into manhood. He is simply fulfilling the cultural role expectations of his ethnic group. The cross-cultural counselor must be able to diagnose clients by recognizing the demands and expectations that are placed on them by their culture. Concurrently, he or she must become cognizant of the demands and expectations that are placed on clients living in a culturally different environment—in essence, becoming a cultural interpreter and mediator. Indeed, Eze legally cannot use head shaving as a punishment, but, by the same token, the professionals working with Eze's family must understand that, from a Nigerian perspective, head shaving is not a form of abuse.

Existential Perspective

Eze is overwhelmed with existential anxiety (May, 1961, 1977; Vontress, 1986a). Acting in accord with his native culture, he continues to face tremendous opposition from his new American environment. As he attempts to carry out his roles as a father, husband, and leader of his family, he struggles to quell the anxiety that is arising from the thwarting of his personal freedom. His ability to oversee the undertakings of his family and guide it accordingly is linked directly to the edicts of others. Without a sense of freedom to guide his family, he loses the meaning he derives from being a father and is growing anxious in the face of an uncontrollable situation.

Belonging. Eze's control over his interpersonal world and sense of belonging appeared to be challenged intensely by the actions and behaviors of the social workers, his daughter's school officials, his residential manager, and his neighbors. Culturally, the interpersonal world that he remembers of his home in Nigeria is one of benevolence, warmth, and closeness of family and neighbors. He experienced an immeasurable level of belonging within his ethnic group. In contrast, his inter-personal experiences in his American community were anything but warm and receptive. Unlike his home community in Nigeria, he did not experience an integration into his American community with the snug-ness of a glove but rather experienced a separateness, or isolation, that was an undeniable source of anxiety.

Nwadiora (1996) found that Nigerian families residing in close prox-imity to other Nigerians or Africans possess a greater "sense of belong-ing" because of their shared commonalities in values as opposed to those who are "isolated." Of course, this is not to suggest that Eze should self-segregate himself from White Americans and situate himself in a community of native Africans—which would not be possible in any case—but that he may consider moving to an international residence that is affiliated with a university or international organization, where he may have more in common with his neighbors, who may feel as alienated in American society as he does.

Responsibility. Eze perceived himself as being a very responsible man who never experienced any difficulty with law enforcement. He is presi-dent of approximately 3,000 people of his ethnic group residing in the Washington, DC, metropolitan area and chief of his ethnic group in Nigeria. In the private, psychological world of Eze, he equated his lead-ership of his people and family with being a responsible and honorable man. Moreover, he saw himself adhering to the age-old traditions of his culture. Not only this, he was working two jobs and attending graduate school simultaneously. As he attempted to uphold his tradition by play-ing the roles demanded by it, he experienced extreme stress and "cul-tural dissonace"—culture clash—as the culture he is in forbids him from abiding by the customs of the culture from which he comes.

Eze was accused by school officials of sexually abusing his daughter, Ada. In his culture, a father's sexual abuse of his daughter is an abomi-nation. Eze believed that the speculation was an attempt to besmear his reputation. The school's allegation represented a devastating blow to his vanity as a leader of his tribal group. In Eze's cultural world, fathers do not sexually abuse their children; rather, they demonstrate love for them by promoting and nurturing their personal well-being. This in-cludes assuming responsibility for one's daughter's mental health.

The psychological testing and classification of his daughter Ada were of grave concern to Eze. Ada's school classified her as mentally re-tarded, as later did a state psychiatric facility. However, the psychiatrist at the state hospital conceded that Ada had "serious emotional prob-lems" but thought that she may have been "malingering"—fooling her teachers to get attention and evade doing school work—rather than suffering from mental retardation. Much like Ada, her sister, Mo, was tested and received an IQ score in the low-average range. But as the case facts indicate, Mo later made the honor roll. Being a very conscientious and caring father, Eze was extremely concerned with the reported mental status of his daughters, in particular, the accuracy of the labels and diagnoses rendered by the psychologist, psychiatrist, and social workers. The testing of Mo and Ada raised some extremely serious questions, as their intelligence and behaviors were measured by culturally insensitive instruments and professionals who seem to have colluded to remove them from their school rather than to remediate their partly language-based difficulties.

The actions and bureaucratic procedures of the social services agency tested Eze's ability to maintain his composure. The agency's communication with Mo and Ada's biological mother was antithetical to Eze's cultural tradition. The facts of the case indicate that in his country "all children belong to the father and his family." Moreover, the concept of stepmother in his culture is alien. His unwanted interpersonal contact with the social services agency surrounding the well-being of his daughters engendered additional stress.

In an attempt to discipline his daughter Mo, Eze "smacked her, and she went to school and reported the incident." He believed that this episode was the beginning of his difficulties with the social services agency. In his culture, corporal punishment is the norm and is, in fact, an expected measure. However, the laws of the United States usually frown on parents who physically discipline their children, although child protective services agencies often do not intervene unless the parents leave visible marks—which, incidentally, was not the case with Eze. Eze's "smacking" of Mo instigated an investigation by child protective services, which was probably prompted by Mo's school, which was at wit's end with her disruptive behaviors and wished to proverbially "call in the cavalry" when all that may have been necessary was a parent–teacher conference, perhaps followed by a family meeting with the school counselor, who might have recommended outpatient psychotherapy for the children.

Eze said that the social workers never consulted with him. "They asked me my name and what I do. They've asked me nothing else about myself," he recalled. The procedures of the social workers excluded him from their casework of his family. In seeing himself as the leader and the ultimately responsible member of his family, Eze felt that his culturally prescribed responsibilities were being taken away. The actions of the social workers adversely affected the parental role that provided him with his meaning in life (Frankl, 1962). In short, the purpose he derived from being a responsible family man was contested by others who were culturally different.

Eze was further embarrassed by the social workers' conferring with Orie and his children but not with him. In his native country of Nigeria, the behaviors of the social workers would be considered as a horrendous slight. Outsiders do not approach individuals in a Nigerian family without first obtaining permission from the head of the family. Of course, the social workers were conducting a sexual abuse investigation of Eze and their indifference to his leadership over his family stemmed from their presumption that he may be a guilty party. Even so, their cultural insensitivity added to the family's distress rather than palliated it.

In summary, Eze's identity is intricately connected to his ethnic culture rather than that of the United States. Any effort by outsiders to usurp his authority as leader of his family presents a threat to his perceived meaning in life. His personal freedom and the sense of purpose he gains from carrying out the cultural roles of man, father, spouse, and chief is being undermined by outsiders and is creating severe confusion and existential anxiety.

DSM-IV (APA, 1994) Perspective

This section attempts to provide a diagnostic perspective of Eze's life by using the *DSM–IV*, including full consideration of the impact of his culture on his psychological state. The proposition that he is a sexual or physical abuser was rejected as a cultural misunderstanding. What follows is a culturally sensitive assessment of his condition:

Multiaxial Diagnosis

Axis I	Adjustment disorder with anxiety (309.24) Client is experiencing ongoing cultural adjustment challenges that are creating anxieties around cultural differences with his residential manager, neighbors, his children's school officials and teachers, social workers, and mental health professionals.
Axis II	No diagnosis
Axis III	No diagnosis
Axis IV	**Economic problems**. The family's income and public assistance are insufficient in meeting the family's basic needs. **Housing problems**. Eze's neighbors are cold and unfriendly, and their residential manager wants them to move. **Problems with primary support group**. Eze has been separated from his extended and immediate family members and communal ethnic group, who provided

social support to him and his family. His separation from his mother and other family and ethnic group members is causing severe psychosocial stress. The lack of support-group relationships represents an interpersonal void in Eze's life.

Occupational problems. Eze's working of two jobs is producing severe stress and lessens his time and ability to manage his family life.

Educational problems. Eze and his wife are students and full-time workers; these two factors are compounding their stress levels in their culturally different American environment. Eze is experiencing severe psychosocial stress concerning the quality of his children's education, their psychological testing and diagnoses, and the behaviors of his daughter Ada's teachers and school officials.

Problems related to the social environment. Eze and his family are living basically in a socially isolated environment among neighbors who are unfriendly, stare in a hostile manner, and complain of their presence in the community, as well as a residential manager who urges them to move.

Other psychosocial problems. Eze is experiencing immense disagreements and conflicts with the social workers and the case procedures employed in working with his family, which excludes his input. Culturally, the behaviors and procedures of the social workers oppose his age-old cultural traditions, as he expects them to respect and honor his position as the head of his family, controller of his wife and children.

Axis V	GAF = 67 (current)

INTERVENTION STRATEGY

Understanding Eze's culture is the key to understanding him. If the counselor ignores Eze's cultural heritage and simply pigeonholes him as "another Black man," this would be a gross therapeutic error. Eze is the product of a unique cultural heritage that bears no resemblance to the culture of African Americans. On the basis of the case information, it appears that a disproportionate amount of Eze's interpersonal stress was caused by the social workers' cultural insensitivity in their investigation of his family, which disregarded his input. Because Eze is the head of his household in the Nigerian tradition, it may be appropriate for his counselor to act as an advocate and "cultural interpreter" in helping the social services agencies to recognize him as the primary contact person in the interviewing of his family. The cross-cultural counselor also can assist Eze in understanding the laws governing the behavior of parents in the United States.

Another intervention strategy would be to assist Eze in reducing his social isolation and stress. Eze and his family are physically and socially isolated from extended family members and their ethnic group. Their isolation is having a very serious impact on their sense of belonging. The counselor could encourage Eze and his family to visit every month Nigerians living in adjacent communities. These visits might assist Eze and his children to socialize with other Nigerians sharing the same values and traditions. As mentioned earlier, the family could consider moving to a multicultural community.

In Eze's attempt to negotiate two different worlds, Nigerian and American, he is confronted with "acculturative stress." The counselor can assist Eze in finding his personal comfort zone in managing his living within two different cultural worlds. Helping Eze to recognize that he may suspend the practice of his traditional customs temporarily and make certain adjustments to American customs might benefit him in reducing his stress. Most important, the counselor can assist Eze in understanding that culture is in part a construction of the individual that must allow itself to be malleable to changing circumstances. Nwadiora (1996) suggested that therapists might assist Nigerian families by encouraging them to eliminate those traditional values that may no longer be of use to them in the American cultural world.

Because Eze is a fundamentalist Christian, the counselor may encourage him to seek the support of other fundamentalist Christians. This intervention strategy might serve two purposes: First, it could provide him the opportunity to connect with others who share many of his cultural and traditional values, and second, his being with other Christians might provide the opportunity to be spiritually renewed and validated by those sharing similar religious values and beliefs. The goal of the counselor would be to assist Eze in developing self-sustaining strategies to reduce his stress and anxiety.

Eze is also experiencing anxiety and stress over the possible Americanization of his children. In an attempt to impede this process, he keeps them at home under lock and key, unless he is going out with them. To lessen his children's isolation, which seems to be at the root of their attention-seeking behaviors, the counselor can recommend that Eze seek the social interaction and presence of other Nigerian families to provide his children the opportunity to be with those sharing many of the same cultural values and traditions. Through Eze and his family's involvement with other Nigerians, they might serve effectively as surrogates for his mother and other family members in the socialization of his children.

DISCUSSION OF THE CASE

Eze experienced severe stress and anxiety as a result of the behaviors of outsiders who "interfered" with his family life. By using IQ tests and other psychometric instruments that have been normed and standardized on American populations, psychologists and psychiatrists rendered some very questionable diagnoses of his daughters. Social workers excluded him from their casework of his family, creating a mammoth cultural insult to him. He experienced much difficulty with his daughter Ada's teachers and school officials and seriously questioned the quality of his children's education. By present accounts, the Okon daughters suffer no discernible mental illnesses but rather appear to be imaginative teenagers who like to "act crazy" when it gets them attention.

Throughout the case, it appears that Eze experienced attacks on his manhood and sense of responsibility as a father and chief of his ethnic group. In his interpersonal world, he continuously faced the total disregard of his cultural identity. His new environment was devoid of a collectivity of adults who could help socialize the children with the values he cherished. Existentially, he was living in an alien and unfamiliar world that created anxiety and uncertainty. His main challenge was to adjust to this world without losing the cultural identity that gives his life meaning.

Many professionals and counseling students who read this case may strongly disagree with its recommendations. To American sensibilities, Eze is an antiquated sexist who is trying to impose on his wife and daughters a sexually repressive belief system that may impede their development as women and human beings. Whereas from an American perspective, Eze can be cast as a Neanderthal, we as Americans must pause to consider how much our own cultural ethnocentricity colors our reaction to this case. Is it wrong for culturally different persons to hold values that we long ago discarded, or must everyone share our progressive thinking?

DISCUSSION QUESTIONS

1. What approach would you use in developing an understanding of Eze's world? In developing your approach, consider how his cultural traditions are affecting his life in the United States.

2. As a cross-cultural counselor, what intervention strategies would you use in assisting Eze in negotiating his new American cultural environment?

3. In an attempt to prevent the Americanization of his children, Eze does not allow them to go out of the house without him. Does his choice to keep them indoors have any impact on their psychosocial development? Discuss the possible outcomes of his keeping his children indoors in conjunction with the implications for counseling.

4. Outline and discuss the counseling strategies you would use in assisting Eze in his working with the social workers, school officials, psychologist, and psychiatrist who have had a significant impact on his family's life.

5. In your review of the case facts, outline and discuss the cultural differences that exist between Eze's Nigerian and American cultural worlds that are creating stress and existential anxiety in his life.

6. According to the case facts, "The school is very concerned about the possible sexual abuse between Ada and her father." Discuss whether the case facts offered enough information to substantiate this assertion and whether the counselor should thoroughly pursue assessing Eze's behavior around the allegation of sexual abuse of his daughter.

7. Discuss what effect the absence of a cultural support group has had on the well-being of Eze and his family.

8. Discuss the cultural implications of Eze's daughters being psychologically tested through the use of standardized American psychometric instruments, especially the use of the WISC–R.

9. Outline and discuss the implications of using the *DSM–IV* in assessing the mental health status of Eze and his family.

10. Outline and discuss the strategies you would use in helping Eze to reduce his stress in maintaining two jobs, socializing his children in a culturally different world, his daughter Ada's institutionalization, his existing on very little income, and living in a very cold and hostile neighborhood. Include in your discussion how Eze's culture might affect your approach as a cross-cultural counselor.

CHAPTER TWELVE

All Uphill From Here: The Challenge of a Life in Chaos

INTRODUCTION

Years of substance abuse had made Nina a gaunt and miserable image of a once-proud African American woman. At 44 years of age, she sought counseling in a moment of desperation. Her estranged husband had struck her across the forehead with a jagged broom handle, leaving a nasty bruise and scar. He was charged with assault and serious battery but was released from prison on a technicality of the law contrived by his "shrewd" defense attorney. Left penniless by her husband's estrangement, Nina was unable to find employment and is currently on probation for past drug charges. She has been incarcerated on at least four occasions for drug peddling, drug possession, and robbery charges.

Previously, Nina was diagnosed with paranoid schizophrenia, depression, and the ominous AIDS virus, HIV. She reported suicidal ideation and a history of several suicide attempts, which involved efforts to take her own life in violent ways. The latest and most serious attempt occurred 6 months ago when Nina deeply slashed both of her wrists with a kitchen meat cleaver and had to undergo several complicated neurosurgical procedures to stitch together the gaping flesh wound, severed tendons, nerves, ligaments, and veins.

Three months ago, Nina began individual therapy in an attempt to surmount her depression and improve the quality of her life by finding a special meaning in it. The therapeutic approach her counselor used was existential therapy. Nina attended a total of 14 weeks of counseling. The initial counseling sessions occurred three times a week because of her unrelenting suicidal ideation. In the last 2 weeks, the sessions were tapered to two per week as she became more committed to living and internalized an ethos of hope. The counselor's sources of information were the client, her mother, her hospital chart, and her criminal record.

The counselor, a young Greek woman who was wiser and more mature than her chronological age would suggest, approached the case holistically. She considered the client's problems, needs, limitations, and strengths with respect to the principles of cross-cultural counseling and the existential worldview. In addition, the counselor used, at her discretion, several techniques derived from other counseling approaches that supported the existential ideas of freedom and responsibility.

Nina's case offers a point of reference for mental health counselors who deal with complicated and seemingly hopeless cases. It also illustrates a successful outcome with an individual who has struggled with a serious mental illness that had led to her utter demoralization. In fact, the central message of this case is that by accepting responsibility for our present life and recognizing our freedom to make better choices, there is hope for spiritual and emotional recovery.

PRESENTING CHALLENGE

Nina was hospitalized 6 months ago following a suicide attempt in which she deeply slashed both of her wrists. She underwent 7 hr of neurosurgical repair of both hands by a special emergency trauma team. She was treated with antidepressant and antipsychotic medications several days after surgery. Because of the seriousness of her suicide attempt, Nina was transferred to a psychiatric hospital under an involuntary order of commitment, where she was treated for 3 months for her psychotic and depressive symptoms. She also received physical therapy for both of her arms. The factors that precipitated Nina's suicide attempt included her recent separation from her husband, her diagnosis of HIV positive, her feelings of isolation and loneliness, her unemployment, her imminent eviction from her apartment as a result of her drug and alcohol abuse, and her knack for getting herself incarcerated at the very moment she was putting her life together.

Over time, Nina began to feel deeper and deeper sadness, depersonalization, isolation, hopelessness, and suicidal ideation. No longer wanting to live, she attempted to commit suicide by slashing her wrists. "I went into the bathroom and with a lot of courage, I slashed my wrists with a meat cleaver," she confided. She reportedly wanted to die. "Blood poured out," she added, "and about 10 minutes later, I got dizzy and felt weak and nauseated, so I laid down on the floor. Ten minutes later, the blood dripped more slowly. I realized I was going to become unconscious and then die, so I called my mother to say 'goodbye' and asked her to forgive me for my wasted life and my moral weakness. Later on, I don't remember when, I woke up in a hospital with doctors and nurses peering at me in amazement that I had opened my eyes."

After her discharge from the psychiatric hospital, Nina moved in with her mother, who is the only person in the family with whom Nina maintains a relationship. While staying with her mother, Nina reported experiencing psychotic and depressive symptoms along with suicidal ideation. Nina's mother referred her to a mental health counselor for psychological treatment. At the time of the referral, the major concern was Nina's risk of another suicide attempt, her threats of violence toward her mother, and the association of these issues with her disorganized mental state, substance abuse, and poor physical health. In Nina's own words, her chief complaint was, "There is no reason for me to live, but I am so stupid I can't even take my own life."

CASE HISTORY

Social History

Nina is a native of the Bronx, New York. She is the second of five children born to a two-parent family. Her father abandoned the family when Nina was 9 years old, and they never heard from him again, although he was rumored to have taken up residence with a "lewd woman" he had met in a nightclub. Nina was raised by her mother and stepfather. There have been allegations against her stepfather for sexual abuse. However, the abuse was never substantiated by a medical examination, nor did a child protective services investigation occur at the time of the alleged abuse.

Reportedly, Nina was a good student in the early years, but she dropped out of school in the ninth grade. Around this time, she became sexually active and started experimenting with drugs and alcohol. She became pregnant at age 15, and the pregnancy was aborted. During this time, she was arrested for illicit drug use and prostitution. After serving a brief sentence in a women's penitentiary, Nina lived on the streets of New York City for approximately 14 years as a homeless drifter, sleeping in subway, bus, and train stations. At times, she lived in homeless shelters or in rented rooms, and she was incarcerated several times for loitering and vagrancy. For the next 14 years, she lived with her boyfriend, a street hustler of stolen goods and a gambler, who is now her husband. After her separation from him and her suicide attempt, she moved in with her mother.

Nina's marriage was riddled with emotional blackmail and physical abuse by her husband, who was arrested for "pummeling" Nina on the head with a soda bottle in a public setting. There were other complaints by the client in her medical record that her husband was physically abusive to her, including charges that he had pushed her out of a moving vehicle and had attempted to push her in front of a subway train but grabbed her at the last minute, as well as other complaints that reflected emotional and physical abuse that bordered on torture.

Substance Abuse History

Nina's substance abuse problem is chronic, having begun at the early age of 13. Her drug of choice was heroin, although she has experimented with cocaine, ethanol, PCP, and hallucinogens. Recently, she had a 2-year period of abstinence from illicit substances and ethanol; however, she finally relapsed in September of 1994. Since then, she has had several drug-related arrests and was charged with the armed robbery of a convenience store, which she held up with a fake plastic gun that was stolen from a toy store. She has been incarcerated on at least four occasions and currently is on probation. Nina has abstained from drugs and alcohol for 6 months since her last suicide attempt.

Mental Health History

Nina was diagnosed with severe depression when she was 17 years old. At the age of 21, she had a "nervous breakdown" followed by a suicide attempt and was hospitalized in a psychiatric hospital. At that time, she was diagnosed with paranoid schizophrenia. She typically displayed symptoms of auditory hallucinations and "dark and ominous" delusions, with the report that a persistent voice from afar beckons her "to watch out for stepdaddy." Since then, she has been hospitalized more than nine times for these illnesses. A year ago, she was hospitalized for detoxification from alcohol and drug abuse and stabilization of her mental illnesses.

Medical History

Nina was diagnosed as being HIV positive 3 years ago, purportedly having contracted the virus through either her intravenous drug use or her forays into prostitution to support her drug habit. Until now, the course of her HIV disease has been relatively uncomplicated. She has not suffered any opportunistic infections secondary to HIV, nor has she had any HIV-related hospitalizations. But the presence of the potentially deadly virus in her body is a grim specter that haunts her and contributes to her demoralization.

Results of Psychological Testing

Nina's most recent neuropsychological testing occurred in 1995. Her cognitive functions appeared within normal limits, her short- and long-term memory were intact, and she was able to provide a coherent and organized account of her life. The Wechsler Adult Intelligence Scale—Revised score indicated that she functions in the superior range of intelligence.

Nina appeared to understand the precursors to her suicide attempt, but appeared emotionally detached from this event. She may be capable of developing emotional insight into her recent difficulties. She said that she felt "very fortunate, if not blessed, by Jesus and the angels" that her suicide attempt did not work. She also reported that she now feels hopeful that counseling and psychiatric treatment may help her. Her judgment appears to be improving, along with her will to live.

Mental Status Examination

Nina is a well-developed, 44-year-old African American female who looks many years older because of the damage endured by her body from years of drug abuse and improper nutrition. She appeared well-groomed, with good hygiene and casual dress. She was cooperative for the interview and motivated to pursue treatment. She made good eye contact and displayed good impulse control. Her speech was of a normal rate, volume, and tone without hesitation or pressure. Her mood was neutral, and her affect was flat. Her thought content was concrete and goal-directed but was overwhelmed periodically with auditory and visual hallucinations and paranoid ideation. She was oriented to person, place, situation, time, and date. She reported suicidal ideation but had not devised an imminent suicide plan. Her judgment and insight were described as "good," which may be more of a wishful prognostication than a reality.

CASE ANALYSIS

Conceptual Perspective

By displaying empathy toward the client and cultural sensitivity, the counselor avoided stereotyping Nina as having a "borderline personality disorder," as so many angry, difficult, and impoverished clients often are labeled. Initially, the counselor noticed that Nina was reluctant to self-disclose. She expressed feelings of mistrust and suspiciousness toward her White, Greek counselor in both her reticent speech and her unrelaxed body language. This phenonenon has been called *historical hostility*, which is defined as the unconscious mistrust and anger toward White counselors arising from their ethnic group's mistreatment of African Americans over history (Vontress & Epp, 1997). Interestingly, Greeks have not been historical oppressors of African Americans, but a light skin color may elicit irrational feelings in some African Americans because it symbolizes the skin color of their historical oppressors.

The early detection of this interpersonal dynamic prompted Nina's counselor to carefully and concertedly establish a close, empathic relationship with her client prior to any exploration of sensitive issues. Hence, *prerapport* needed to take place to palliate any feelings of historical hostility. The client needed to overcome the dangerous impediment of viewing the counseling dyad as an oppressor–oppressed relationship. For an effective and equal therapeutic alliance to develop, it was important that Nina did not have feelings of hatred or inferiority toward her White counselor.

Another important factor contributing to Nina's issues was her poverty. She was unemployed and lived from day to day with whatever money she could panhandle, borrow from her mother, or charm from a passing friend or acquaintance. She was a high school dropout who had lived the majority of her life in a criminal subculture: Clearly, she was not the kind of employee an organization would welcome. She faced difficulties in her relationships with family and friends, and her attitude toward life was pessimistic and hopeless. The combination of these multiple stressors was as if a noose made of a heavy ball and chain had been wrapped around Nina's neck, and with this burden she had been cast unmercifully into the turbulent sea of life.

Culture was a significant influence in Nina's life. During the counseling sessions, Nina frequently repreated the phrase "in my culture." Although she seemed alienated from her African American subculture's urban environment of poverty and violence, she appeared to be strongly connected with her culture's spiritual environment, the Baptist church. She often mentioned how important the church was to her and the good relationship she had developed with her handsome and charismatic minister, whom she would consult about her personal problems on occasion but not quite enough to help her alter her ways.

In Nina's culture, family and familial bonds were very important. However, that attitude clashed with the individualism of the American popular culture that she also had internalized. Nina seemed to be affected by both trends and was struggling to choose the one that was right for her. During her development, she received conflicting messages regarding this issue. From the church and her parents, she heard how important it is to be close to your family and to stay connected with family members. On the other hand, she often saw her younger relatives, as well as her aunts and uncles, "doing their own thing," without taking account of the family's wishes. Nina always wanted to be close to her family. She was taught that this was the way it was supposed to be. Yet she felt disconnected from her family when her father abandoned her and her mother brought home a new husband, who was abusive to her and the other children. Nina's mother liked to talk about family values, but she acted with great hypocrisy when she did not wish to diminish her own satisfaction by sending away a man who was abusive to her family.

Existential Perspective

Behind the curtains of depression and hopelessness, Nina was striving for hope, love, and meaning in her life. Her current life was in a shambles and offered her no direction. Her counselor needed to reacquaint her with the basic existential reality of life: We all suffer in one way or another. That way, Nina would not condemn herself for an early life wasted on drugs and criminality, which was her particular burden. Yet a grim past can be the springboard for a better life in the future; and Nina's counselor wanted to operate as the facilitator of Nina's self-reflection in the pursuit of better living. Once Nina could confront her painful past, she could derive meaning from it and find her way to recovery and happiness. By denying the absurdity of her past, she was creating a psychological impediment to her discovery of a life that was free of drugs and full of meaning.

It was important for Nina to view her continuous suffering from a positive perspective and to realize that through suffering one can grow. Crisis and suffering help us connect better with ourselves and experience the process of self-actualization. When the time of crisis is over, we are able to evaluate all the factors that contributed to the crisis to gain a better understanding of ourselves and our environment, to appreciate the value of what we have, and to allow ourselves to enjoy life fully. Joy always tastes better after one has experienced misery.

Another essential truth that Nina had to realize was that crisis and suffering do not last forever. Our success in dealing with a crisis does not depend on how quickly we go through it but on how we deal with it and how much we benefited as persons from our painful experience. At this point in her life, Nina had to learn to appreciate and understand the meaning of "courage." It takes courage to be, and it takes courage to remake ourselves into better human beings.

Humans cannot live alone, totally disconnected from their social and natural environment. Aristotle (1943/1971, p. 219) remarked, "Whoever lives completely alone is either a god or a beast." Nina had to realize that her mental health and substance abuse problems did not happen all of a sudden without any reason. Many factors needed to be examined, especially the four basic existential relationships in Nina's life:

1. *Her relationship with herself.* Did she love herself?
2. *Her relationship with other people.* Could she appreciate the importance of her family and friends?
3. *Her relationship with the physical world.* Was she in harmony with her physical environment?
4. *Her relationship with the spiritual world.* How did she understand God and her purpose in the universe?

After examining these four spheres of Nina's life, one could easily see that she was experiencing problems in all of them except the fourth one, the spiritual, which appeared to be more fulfilling than the others. However, that relationship needed to be explored and expanded as well. The basic relationships of Nina's world were seriously disturbed, as was her mental health. Nina was experiencing what the German existentialists called "stuck existence." The "unfolding," or "blossoming," of those four relationships was "stuck" and needed improvement for Nina's mental health to improve.

Nina needed to be confronted with the fact that life is short, and the question of whether she cared to live her entire life as a criminal, drug addict, and homeless drifter needed to be posed quite bluntly. Humans often appreciate life more when they are reminded of the existence of death. Death is the final stop sign beyond which there is no more road to travel. Nina had to decide which path in life she cared to follow. She was free to stay on the course she had previously traveled or she could choose a path that may yield greater happiness—or, even, greater misery. That is the risk choice entails. But considering that Nina's life was already so bleak, any choice would be better than the ones she had made. She was heading toward a self-destruction of her own choosing.

DSM–IV (APA, 1994) Perspective

If one were to diagnose Nina from a *DSM–IV* perspective only, one would be struck by the severity of her psychopathology that eclipses her many strengths and existing relationships. Currently, Nina is very challenged, but with supportive psychotherapy and the proper medication, eventually, she can lead a virtually normal life. The important point is not to let an ominous *DSM–IV* diagnosis become the condemnation of a client's potential.

Because often there is some subjectivity in making a diagnosis and deciding what to include in it, one possible diagnostic summary of Nina's condition may read as follows:

Multiaxial Diagnosis

Axis I	Schizophrenia, paranoid type (295.30) Major depressive disorder, recurrent (296.24) Polysubstance dependence (304.80)
Axis II	No diagnosis
Axis III	Self-inflicted wounds with nerve damage of right wrist HIV Infection
Axis IV	Unemployment Financial stress Legal problems and previous incarcerations
Axis V	GAF = 55 (current)

INTERVENTION STRATEGY

From the first session with Nina, her counselor realized that she had to deal with a cross-cultural counseling relationship and its potential pitfalls. To avert a poor outcome, considering the underlying historical hostility that Nina was experiencing toward White people, the counselor did not challenge, but instead entered, the client's worldview. To enable that process, the counselor devised her own cross-cultural counseling technique, entitled the "Bipolar Cross-Cultural Counseling Exploration Method." According to this method, which is an eclectic synthesis of cross-cultural counseling theory, the counselor focused simultaneously on two areas: (a) exploration of the client's *specific culture* and (b) exploration of the *specific client* through the culture.

It should be noted that the word *specific* in the bipolar method is very meaningful because the underlying assumption of this method is that every client is *unique* and *different* despite the similarities that he or she has with individuals who belong to the same culture. That is to say that in every culture, people share common values and beliefs, but every culture also is composed of many *subcultures* that have differences among them. Therefore, in Nina's case, the counselor began her intervention with the idea that (a) All African American clients are *not alike* despite the fact that they share common characteristics and behaviors and (b) within the African American culture, there are *many subcultures* that have many important differences. In sum, Nina lives within the confluence of two cultural currents: the African American culture and the American drug culture. This is the cultural backdrop of Nina's complicated issues.

Nina's case was a complex puzzle that seemed unsolvable. She was experiencing many serious problems: major depression and suicidal ideation, periodic hallucinations, substance abuse, HIV infection, unemployment, separation from her spouse, and the possibility of incarceration. Because of the case's complexity, Nina's counselor prioritized her issues to determine which one should be given most attention during the counseling process. The counselor determined that Nina should receive treatment for her depression and suicidal ideation first because these essentially were life-threatening, and then for the other issues, each as daunting as the other, in their turn.

A focus on Nina's depression was not an attempt at reductionism. Her counselor recognized that Nina's problems were interrelated. For example, her rigid thinking and HIV status contributed to her depression, and her depression contributed to her chemical dependency, which was an ineffective means of self-medicating. It was essential that her presenting problems be viewed holistically. Viewing issues in this way does not preclude chopping them into manageable pieces for therapeutic attack, especially when one of the issues is as dire as suicidal ideation.

Nina's counselor wanted her input in prioritizing her issues. To facilitate this process, the counselor used one of her own techniques, the "Archer's Target Exercise." Nina was asked to label each ring of a target by giving it the name of an issue she was facing. At the "bull's-eye," Nina was instructed to place her most significant issue. Then she had to rank every remaining issue closer to or further from the "bull's-eye" according to its significance. On the Archer's Target, each consecutive ring receives its value from the relative value of its adjoining ring. The relationship among the rings in the Archer's Target represents Nina's own perception of the relative importance of her life's challenges.

Following the exercise, Nina was able to view a concise map of her issues. Being able to visualize her issues in simple and concrete form, Nina gained a better understanding of them while simultaneously stepping out of her situation and viewing it more objectively. The whole process helped her to confront her issues and allowed a treatment plan to be developed.

Nina's counselor conceptualized her case from the perspective of existential theory. To Nina's chief complaint that "there is no reason for me to live," her counselor decided to make the following suggestion: "Well, Nina, let's search for a reason for you to live." Nina's counselor wished to use Frankl's logotherapy—a powerful therapy based in the search for life's meaning (Frankl, 1967). The objective was to help Nina discover her meaning in life by combining three approaches to living: (a) finding meaningful work or doing a good deed, (b) experiencing the simple pleasure of loving another human being and nature, and (c) learning from life's inevitable suffering.

Nina's life experience and education were far removed from the philosophy of existentialism. Hence, the counseling intervention could not be effective without the appropriate preparation of the client. Nina had to be taught the relevance of existential thought to her own life—how this highbrow European philosophy could be of value to a high school dropout. Her instruction in existential theory was centered around the following areas:

- *Human nature.* How does the client perceive human nature: as simply being good, as a combination of being good and bad, or as simply being bad? Does her view of human nature influence her relationships with others?
- *Social relationships.* How does the client understand her interpersonal relationships with others? Where and how does she find loving relationships?
- *Nature.* How does the client perceive her relationship with nature? Does she spend sufficient time in natural spaces, or is she confined to the noise, haste, and concrete of an urban existence?
- *Time.* How does the client perceive the passage of time? Is she fixated on the past? Or can she allow herself the freedom that present- and future-oriented thinking allows?
- *Activity.* How does the client search for meaning in her life? Does she focus on "being" by preferring activities that allow for a spontaneous expression of self or on "scheduling" by rigidly planning one's existence rather than "going with the flow"?

While exploring Nina's worldview, the counselor used the *Socratic method.* The counselor used a directive approach but did not act as a drill sergeant or interrogator. She chose to behave as Nina's helper and facilitator—a gentle, but earnest, interviewer—because she wanted Nina to be in charge of the exploration process. The Socratic method often is called the *midwife's technique,* because a midwife helps a woman at the time of a baby's delivery by using her knowledge and skill just as the counselor assists a client at a time of self-reflection to deliver his or her own truth and self-awareness. Each professional, whether a midwife or counselor, is the facilitator of another's accomplishments rather than a surrogate who assumes another's responsibility.

The counselor taught Nina the existential meaning of "choice," "freedom," and "responsibility." The underlying objective of this counseling strategy was for the client to recognize that she is free to choose the way she wants to live her life and is thus responsible for her own happiness. Among the daily homework assignments that Nina had to follow was the repetition of the phrase "As long as I breathe, I have a choice." This strategy proved to be extremely therapeutic, if simple in its conception.

DISCUSSION OF THE CASE

Nina's response to counseling was more satisfactory than expected. She followed through with the counselor's recommendations and showed significant improvement in all the areas of her life. As a result of therapy, she was able to overcome the severe depression she was experiencing and began to find some enjoyment in life. She also gained insight about her mental illness and substance dependency and a better understanding about herself and her surroundings. Initially, Nina's case seemed impossible, and it was thought that she would be just another human life that was demoralized beyond repair and inaccessible to psychotherapy. But the resilience of the human spirit cannot be predicted; and this case may serve as a reminder to counselors that the cases that seem most hopeless often surprise us with magical transformations.

DISCUSSION QUESTIONS

1. How could Nina's counselor have established better rapport with her?
2. What resistances to self-disclosure might the counselor predict in working with a cross-cultural client such as Nina?
3. Was historical hostility a real impediment in this case?
4. Could you empathically enter the world of a drug addict without making a moral judgment of this behavior?
5. What role will insight play in Nina's recovery? Is it really important?
6. Can Nina transcend her past to find a meaning in life?
7. Nina is HIV positive. From an existential perspective, how would one view death and finiteness? How might the counselor work with Nina's fears about death and nonbeing?
8. Nina thinks about committing suicide as a way out of a life without meaning. How can a counselor help her find meaning in her life?
9. Nina reports having a strong faith in God. How can her spirituality be helpful to the treatment of her suicidal ideation and depression?
10. In Nina's case, the counselor decided that her suicidal ideation and depression are the issues that should be treated first. However, the counselor's perspective is that all of the issues she faces are interconnected and should be viewed holistically. What is your opinion of the counselor's approach? If you do not agree, what would you do differently and why?

CHAPTER THIRTEEN

Final Reflections

The title of this book is *Cross-Cultural Counseling: A Casebook*. The word *cross* is used to define the action of people meeting one another, of moving from one side to another, or of entering into the other's space. Counseling is used to suggest generic holistic helping. The assistance may be social, psychological, physical, or spiritual, or a combination of all of the above. The word *multicultural* is not used in the title because it only signifies "many" and therefore fails to communicate the idea of counselors from one culture helping clients from another, or vice versa. Psychotherapy is not used because it often connotes an exclusive focus on psychological helping.

The cases presented in this book are instructive to counselors whose clients are culturally different either because they are natives of foreign countries or because they, although U.S.-born, are members of minority groups that have not assimilated fully into the mainstream culture. They continue to live in enclaves in which the culture of their forebears is perpetuated generation after generation. It is not unusual to encounter second- and third-generation descendants of immigrants living in ethnic communities in which they communicate only in the language of their grandparents and feel like outsiders in the United States, their birth country.

Even though today there is considerable discussion of cultural differences, it is important to recognize that people are more alike than they are different. Besides, clients often consult counselors about problems in living that have nothing to do with their race, ethnicity, or cultural origin. Concerns about learning, loving, living, and dying are human problems that transcend culture. We therefore reject the tendency to stereotype clients according to the racial, ethnic, or cultural group into which they were born. In cross-cultural counseling, stereotyping is best referred to as the "groups approach." Instead, we advocate a conceptual approach to helping in which the focus is always on the individual, not on the person's racial, ethnic, or cultural group of origin. That is, counselors should consider various psychosocial constructs as they relate to clients.

For example, it may be important to determine to what extent clients are acculturated to the host or dominant culture. This determination has implications for how counselors decide to help clients. In general, they may feel free to use their usual counseling procedures with assimilated clients. On the other hand, they are apt to be challenged by clients who do not fit comfortably into the host or dominant culture because of cultural reasons. Often such clients experience a great deal of cultural anxiety. In the case of international sojourners, the anxiety may not be so much a product of their being in a strange country, in which they must eat food that is new to the palate and speak a foreign language, as it is a result of the sudden loss of status they experience.

On American college campuses, individuals from upper-class families who are accustomed to deference back home usually are lumped into a general category, "foreign students," and treated as if they were inferior to native English-speaking peers. In like manner, in much of the multicultural or cross-cultural counseling literature, U.S.-born clients are discussed by categories or groups. Readers find chapters in books devoted to the "African American," "Native American," "Asian American," and so on, as if to suggest that people in each group are culturally the same. The practice is at best antitherapeutic: It departs from the basic principle of counseling that each client should be viewed as a unique individual.

THE COUNSELING ENTERPRISE

Mental health problems should always be understood in cultural context. In like manner, attempts to find solutions to difficulties must take into consideration the culture in which the remedies are to be played out. Culture dictates whom to consult when outside help is needed to assist in the resolution of problems in living. Culture also prescribes acceptable methodologies for remedies. In the United States, counselors generally follow culturally prescribed methods of helping clients that may need to be modified creatively with the culturally different.

Counselors

Effective cross-cultural counselors are people with a broad view of humanity. They see people as people, all deserving equal respect and assistance with their movement through life. They try to free themselves through learning, living, and loving from the prejudices that set people apart. In recognizing that they are made of the same ingredients as their clients, they resist the notion that they are superior to their clients. They, therefore, approach their clients with personalism, not objective aloofness. A human-to-human encounter is therapeutic for all clients, regardless of their cultural background. Although most of the counselors who reported cases in this book are European Americans, they encountered no problems in relating to, diagnosing, or intervening on behalf of their culturally different clients.

Diagnosis

The human personality is a spirit. It is illusive. It cannot be reduced and dissected for precise measurement by the rules of science. Understanding and changing it is an inexact science at best. In this book, each case was analyzed in three ways—the conceptual approach, the existential approach, and the *DSM–IV* (APA, 1994) approach—because we feel that cross-cultural counselors should view their clients in as many ways as possible before assigning a diagnostic label to them. Labels, once assigned, are not easy to remove. Often they continue to harm clients for the rest of their lives. We recommend that counselors take as much time as needed to understand the stressors that may be causing clients difficulties, even though they may feel pressured to provide a diagnostic label after the first interview. We suggest that cross-cultural autobiographies be used to get to know clients. It also is helpful to consult significant others when they are available. If counselors use the *DSM–IV* diagnostic labels, it is recommended that the qualifiers *tentative* or *rule out* be placed after the code until they have had enough time to confirm their first impressions.

Therapeutic Plans

Diagnoses cannot be divorced from therapeutic plans. Incorrect diagnoses almost always lead to incorrect intervention recommendations. In working with culturally different clients, it is best to check with clients to see what they think about the plan of attack that has been developed to help them. Along with the plan, counselors who receive third-party reimbursement in community settings are expected to indicate a treatment timetable. This expectation often is required after a single interview in order to obtain authorization to provide extended therapy for clients. Counselors who feel that such an expectation is unrealistic usually write "something" to allow the therapy to proceed until they can provide a more firm diagnosis. Be careful not to write "something" that is stigmatizing for the client and serves only the counselor's financial benefit.

Methodology

The methodology used by counselors who described their cases in this book can best be called a Socratic dialogue. It is a *maieutic approach* in which they help clients to give birth to themselves. They are midwives who assist individuals to discover who they are as they unfold in the natural, social, and spiritual environments that are home for them as long as they live. The unfolding is a continuous process; therefore, problems in living may develop at any stage of existence.

There are no specific techniques for counseling culturally different clients. Individuals are each genetically unique and arrive in the world at different places and times. What they absorb from their surroundings makes them singular human beings. It therefore seems unreasonable to posit a theory that is therapeutic for all clients, regardless of their cultural origin.

CONCLUSION

In this book, we advocated an existential approach to helping. We developed a perspective on human existence that is universally comprehensive. Human beings are confronted with essentially the same problems in living, even though there are variations on basic themes that are endemic to the species. Although current psychotherapeutic helping models are useful, they are the products of the creative imagination of single theorists who, in the search for meaning and direction in their own lives, developed recipes for existence that they offered for everybody else. The theoretical prescriptions are culture-specific because the theory builders were each products of a single culture.

Existential therapeutic philosophy is an umbrella view of human beings and their problems in the world. It encourages a comprehensive self-discovery. Humans are constantly evolving. They also suffer a great deal in the process. However, there is no pill to ease the pain in their lives. Nor is there a compendium of simple solutions to life's problems. The greatest help in living comes from the understanding and companionship provided by fellow travelers—known as "counselors"—each of whom helps his or her clients differently because, like their clients, each is cut from a different existential cloth. The meeting of counselor and client creates a limitless font of courage and love that is the ultimate source of healing.

REFERENCES

Ali, A. Y. (1983). *The holy Qur'an: Text, translation, and commentary*. Brentwood, MD: Amana.

American Psychiatric Association. (1994). *Diagnostic and statistical manual of mental disorders* (4th ed.). Washington, DC: Author.

Angeles, P. A. (1981). *Dictionary of philosophy*. New York: Barnes & Noble.

Anikeeff, A. M. (1951). *Reciprocal empathy: Mutual understanding among groups*. Lafayette, IN: Purdue University, Division of Educational Reference.

Annas, J. E. (1992). *Hellenistic philosophy of mind*. Berkeley: University of California Press.

Arbuckle, D. (1975). *Counseling and psychotherapy: An existential–humanistic view*. Boston: Allyn & Bacon.

Bayer, R. (1987). *Homosexuality and American psychiatry*. Princeton, NJ: Princeton University Press.

Becker, H. (1950). Sacred and secular societies. *Social Forces, 28,* 361–376.

Bedford, M. (1972). *Existentialism and creativity*. New York: Philosophical Library.

Bielefeldt, H. (1995). Muslim voices in the human rights debate. *Human Rights Quarterly, 17,* 587–617.

Binswanger, L. (1962). *Existential analysis and psychotherapy*. New York: Dutton.

Boss, M. (1963). *Psychoanalysis and daseinsanalysis*. New York: Basic Books.

Breggin, P. (1997). *The heart of being helpful: Empathy and the creation of a healing presence*. New York: Springer.

Breggin, P. R., & Breggin, G. R. (1994). *Talking back to Prozac: What doctors aren't telling you about today's most controversial drug*. New York: St. Martin's Press.

Brett, G. S. (1963). *Psychology: Ancient and modern.* New York: Cooper Square Publishers.

Buber, M. (1964). *I and thou* (W. Kaufman, Trans.). New York: Scribner.

Buber, M. (1970). I and thou. In M. Friedman (Ed.), *The worlds of existentialism: A critical reader* (pp. 216–235). Chicago: University of Chicago Press.

Bugental, J. F. T. (1965). *The search for authenticity: An existential-analytic approach to psychotherapy.* New York: Holt, Rinehart & Winston.

Bugental, J. F. T. (1976). *The search for existential identity: Patient–therapist dialogues in humanistic psychotherapy.* San Francisco: Jossey-Bass.

Bulka, R. P. (1979). *The quest for ultimate meaning: Principles and applications of logotherapy.* New York: Philosophical Library.

Carrithers, M. (1992). *Why humans have cultures: Explaining anthropology and social diversity.* New York: Oxford University Press.

Chelune, G. J., & Associates. (Eds.) (1979). *Self-disclosure: Origins, patterns, and implications of oneness in interpersonal relations.* San Francisco: Jossey-Bass.

Christian, J. L. (1977). *Philosophy: An introduction to the art of wondering* (2nd ed.). New York: Holt, Rinehart & Winston.

Cottam, R. (1979). *Nationalism in Iran.* Pittsburgh, PA: University of Pittsburgh Press.

Crimbaugh, J. C. (1975). *Logotherapy as a bridge between religion and psychotherapy.* Paper found on The Educational Resources Information Center (ERIC).

Dana, R. H. (1993). *Multicultural assessment perspectives for professional psychology.* Boston: Allyn & Bacon.

Delamarre, B. (1996). *L'existence: La mort, le bonheur* [Existence: Death, happiness]. Paris: Ellipses/Edition Marketing S. A.

Dewey, J. (1959). The unity of the human being. In H. Peterson (Ed.), *Essays in philosophy* (pp. 381–400). New York: Pocket Books.

Diallo, Y., & Hall, M. (1989). *The healing drum: African wisdom and teachings.* Rochester, VT: Destiny Books.

Doll, E. A. (1953). *The Measurement of Social Competence Manual for the Vineland Social Maturity Scale.* Circle Pines, MN: American Guidance Service.

Donceel, J. F. (1961). *Philosophical psychology* (2nd ed.). New York: Sheed & Ward.

Draguns, J. G. (1989). Dilemmas and choices in cross-cultural counseling: The universal vs. the culturally distinctive. In P. G. Pedersen, J. G. Draguns, W. J. Lonner, & J. F. Trimble (Eds.), *Counseling across cultures* (3rd ed., pp. 3–21). Honolulu: University of Hawaii Press.

Dube, S. C. (1988). Cultural dimensions of development. *International Social Science Journal, 40,* 505–511.

Elungu, P. E. A. (1984). *L'éveil philosophie africain* [The awakening of African philosophy]. Paris: Editions L'Hamattan.

Epicurus. (1994). *A letter on happiness* (R. Waterfield, Trans.). San Francisco: Chronicle Books. (Original work published c. 271 BC)

Epp, L. (1998). The courage to be an existential counselor: An interview of Clemmont Vontress. *Journal of Mental Health Counseling, 20*(1), 1–12.

Fischer, H. (1965). *Theorie der kulter* [Cultural theory]. Stuttgart, Germany: Seewald Verlag.

Flam, L. (1970). *La philosophie au tourant de notre temps* [Philosophy at the turn of the century]. Paris: Presses Universitaires de France.

Frank, J. D. (1961). *Persuasion and healing.* Baltimore: Johns Hopkins University Press.

Frankl, V. (1978). *The unheard cry for meaning.* New York: Simon & Schuster.

Frankl, V. E. (1962). *Man's search for meaning.* Boston: Beacon Press.

Frankl, V. E. (1967). *Psychotherapy and existentialism: Selected papers on logotherapy.* New York: Simon & Schuster.

Frankl, V. E. (1975). *The unconscious god.* New York: Simon & Schuster.

Freud, S. (1955). Group psychology and the analysis of the ego. In J. Strachey (Ed. and Trans.), *The standard edition of the complete works of Sigmund Freud* (Vol. 18, pp. 67–143). London: Hogarth Press. (Original work published 1921)

Fromm, E. (1976). *Man for himself: An inquiry into the psychology of ethics.* New York: Rinehart & Winston.

Funk, R. (1982). *Erich Fromm: The courage to be human.* New York: Continuum.

Glasser, W. (1965). *Reality therapy: A new approach to psychiatry.* New York: Harper & Row.

Gough, H. (1971). Some reflections on the meaning of psychodiagnosis. *American Psychologist, 26,* 160–167.

Gross, M. L. (1978). *The psychological society.* New York: Random House.

Hadas, M. (1958). *The Stoic philosophy of Seneca: Essays and letters.* New York: Norton.

Hall, C. S., & Lindzey, G. (1957). *Theories of personality.* New York: Wiley.

Hamilton, E., & Huntington, C. (Eds.). (1987). *The collected dialogues of Plato, including the letters.* Princeton, NJ: Princeton University Press.

Hammer, D. H. (1993). A linkage between DNA markers on the x chromosome and male sexual orientation. *Science, 261,* 321–327.

Helms, J. E. (1992). Why is there no study of cultural equivalence in standardized cognitive ability testing? *American Psychologist, 47,* 1083–1101.

Huff, T. (1993). Science & civilizations: East and West. *Culture and Society, 31*(1), 77–79.

Jackson, M. L. (1987). Cross-cultural counseling at the crossroads: A dialogue with Clemmont F. Vontress. *Journal of Counseling and Development, 66*(1), 20–23.

Jackson, M. L. (1995). Multicultural counseling: Historical perspectives. In J. C. Ponterotto, J. M. Casas, L. A. Suzuki, & C. M. Alexander (Eds.), *Handbook of multicultural counseling* (pp. 3–16). Thousand Oaks, CA: Sage.

Jaynes, J. (1976). *The origin of consciousness in the breakdown of the bicameral mind.* Boston: Houghton Mifflin.

Johnson, A. H. (1977). *Philosophers in action.* Columbus, OH: Charles E. Merrill.

Johnson, R. E. (1971). *Existential man: The challenge of psychotherapy.* New York: Pergamon Press.

Jourard, S. M. (1964). *The transparent self.* Princeton, NJ: Van Nostrand.

Klinger, E. (1977). *Meaning and void: Inner experiences and the incentives in people's lives.* Minneapolis: University of Minnesota Press.

Koestenbaum, P. (1971). *The vitality of death: Essays in existential psychology and philosophy.* Westport, CT: Greenwood Press.

Kopp, S. B. (1972). *If you meet the Buddha on the road, kill him: The pilgrimage of psychotherapy patients.* New York: Bantam Books.

Lambert, R. G., & Lambert, M. J. (1984). The effects of role preparation for psychotherapy in immigrant clients seeking mental health services in Hawaii. *Journal of Community Psychology, 12,* 263–292.

Lao Tsu. (1972). *Tao te ching* (G. Feng & J. English, Trans.). New York: Random House.

Lavely, J. H. (1967). Personalism. In P. Edwards (Ed.), *The encyclopedia of philosophy* (Vol. 6, pp. 107–110). New York: Macmillan/Free Press.

Lee, C. C. (1997). *Multicultural issues in counseling: New approaches to diversity* (2nd ed.). Alexandria, VA: American Counseling Association.

Lee, C. C., & Richardson, B. L. (1991). *Multicultural issues in counseling: New approaches to diversity.* Alexandria, VA: American Association for Counseling and Development.

LeVay, S. (1991). A difference in hypothalamic structure between heterosexual and homosexual men. *Science, 253,* 1034–1040.

Lindenauer, G. G. (1970). Loneliness. *Journal of Emotional Education, 10*(3), 87–94.

Loomis, C. (1940). *Fundamental concepts of society*. New York: American Book.

Lowen, A. (1969). *The betrayal of the body*. Toronto, Ontario, Canada: Macmillan.

Lowen, A. (1980). *Fear of life*. New York: Macmillan.

Macquarrie, J. (1977). *Existentialism*. New York: Pelican Books. (Original work published 1972)

Maslow, A. H. (1971). *The farther reaches of human nature*. New York: Viking Press.

Masolo, D. A. (1994). *African philosophy in search of identity*. Bloomington: Indiana University Press.

May, R. (Ed.). (1961). *Existential psychology*. New York: Random House.

May, R. (1967). *Existential psychotherapy*. Toronto, Ontario, Canada: CBC.

May, R. (1975). *The courage to create*. New York: Norton.

May, R. (1977). *The meaning of anxiety* (Rev. ed.). New York: Norton.

May, R. (1991). Existence: A new dimension in psychiatry and psychology. In J. Ehrenwald (Ed.), *The history of psychotherapy* (pp. 388–393). Northvale, NJ: Jason Aronson.

Missinne, L. E., & Wilcox, V. (1981). *Frankl's theory and therapy*. Paper presented at the annual conference of the Western Gerontological Society, Seattle, WA.

Moles, A. A. (1967). *Sociodynamique de la culture* [Sociodynamics of culture]. La Haye, France: Mouton Paris.

Morano, D. V. (1973). *Existential guilt: A phenomenolagical study*. Assen, the Netherlands: Van Gorcum.

Moulyn, A. C. (1982). *The meaning of suffering: An interpretation of human existence from the viewpoint of time*. Westport, CT: Greenwood Press.

Mounier, B. (1992). *Le personnalisme* [Personalism]. Paris: Presses Universitaires de France.

Mounier, E. (1947). *Introduction aux existentialismes* [Introduction to existentialism]. Paris: Société des éditions Denobel.

Nauman, S. E., Jr. (1971). *The new dictionary of existentialism*. New York: Philosophical Library.

Netton, I. (1992). *A popular dictionary of Islam*. Atlantic Highlands, NJ: Humanities Press.

Nwadiora, E. (1996). Nigerian families. In M. McGoldrick, J. K. Pearce, & J. Giordano (Eds.), *Ethnicity & family therapy* (2nd ed., pp. 129–138). New York: Guilford Press.

Ochanine, D. (1938). *La sympathie et ses trois aspects: Harmonie, constrainte, délivrance* [Sympathy and its three aspects: Harmony, restraint, relief.] Paris: Libraire Le Rodstein.

Ofman, W. V. (1976). *Affirmation and reality: Fundamentals of humanistic existential therapy and counseling.* Los Angeles: Western Psychological Services.

Okolo, C. (1992). Self as a problem in African philosophy. *International Philosophical Quarterly, 4,* 477–485.

Oseghare, A. S. (1992) Sagacity and African philosophy. *International Philosophical Quarterly, 32,* 94–104.

Pachuta, D. M. (1989). Chinese medicine: The law of five elements. In A. A. Sheikh & K. S. Sheikh (Eds.), *Eastern and Western approaches to healing* (pp. 64–90). New York: Wiley.

Paniague, F. (1994). *Assessing and treating culturally diverse clients: A practical guide.* Thousand Oaks, CA: Sage.

Ponterotto, J. G., Casas, M. J., Suzid, L. A., & Alexander, C. M. (1995). *Handbook of multicultural counseling.* Thousand Oaks, CA: Sage.

Puligandla, R. (1975). *Fundamentals of Indian philosophy.* New York: Abingdon Press.

Redfield, P. (1947). The folk society. *American Journal of Sociology, 52,* 293–308.

Reese, W. L. (1980). *Dictionary of philosophy and religion.* Atlantic Highlands, NJ: Humanities Press.

Ricken, F. (1991). *Philosophy of the ancients.* Notre Dame, IN: University of Notre Dame Press.

Rogers, C. R. (1961). *On becoming a person.* Boston: Houghton Mifflin.

Rogers, C. R. (1995). *A way of being.* New York: Houghton Mifflin. (Original work published 1980)

Rychlak, J. F. (1979). *Discovering free will and personal responsibility.* New York: Oxford University Press.

Rychlak, J. F. (1981). *Introduction to personality and psychotherapy: A theory construction approach.* Boston: Houghton Mifflin.

Sardar, Z. (1993). Paper, printing, and compact disks: The making and unmaking of Islamic culture. *Media, Culture, and Society, 15,* 43–59.

Sartre, J. P. (1957). *Existentialism and human emotions.* New York: Wisdom Library.

Sartre, J. P. (1972). *No exit & the flies.* New York: Knopf.

Sartre, J. P. (1996). *L'existentialisme est un humanisme* [Existentialism is humanism]. Paris: Gallimard.

Satir, V. (1988). *The new peoplemaking.* Mountainview, CA: Science & Behavior Books.

Selye, H. (1956). *The stress of life.* New York: McGraw-Hill.

Servan-Schreiber, J. L. (1987). *The return of courage.* New York: Addison-Wesley.

Shaku, S. (1987). *Zen for Americans.* New York: Dorset Press.

Staniforth, M. (1964). *Marcus Aurelius: Meditations.* New York: Penguin Books.

Stumpf, S. E. (1975). *Socrates to Sartre: A history of philosophy* (2nd ed.). New York: McGraw-Hill.

Sue, D. W. (1981). *Counseling the culturally different: Theory and practice.* New York: Wiley.

Sue, S., & Zane, N. (1987). The role of culture and cultural technique in psychotherapy: A critique and reformulation. *American Psychologist, 37,* 1239–1244.

Suzuki, D. T. (1959). *Zen and Japanese culture.* New York: MJF Books.

Talbot, P. A. (1967). *Tribes of the Niger delta: Their religions and customs.* New York: Barnes & Noble.

Triandis, H. C. (1994). *Culture and social behavior.* New York: McGraw-Hill.

Tumin, M. M. (1973). *Patterns of society: Identities, roles and resources.* Boston: Little, Brown.

Turner, V. M. (1986). Body, brain, and culture. *Cross Currents, 36,* 156–178.

Ungersma, A. J. (1961). *The search for meaning: A new approach in psychotherapy and pastoral psychology.* Philadelphia: Westminster Press.

van Deurzen-Smith, A. (1988). *Existential counseling in practice.* Thousand Oaks, CA: Sage.

van Kaam, A. (1962). Counseling from the viewpoint of existential psychology. *Harvard Educational Review, 32,* 403–415.

Vontress, C. E. (1979). Cross-cultural counseling: An existential approach. *Personnel and Guidance Journal, 58,* 117–122.

Vontress, C. E. (1986a). Existential anxiety: Implications for counseling. *American Mental Health Counselors Association Journal, 8,* 100–109.

Vontress, C. E. (1986b). Social and cultural foundations. In M. D. Lewis, P. Hayes, & J. A. Lewis (Eds.), *An introduction to the counseling profession* (pp. 215–250). Itasca, IL: Peacock.

Vontress, C. E. (1991). Traditional healing in Africa: Implications for cross-cultural counseling. *Journal of Counseling and Development, 70*(1), 242–249.

Vontress, C. E. (1996). A personal retrospective on cross-cultural counseling. *Journal of Multicultural Counseling and Development, 24*(3), 156–166.

Vontress, C. E., & Epp, L. R. (1997). Historical hostility in the African American client: Implications for counseling. *Journal of Multicultural Counseling and Development, 25*(3), 170–184.

Wade, P. (1993). Race, nature and culture. *Man, 28,* 17–34.

Watts, A. (1995). *The Tao of philosophy: The edited transcripts.* Boston: Charles E. Tuttle.

Watts, A. (1996). *Buddhism: The religion of no-religion: The edited transcripts.* Boston: Charles E. Tuttle.

Wechsler, D. (1981). *Manual for the WISC–R.* New York: Psychological Corporation.

West, C. (1993). *Race matters.* Boston: Beacon Press.

Wild, J. (1979). *The challenge of existentialism.* Westport, CT: Greenwood Press.

Wolff, R. P. (1976). *About philosophy.* Englewood Cliffs, NJ: Prentice Hall.

Yalom, I. (1980). *Existential psychotherapy.* New York: Basic Books.

Zimmer, H. (1974). *Philosophies of India.* Princeton, NJ: Princeton University Press. (Original work published 1951)

INDEX

C